MODERN MARXISM

A GUIDE FOR CHRISTIANS IN A WOKE NEW WORLD

DISCLAIMERS

Portions of this work have appeared previously on AnswersInGenesis.org as blog posts or articles by the author.

Aside from minor word processor suggestions, no part of this manuscript was generated by large language models or other artificial intelligence.

This work cites a wide variety of sources representing a broad array of theological, political, and philosophical perspectives that do not necessarily reflect the views of the author or of Answers in Genesis.

COPYRIGHT

ISBN: 978-1-9844-1446-5
Product ID: 3000647

Author: Patricia Engler

Cover Design: Michaela Duncan
Interior Layout: Michaela Duncan
Appendix Map Design: Justine Foster

Editors: Gary Vaterlaus, Evonne Krell, Gretchen Doolittle, Ryan Freeman, Sarah Zornes

Content Reviewers: Bryan Osborne, Joe Owen, Dr. Georgia Purdom

Production: Dan Zordel, Shonda Snelbaker, Jenn Reed, Joel Leineweber, Justine Foster, Andrew Schwab, Ian McEwen

Text edition 2024.

Printed in the United States of America

TABLE OF CONTENTS

IMAGE CREDITS

Cover: Circuit board pattern and front cover fist from Getty Images.

Part One Divider: Protest on page x from Patricia Engler, snake on page xi from Answers in Genesis.

Chapter 1: Clouds on page xii from Unsplash. Flag image on page xii from Getty Images. Protest image on page 2 from Patricia Engler.

Chapter 2: Marx's face on page 24 from Getty Images, skull from Unsplash, snake images from Answers in Genesis.

Chapter 3: Rousseau, colosseum, Notre Dame, protesters, and storm images on page 52 from Getty Images.

Chapter 4: Pen, paper, and flower images on page 80 from Getty Images.

Chapter 5: Chain images on page 110 from Getty Images. Sigmund Freud image on page 110 public domain.

Part Two Divider: Church, bullet, and Pinocchio on page 144 from Getty Images. Clouds on page 145 from Unsplash.

Chapter 6: Church on page 146 from Getty Images. Landscape on page 146 from Unsplash.

Chapter 7: Brain and marionette images on page 170 from Getty Images.

Chapter 8: Towers in the center and lower right and left corners and all images of viruses on page 202 are from Getty Images. Candle and towers on upper left and upper right on page 202 from Unsplash.

Part Three Divider: Rose image on page 230 from Getty Images. Wolf on page 231 from Unsplash.

Chapter 9: Barbed wire, sheep, and teardrops on page 232 from Unsplash.

Chapter 10: Right ring on page 258 from Unsplash. Left ring, hands, and circuit board pattern on page 258 from Getty Images.

Chapter 11: Shattered glass, crown of thorns, and dove on page 284 from Getty Images.

Appendices Divider: Map on page 300 and cityscape on page 301 from Getty Images.

Appendix C: Bailey image on page 341, Besant, Blake, and Blavatsky images on page 342, Engels and Fourier images on page 343, Freud, Hegel, Marx, and Owen images on page 345, and Reich, Rousseau, Shelley, and Solzhenitsyn images on page 346 are from the public domain. Darwin, Diocletian, Firestone, and Lenin images on pages 342–346 from Getty Images. Freire image on page 343, Fromm image on page 344, Horkheimer and Marcuse images on page 345, and Teilhard image on page 346 are from Wikimedia via ShareAlike3License. Their contrasts and colors were modified via Photoshop. Map on page 349 from FreePik.

ACKNOWLEDGMENTS

All glory belongs to "one God, the Father, from whom are all things and for whom we exist, and one Lord, Jesus Christ, through whom are all things and through whom we exist" (1 Corinthians 8:6). He has brought together all the pieces that resulted in this book reaching you.

On that note, I'd like to thank you (yes, you), the reader, for picking up this resource. I pray that God will use these pages to equip and encourage you to the fullest extent of his purposes.

I am also especially grateful to the intellectuals cited throughout this book, whose works proved instrumental to my research, helping me identify key issues to highlight, thinkers to investigate, and locations to visit.

My deep appreciation extends further to the Christian authors whose stories and insights regarding persecution appear in part three of this book, corroborating themes from my global student interviews.

Here are just some of the others I'd like to thank:

- To the families, friends, and strangers who helped me during my European research journey—thank you for your hospitality, fellowship, and kind assistance in everything I needed, from finding Christian contacts to escaping assorted predicaments.
- To the Christians I interviewed in connection with this book—thank you for taking the time to share your stories, insights, and practical advice for other believers.

- To Dr. Georgia Purdom, Bryan Osborne, Joe Owen, and others who read this book in its early phases—thank you for the care you invested in reviewing this work and for your support along the journey.
- To the editing, design, and publishing team members at Answers in Genesis, including Evonne Krell, Gary Vaterlaus, Gretchen Doolittle, Ryan Freeman, Sarah Zornes, Andrew Schwab, Ian McEwen, Joel Leineweber, Justine Foster, Jenn Reed, Michaela Duncan, Dan Zordel, Shonda Snelbaker, and others involved in this project—thank you for the hours you invested in preparing this book to become a polished tool ready for use. Thank you also to Ken Ham for your role in this book.
- To the friends, colleagues, and supporters who have cheered me on—thank you for your encouragement, presence, and prayers along the way.
- To my family—thank you for your counsel, prayers, and encouragement to keep adventuring wherever God leads.

DEDICATION

To my brothers and sisters in Christ,

and to Jesus our Creator,

with love.

1 Corinthians 16:13–14

FOREWORD

BY KEN HAM

When you picked up this book, you may have wondered, "Why is Answers in Genesis tackling Marxism and wokeism?" After all, what do communism, socialism, and radical cultural revolution have to do with Genesis? Well, as you'll discover, a lot!

You see, the battle in the West against the resurgence of "the isms" is really just a different version of the same battle that's been raging since the garden of Eden: Did God really say? At the heart of that question is a desire to be our own gods, decide truth for ourselves, and use our own wisdom to usher in a utopia based on our knowledge of good and evil. Really, it's a battle over two foundations: man's word or God's Word.

If that sounds familiar, it's because I've been highlighting the foundational nature of the so-called "culture wars" for decades now. All of the societal ills—the division, violence, and shocking immorality pervading our culture today—are symptoms of the same problem: starting our thinking on man's word rather than God's Word.

If man determines truth, then anything goes. It's like what we read in Judges 17:6: "In those days there was no king in Israel. Everyone did what was right in his own eyes." In other words, when there is no ultimate authority ("no king" but being one's own god), everyone does what he thinks is right. Truth becomes relative, and human wisdom reigns supreme.

This worldview, based on the foundation of man's word, is at war with the biblical worldview, which is grounded on the authority of God's Word, beginning in Genesis. God's Word says there is an objective standard, right and wrong are determined by God, and true wisdom begins with him.

This is why there is no neutrality; Marxism, communism, and socialism are not neutral philosophies Christians can borrow and then "Christianize" by sprinkling a few Bible verses on top. They are worldviews grounded in man's word that stand in direct opposition to God and his truth.

And this is why Answers in Genesis' Patricia Engler is tackling this issue—because the answers to Marxist thinking are in Genesis! You see, Genesis is the foundation for our Christian worldview, all doctrine, the gospel, and, in fact, everything. So yes, when it comes to fighting "the isms," we'll be going back to Genesis to see what the Creator says about human nature, our purpose and meaning, and why the world is the way it is.

As history has clearly shown, Marxism, communism, and socialism are deadly ideologies. But sadly, they've come back in vogue. We need Christians who can rightly apply the biblical worldview to this vital issue and teach others to do the same.

> See to it that no one takes you captive by philosophy and empty deceit, according to human tradition, according to the elemental spirits of the world, and not according to Christ. (Colossians 2:8)

Ken Ham

Ken Ham
Founder CEO
Answers in Genesis, Creation Museum, and Ark Encounter

KEY DIFFERENCES BETWEEN GOD'S WORD AND MARXISM + HISTORICAL FACTS TO HELP UNDERSTAND TODAY'S CULTURE

PART ONE

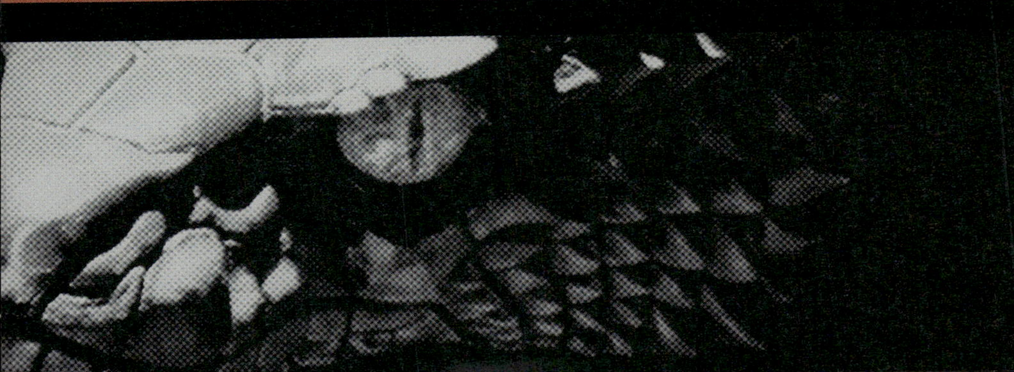

MATTHEW 7:24-25

EVERYONE THEN WHO HEARS THESE WORDS OF MINE AND DOES THEM WILL BE LIKE A WISE MAN WHO BUILT HIS HOUSE ON THE ROCK. AND THE RAIN FELL, AND THE FLOODS CAME, AND THE WINDS BLEW AND BEAT ON THAT HOUSE, BUT IT DID NOT FALL, BECAUSE IT HAD BEEN FOUNDED ON THE ROCK.

CHAPTER 1

THE GATHERING STORM

WHAT SHOULD CHRISTIANS MAKE OF THIS CHANGE IN THE WEATHER?

The signs were everywhere. Posters, flags, and banners swirled with the protesters in the plaza where I stood, speechless. I hadn't expected to run into anything quite like this. Not today. Not during my lifetime. And especially not here.

Less than 50 years ago, the Berlin Wall had stood not two miles from this place. I'd heard about how people went to desperate lengths to escape the communism within that wall—or die trying. I'd heard about how the crowds had cheered, tears streaming down their faces, when the wall fell. And now I heard crowds cheering again. But this time, they were cheering **for** communism.

All around me, people applauded. Banners waved. Somewhere, a German speech was echoing from a megaphone. And everywhere, I saw flags. Their emblems ranged

The protest I ran into in Berlin

from communist organization logos to rainbow banners to—of all things—the Soviet hammer-and-sickle insignia. Not far away, teenagers representing the Socialist German Workers Youth held a sign which translated to, "Your war, our dead. Peace to the workers. War to capitalism."

Ironic, I thought, **that I've stumbled into a communist protest the one day I visit this campus**. Karl Marx, who popularized communism, had studied here at the University of Berlin. Now, nearly two centuries later, I had come to Marx's *alma mater* while backpacking around Europe to research the history and consequences of Marxist thinking. And these flags on Marx's former campus were not the first signs I'd encountered of a Marxist revival in Western culture.

Only a month earlier, at a university in London, I'd spotted a poster for a "Marxism 2022" event promising a "festival of socialist ideas." And a few weeks before that, I'd glimpsed a sign in Northern Ireland that stated, "Sectarianism, climate change, gender violence . . . we can't live

with capitalism!" Those words had reminded me of a similar message I'd seen nearly four years prior at a Canadian university. The poster had invited students to join Canada's Young Communist League, declaring, "Capitalism is war, racism, climate crisis, xenophobia, student debt, poverty wages, patriarchy, colonialism, unemployment, and precarious work."

In Canada, the UK, and Germany, these messages represented just a few (literal) signs of a larger storm we're watching unfold across the globe. It's a phenomenon that exploits cultural issues to promote an anti-biblical belief system rooted in Marxism, as upcoming chapters of this book will demonstrate. It's an agenda that tells us we can (and must) become our own creators, saviors, and authorities for truth. And it's a religion whose followers demand that others not only **stay out of the way** but also **actively support the cause**.

This religion divides people into identity groups labeled "oppressor" or "oppressed." Humanity's only hope, according to this doctrine, lies in the oppressed overthrowing the oppressors. And it's no secret that popular messages in today's Western culture paint biblical Christianity as "oppressive." It's also no secret that open hostility against Christianity has been escalating. Our world longs for hope but increasingly seeks to vilify, censor, and marginalize followers of the only one who can deliver this hope. As the pressure builds, Christians who never imagined this kind of storm would rise so soon or so close to home confront the question "Now what?"

THIS RELIGION DIVIDES PEOPLE INTO IDENTITY GROUPS LABELED "OPPRESSOR" OR "OPPRESSED."

That's where this book comes in. Drawing insights from Scripture, history, and Christians who have "been there," this three-part survival guide helps Christians understand and respond to these cultural changes. The journey begins here in **part one**, which reveals key differences between God's Word and Marxism and uncovers historical facts relevant to understanding culture today. **Part two** exposes common strategies that revolutionary agendas wield when trying to replace Christian-influenced societies with secular totalitarian regimes. **Part three** offers practical tools for Christians to respond by living out an uncompromised biblical view in today's culture.

But first, a caveat. This book is not implying, as a conspiracy theorist manifesto might, that any particular agency is engineering a "hard totalitarian" global takeover. This book will document how today's social conditions, however they may have arisen, contribute to creating a society that's easy to manipulate, monitor, and control in ways that social commentator Rod Dreher would call "soft totalitarianism."[1] Let's look closer at what totalitarianism is, what its "hard" and "soft" varieties entail, and how it's infiltrating our society.

A WAR OF WORLDVIEWS

At its core, totalitarianism is a system of governance that results when **someone** or **something** tries to take God's place as the authority for truth. As Rod Dreher aptly defined it, "A totalitarian state is one that aspires to nothing less than defining and controlling reality."[2]

Dreher explains that this quest for total power sets **totalitarianism** apart from **authoritarianism**. Authoritarianism is a dictatorship that controls political and civil life. But

totalitarianism goes further as an attempt to control **everything**—not just people's behavior but also their thoughts, emotions, and objective truth itself.

How do totalitarian regimes set about this task? Here's where the **hard** and **soft** versions come in. Dreher differentiates hard totalitarianism, embodied in the Soviet Union with its gunmen and gulags, from a kinder-spoken—but no less nefarious—variety. While hard totalitarianism attempts to seize and sustain control via brute force, soft totalitarianism wields a subtler strategy.

WHILE HARD TOTALITARIANISM ATTEMPTS TO SEIZE AND SUSTAIN CONTROL VIA BRUTE FORCE, SOFT TOTALITARIANISM WIELDS A SUBTLER STRATEGY.

Like a scammer smooth-talking a group of victims into handing over everything they own, soft totalitarianism charms its way past society's defenses. It rebrands words like **justice**, **equity**, **liberation**, and **tolerance** to summon support and silence argument. It paints pictures of frightful scenarios and assures us only one solution exists: to do everything we're told, without question. It promises safety, comfort, and convenience for the small price of privacy, freedom, and personal convictions. And no less than its ironfisted counterpart, soft totalitarianism seeks to coronate humans in God's place as the authority for truth.

What are some of the ways we're witnessing soft totalitarianism sweep through Western cultures? We can begin to see the answer by thinking about two aspects of totalitarian control: the top-down control of "social credit" systems and the bottom-up control of "cancel culture." Let's zoom in on both of these aspects, focusing especially on social credit systems and their rising influence in the West.

HOW SOCIAL CREDIT SYSTEMS WORK

To illustrate what social credit systems entail, let me invite you back a few years to a conversation I experienced while visiting a communist country in Asia. Having recently graduated from a secular university, I was backpacking 360° around the world in 180 days interviewing other Christian students about how they kept their faith during non-Christian higher education.[3] God had opened the door for me to visit believers in this communist nation—on two conditions. First, I couldn't name the country online. And second, I needed to stay at a hotel to avoid drawing attention to local Christians.

Why the secrecy? Because this country welcomes the gospel like swimming pools welcome sharks. Totalitarian systems cannot tolerate citizens holding to a truth authority **above** the regime. So Christians who follow God's Word **over** communist nations' mandates often find themselves labeled "enemies of the state." And the believers in the nation I visited were no exception.

> **THIS COUNTRY WELCOMES THE GOSPEL LIKE SWIMMING POOLS WELCOME SHARKS.**

Local students had already told me how Christians faced significant social pressures and couldn't work government jobs. But hostility against believers didn't stop these students from evangelizing at their local campus, where I now met with a Christian physics student across a cafeteria table.

> "It's quite dangerous to share your faith in the school," he said. "The law is that you can **maintain** your faith, but you cannot **share** your religion or

invite people to it. If you do, and the teacher knows about it, you will get in trouble."

"What would happen?" I asked.

"They would call you to their office and tell you that Christians are not good and that Christians will take your brain." Here, the physics student waved one hand in the air as if writing a signature. "Then the school will make you sign a promise that you will stop sharing your faith."

Every student, he explained, has a "behavior score." Ways to lose points from this score include missing class, littering on campus, and sharing your faith after being warned to stop.

"If you lose all your points, then what?" I asked.

"You have no right to continue studying in the university."

"So you might have to stop studying if you keep sharing the gospel?"

"Yes, if the teacher knows."

This student's story about "behavior scores" shows how social credit systems work. An authoritative agency—whether a state, an organization, or in this case, a school—allocates social credit "points" to its members based on their behavior. Members gain (or at least **keep**) privileges for "good" behavior and lose privileges for "bad" behavior.

Social credit systems help totalitarian regimes achieve their goals of control on at least two levels. First, assuming the ability to define what's "good" or "bad" in such a micromanaged, easily enforceable way gives a regime the instant appearance of having power over moral truth. Second, this illusion of power lets the regime turn freedoms into privileges. The natural human desire to keep those "privileges," and the fear of losing them, become formidable instruments of persuasion—and therefore control—in the regime's hands.

PEOPLE LIVING UNDER COMMUNISM TODAY MAY LOSE POINTS FOR BEHAVIORS LIKE SLOPPY DRIVING.

We can see such systems operating on the largest, most obvious scales in "hard totalitarian" nations. For instance, *Business Insider* reported that people living under communism today may lose points for behaviors like sloppy driving, playing video games for too long, or sharing "fake news" online.[4] A low social credit score can bar a person from travel, higher education, and well-paying employment. On the flip side, "good citizens" can easily access these assets and gain rewards ranging from discounted utility bills to boosted online dating profiles. And always, people live aware that their actions are being surveilled and recorded, with imminent consequences for not conforming to the authorities' definition of "good."

But these systems only operate in openly communist countries.

Right?

Not necessarily.

THE GROWING PUSH FOR SOCIAL CREDIT

To glimpse the rise of social credit systems' influence in the West, check out the report called *Capital and Debt Today*, which has quietly inhabited the Government of Canada's website since around 2017.[5] A red flag signaling the report's controversial contents appears in the opening disclaimer: "This document does not represent an official policy position of the Government of Canada."[6] Instead, the disclaimer continues, the report resulted from a group of public servants the government invited to "explore policy issues relating to diversity and inclusion" as part of a program designed to "drive a culture change within the public service."[7]

What did the report say? A figure in the document summarizes, "Linkages between ownership and social status are becoming unstable. Ownership could be displaced or augmented by access to service. Social credit may become a more powerful determinent *[sic]* of socio-economic inclusion."[8] In other words, instead of **owning** things, people would **access** items and services based on having social credit. This system is, by definition, a sort of communism. And a Western nation—my homeland—is pushing for it.

> **INSTEAD OF OWNING THINGS, PEOPLE WOULD ACCESS ITEMS AND SERVICES.**

But this push is by no means limited to Canada. For years, major global attention has focused on advancing a "sharing economy," which some commentators suggest "could bring about the end of capitalism."[9] The sharing economy, which centers on "the sharing of underutilized assets" like cars or cottages, overlaps significantly with an access economy model.[10] In fact, a 2015 article for *Harvard Business Review* states, "The sharing economy isn't really a 'sharing' economy at all; it's an access economy."[11]

WEF = THE WORLD ECONOMIC FORUM

To glimpse the size of force behind the push for this economy, we can look at the World Economic Forum (WEF). What exactly is the WEF? According to the Forum's website, "The World Economic Forum is the International Organization for Public-Private Cooperation. The Forum engages the foremost political, business, cultural and other leaders of society to shape global, regional and industry agendas."[12] The WEF is a global organization bent on shaping not only global agendas but also the young people who will be global leaders. In fact, the WEF runs a Young Global Leaders program, with alumni ranging from heads of nations to social media CEOs.[13] To call the WEF a big deal would be like saying the ocean seems a little damp.

So what does the WEF have to do with the access economy? Apparently quite a bit. Back in 2012, for instance, the WEF launched a group called the Young Global Leaders Sharing Economy Dialog.[14] This group consisted of high-profile members "committed to advancing the discussion and practice of the sharing economy around the world."[15] A report from 2013 stated that the group was "positioning the sharing economy at the centre of the global agenda."[16] Tellingly, the report concluded that the group's work "offers keen insight into 'access over

SO WHAT DOES THE WEF HAVE TO DO WITH THE ACCESS ECONOMY?

ownership' and the reinvention of traditional market behaviours—such as renting, lending and swapping—through technology."[17]

There's more. In 2016, the WEF and the China Council for International Cooperation on Environment and Development "brought together business leaders . . . academics and government officials from China and around the world to discuss the technology that is driving the transition towards the sharing economy and the effect this is likely to have on society."[18] The WEF's report from this meeting declared,

> China has an opportunity to lead the way in making well-informed policy decisions that provide the right regulatory framework for the sharing economy. Moreover, there is a secondary set of opportunities. The digital platforms on which the sharing economy is based produces huge amounts of data which can help governments in various ways, from environmental monitoring to improved urban planning.[19]

Interesting, eh? We already saw what *Business Insider* reported about China's social credit system driven by digital surveillance within an access economy. So the fact that the WEF endorses China leading the way in developing data-driven sharing economies is striking, to say the least.

Political concerns aside, aspects of a sharing economy based in social credit systems might not sound like such a bad idea at first glance. But a key problem lies in the question "Who determines what being a 'good citizen' means?" In secular countries like Canada, it's not a stretch to suspect that being "good" would require conforming to "policy issues relating to diversity and inclusion" in ways that violate God's Word. We already see this outcome unfolding in another type of social credit system that assigns behavior points not to individuals but to organizations. In this case, the behavior points bear a more impressive title: ESG scores.

ESG SCORES

ESG stands for Environmental, Social, and Governance criteria. So ESG scores measure whether companies exhibit "good behavior" in terms of these criteria.[20] However, the standard for defining "good" is not God's Word but human opinion, with "good" meaning anything from "combatting climate change"[21] to "promoting diversity and inclusion."

ESG = ENVIRONMENTAL, SOCIAL, AND GOVERNANCE

These man-made ideas about what counts as "good" not only may run contrary to God's Word but can also promote Marxist-informed thinking. For example, companies may be able to boost their ESG scores by hiring a more "diverse" staff. But in this context, the concept of diversity rests not on the biblical teaching that all humans are made in God's image but in Marxist ideas that divide society into oppressed and oppressor identity groups.[22] The more oppressed identities a company includes (say, women or LGTBQ individuals), the better the company's diversity metrics for ESG scoring purposes.

As investors and financial organizations increasingly base their decisions on ESG scores, companies face rising pressure to maintain high ESG "social credit." By spring of

2023, over 5,000 investors (representing $121 trillion USD) had pledged to factor ESG into their decisions.[23] To confirm this pledge, these investors signed a set of United Nations-backed statements known as the Principles for Responsible Investment.[24] A recent article in the journal *Financial Management* concluded ESG is here to stay, adding,

> Now is the peak of ESG. It's front and center in the minds of executives, investors, regulators, business students, and even the public. Major corporations are appointing Chief Sustainability Officers to the C-suite, justifying strategic decisions based on their ESG impact, and tying executive pay to ESG metrics.[25]

The problem is that ESG metrics pressure organizations to align with man-made, changeable definitions of "good" that can go against God's Word. Effectively, whoever can influence these metrics holds the power not only to define "good" but also to enforce that definition in ways that impact the economy.

We can see a related set of consequences unfolding **within** organizations as well, illustrated by another document the WEF published. Its title? The "Diversity, Equity, and Inclusion 4.0"[26] tool kit. Before examining this tool kit, it's worth taking a step back to better understand the agendas of the WEF.

THE WORLD ECONOMIC FORUM: GLOBAL AGENDAS

Importantly, messages from the World Economic Forum's leaders reveal several ways the WEF strives to shape global agendas in directions running contrary to God's Word. For instance, the WEF's website features scores of articles championing "diversity, equity, and inclusion" defined in ways that require celebrating unbiblical views of gender, identity, and marriage. One such article published by the WEF concluded:

> The global LGBTQ+ community is up against well-organized and well-funded campaigns by the enemies of equality—an unholy axis of religious fundamentalist groups and populist conservative politicians. The stakes are high and business has a unique role to play. This is about more than Pride flags and rainbow logos. It's about what it means to run a good business.[27]

Just like the communist country I visited labels Christians "enemies of the state," this quote reveals a similar situation unfolding in nations that treat "equality" as the state religion. The quote also illustrates how culture paints "religious fundamentalists" ("biblical Christians") as **oppressors** and groups like the LGTBQ community as **oppressed**—consistent with a Marxist worldview, which sees society in terms of opposing identity groups. Finally, this quote shows how easily humans can redefine "good." Under the new definitions, "running a good business" or "being a good citizen" becomes adhering to man-made definitions of morality above God's Word.

This push for diversity and inclusion isn't the only way the WEF and its members embrace an unbiblical worldview. Beginning from an evolutionary view that **people created God**, WEF conference speaker Professor Yuval Harari argues that "the new human agenda" involves applying technology to become "like God."[28] WEF founder Klaus Schwab has argued that we must use technology to "catalyse a new cultural renaissance" that will let us feel part of "a true global civilization."[29] This renaissance, according to Schwab, will "lift humanity into a new collective and moral consciousness based on a shared sense of destiny."[30] Although vaguely phrased, these buzzwords translate to calling for a cultural revolution toward a more collectivistic, globalist system.[31]

THESE BUZZWORDS TRANSLATE TO CALLING FOR A CULTURAL REVOLUTION TOWARD A MORE COLLECTIVISTIC, GLOBALIST SYSTEM.

Highlighting the potential nature of this system, the WEF created shockwaves by releasing a video predicting that by 2030 "you will own nothing. And you will be happy."[32] To own nothing and be "happy" would presumably require a social credit-based "access economy" similar to the one described in the Canadian Capital and Debt report.

Notably, the WEF already promotes the social crediting of organizations via ESG scores.[33] One of the WEF's Board of Trustee members, Laurence Fink, is also the CEO of BlackRock—the investment firm that manages more wealth than any other and is a leading force promoting ESG investing.[34] But the WEF helps promote a version of social credit systems **within** organizations too. That's where the diversity and inclusion tool kit published by the WEF comes in.

DIVERSITY, INCLUSION, AND TOTALITARIANISM

This tool comprises a series of recommendations in a WEF-sponsored document, "Diversity, Equity and Inclusion 4.0: A Toolkit for Leaders to Accelerate Social Progress in the Future of Work."[35] Right from its preface, the document stated, “Ensuring racial justice, gender parity, disability inclusion, LGBTI equality and inclusion of all forms of human diversity needs to be the ‘new normal’ in the workplace set to emerge from the COVID-19 crisis.”[36] Ingraining this new normal, according to the document, “requires an organization-wide effort from the most senior leaders of the organization . . . as well as by all managers of personnel and by all employees.”[37] The document continues,

> A systemic transformation that creates a diverse, equitable and inclusive company spans the breadth of the company itself—its brand, its working culture, organizational processes, recruitment, reward and performance management as well as inclusive and accessible working facilities. If managed well, such an approach can be supported greatly by the appropriate use of relevant new technology tools.[38]

Ensuring that *all* personnel and *all* activities across the *entire* organization conform to the assigned redefinitions of morality echoes a totalitarian mentality. But in this case, the mentality exists within a business instead of a state. In both cases, enforcing this mentality requires a system which combines heightened surveillance with social credit—a system new technologies make increasingly possible.

For instance, the tool kit advocates for technologically measuring “behaviours which create exclusion.”[39] The document stated, “Machine Learning and Natural Language Processing technologies provide anonymized analysis of employee interaction or communication channels . . . and can evaluate biases and exclusionary behaviour.”[40] Despite the reference to keeping these analyses anonymous, the document suggested that using AI to analyze employees' behavior and dispositions can provide "insight into target areas for further diversity, equity and inclusion training" and supply "input for further coaching and development."[41] The document also recommended that organizations "train and incentivize managers and employees to enhance inclusion and belonging in their daily interactions."[42]

USING AI TO ANALYZE EMPLOYEES' BEHAVIOR AND DISPOSITIONS

So this tool kit published by the WEF encourages organizations to incentivize conformity to inclusion policies (being "good") and to technologically monitor those who need "further training." The WEF, notably, is also taking the initiative to help *facilitate the regulation* of these new technologies on a global level.[43]

Such technologies—and society's increasing dependence on them—enable unprecedented surveillance capabilities.[44] Armed with these new technological powers, organizations and governments would have little problem determining individuals' social credit scores for top-down control.

CANCEL CULTURE

But control in totalitarian systems can also work from the bottom up. When a society buys into totalitarianism, its everyday citizens play a role in keeping the system running. They do so by censoring, reporting, or otherwise punishing their peers who fail to conform with the going definition of "being good." Enter cancel culture.

Though virtually unheard of only a few years ago, the term "cancel culture" has become quite the catchphrase. This term describes how society suppresses, shuns, and silences those who disqualify as "good citizens." Here, a social media franchise deplatforms a celebrity for a post expressing a personal view that contradicts the vogue idea of "truth." There, an organization fires employees who refuse to conform with unbiblical diversity and inclusion policies. And everywhere, Christians begin to lower their voices for fear of being "canceled."

Rod Dreher quotes a professor who, having emigrated to America from the former Soviet Union, has noticed present-day Americans lowering their voices this way, glancing around for eavesdroppers, when expressing conservative opinions. "I grew up like this," the professor told Dreher, "but it was not supposed to be happening here."[45]

SIGNS OF A STORM

Ultimately, whether through bottom-up cancel culture, top-down social credit systems, or other control strategies we'll explore in future chapters, a form of totalitarianism is happening in the West. Like the Marxist protest banners I saw outside Berlin University, or like gathering thunderclouds signaling severe weather, the signs of totalitarianism's impending resurgence are everywhere. Christian commentators have been remarking for years on the gathering storm, and the sky doesn't show signs of clearing any time soon. Still, these events do not have to catch Christians off guard. Scripture tells us,

> But understand this, that in the last days there will come times of difficulty. . . . Indeed, all who desire to live a godly life in Christ Jesus will be persecuted, while evil people and impostors will go on from bad to worse, deceiving and being deceived. But as for you, continue in what you have learned and have firmly believed, knowing from whom you learned it

> and how from childhood you have been acquainted with the sacred writings, which are able to make you wise for salvation through faith in Christ Jesus. (2 Timothy 3:1, 12–15)

Little decisions we start making now can go a long way in preparing us to be faithful believers who "continue in what [we] have learned and have firmly believed," standing on the truth of God's Word with zero compromise. And taking that stance requires understanding, internalizing, and committing to the authority of God's Word. Then when storms hit close to home, our lives will already be grounded on the rock-solid foundation of our Creator's Word (Matthew 7:24–25). We must trust the one who promised, "My counsel shall stand, and I will accomplish all my purpose" (Isaiah 46:10).

What *does* this foundation of Scripture say, and how does a biblical view differ from the secular Marxist one pervading society? That's what we'll investigate next.

ENDNOTES

1. Rod Dreher, *Live Not by Lies: A Manual for Christian Dissidents* (New York: Sentinel, 2020), 7–8 (ebook version).

2. Dreher, *Live Not by Lies*, 7 (ebook version).

3. Dreher, *Live Not by Lies*, 7–8 (ebook version).

4. The key takeaways from this research are available in my book *Prepare to Thrive: A Survival Guide for Christian Students* (Answers in Genesis, 2022).

5. Katie Canales and Aaron Mok, "China's 'Social Credit' System Ranks Citizens and Punishes Them with Throttled Internet Speeds and Flight Bans if the Communist Party Deems Them Untrustworthy," *Business Insider*, last updated November 28, 2022, businessinsider.com/china-social-credit-system-punishments-and-rewards-explained-2018-4?op=1.

6. Gacia Assadourian et al., *Capital and Debt* (Ottawa: Canada Beyond 150, 2018). Accessed May 2024 from Government of Canada, "Capital and Debt: Final Report," catalogue number CP22-167/1-2018E-PDF, publications.gc.ca/site/eng/9.860847/publication.html. Formerly available (accessed August 2023) at canadabeyond150.ca/reports/capital-and-debt.html.

7. Assadourian et al., *Capital and Debt*, 1.

8. The full disclaimer states, "This document does not represent an official policy position of the Government of Canada. Instead, it records the work of a sub-group of new public servants who participated in Canada Beyond 150, a professional development program co-championed by the Privy Council Office and Policy Horizons Canada. The program was designed to support the development of new public servants, and to drive a culture change within the public service. The participants were invited to use foresight, design thinking and engagement tools to explore policy issues relating to diversity and inclusion." Assadourian et al., *Capital and Debt*, 1.

9. Assadourian et al., *Capital and Debt*, 4.

10. Chris Martin, "The Sharing Economy Could End Capitalism—But That's Not All," *The Conversation*, July 29, 2015, theconversation.com/the-sharing-economy-could-end-capitalism-but-thats-not-all-45203.

11. April Rinne states that the access economy "overlaps with" the sharing economy but that "sharing is by no means requisite" to access economies. In other words, not all access economies are necessarily sharing economies. (See April Rinne, "What Exactly is the Sharing Economy?" Economic Growth, World Economic Forum, December 13, 2017, weforum.org/agenda/2017/12/when-is-sharing-not-really-sharing/.) However, Giana Eckhardt and Fleura Bardhi suggest that the sharing economy is by nature an access economy (see reference #13 below).

12. Giana Eckhardt and Fleura Bardhi, "The Sharing Economy Isn't About Sharing at All," Economics, *Harvard Business Review*, January 28, 2015, hbr.org/2015/01/the-sharing-economy-isnt-about-sharing-at-all.

13. Giana Eckhardt and Fleura Bardhi, "The Sharing Economy Isn't About Sharing at All," Economics, *Harvard Business Review*, January 28, 2015, hbr.org/2015/01/the-sharing-economy-isnt-about-sharing-at-all.

14. Giana Eckhardt and Fleura Bardhi, "The Sharing Economy Isn't About Sharing at All," Economics, *Harvard Business Review*, January 28, 2015, hbr.org/2015/01/the-sharing-economy-isnt-about-sharing-at-all.

15. The Forum of Young Global Leaders, "Young Global Leaders Circular Economy Innovation & New Business Models Dialogue," World Economic Forum, 2013, www3.weforum.org/docs/WEF_YGL_CircularEconomyInnovation_PositionPaper_2013.pdf.

16. Forum of Young Global Leaders, "Young Global Leaders Circular Economy."

17. Forum of Young Global Leaders, "Young Global Leaders Circular Economy."

18. Forum of Young Global Leaders, "Young Global Leaders Circular Economy."

19. World Economic Forum, "Understanding the Sharing Economy," December 2016, www3.weforum.org/docs/WEF_Understanding_the_Sharing_Economy_report_2016.pdf.

20. World Economic Forum, "Understanding the Sharing Economy," 9.

21. Mark Bergman et al., "Introduction to ESG," Harvard Law School Forum on Corporate Governance, August 1, 2020, corpgov.law.harvard.edu/2020/08/01/introduction-to-esg.

22. For information on the problems with many secular interpretations of climate issues, see the resources available at AnswersInGenesis.org/environmental-science/climate-change.

23. Maddie Wollerton Blanks and Rashada Whitehead, "Measuring Diversity and Inclusion: Part of the 'G' in ESG," Diversity and Inclusion, GrantThorton, July 6, 2022, grantthornton.global/en/insights/articles/measuring-diversity-and-inclusion-part-of-the-g-in-esg; Bergman et al., "Introduction to ESG"; George Serafeim, "Social-Impact Efforts That Create Real Value," Sustainable Business Practices, *Harvard Business Review*, September–October 2022, hbr.org/2020/09/social-impact-efforts-that-create-real-value; Robin Pomeroy, "ESG—How Can We Measure How 'Good' Companies Are?" Stakeholder Capitalism, World Economic Forum, April 25, 2022, weforum.org/agenda/2022/04/esg-metrics-radio-davos.

24. Principles for Responsible Investment, *Signatory Update*: October–December 2023, accessed May 7, 2024, www.unpri.org/download?ac=20150.

25. Atkin, "Quarterly Signatory Update."

26. Alex Edmans, "The End of ESG," *Financial Management* 52, no. 1 (2023): 3–17, doi.org/10.1111/fima.12413.

27. World Economic Forum, "Diversity, Equity and Inclusion 4.0: A Toolkit for Leaders to Accelerate Social Progress in the Future of Work," June 2020, www3.weforum.org/docs/WEF_NES_DEI4.0_Toolkit_2020.pdf. The tool kit contains a disclaimer that the contents are not necessarily official views of the WEF, but the WEF facilitated its development and published it.

28. Dominic Arnall, "Has Business Reached 'Peak Pride'?" World Economic Forum, June 23, 2023, weforum.org/agenda/2023/06/has-business-reached-peak-pride.

29. He wrote, "So we may well think of the new human agenda as consisting really of only one project (with many branches): attaining divinity." (N. Yuval Harari, *Homo Deus: A Brief History of Tomorrow* [London: Random House, 2016; originally published in Hebrew by Divir, 2015], 46.)

30. Klaus Schwab, *The Fourth Industrial Revolution* (Geneva: World Economic Forum, 2016), 114.

31. Schwab, *The Fourth Industrial Revolution*, 114.

32. The WEF has expressed interest in developing a global digital currency system, stating in a news release, "Creating an inclusive, integrated global digital currency

system requires dialogue across stakeholders ranging from finance ministers to open source developers, and the World Economic Forum is in an ideal position to facilitate this important conversation." (Amanda Russo and Aylin Elci, "Governing the Coin: World Economic Forum Announces Global Consortium for Digital Currency Governance," World Economic Forum, January 2020, weforum.org/press/2020/01/governing-the-coin-world-economic-forum-announces-global-consortium-for-digital-currency-governance.)

33. World Economic Forum (@wef), "8 Predictions for the World in 2030," Twitter, April 9, 2018, twitter.com/wef/status/983378870819794945.

34. E.g., see Naïm Abou-Jaoudé, "Here's Why We Must Not Lose Sight of the Importance of ESG, Despite the Recent Backlash," January 3, 2023, weforum.org/agenda/2023/01/the-importance-of-esg-sustainable-future-davos-2023.

35. World Economic Forum, "Leadership and Governance," About Us, World Economic Forum, accessed May 3, 2024, weforum.org/about/leadership-and-governance; Matthew Goldstein and Maureen Farrell, "BlackRock's Pitch for Socially Conscious Investing Antagonizes All Sides," *The New York Times*, December 23, 2022, nytimes.com/2022/12/23/business/blackrock-esg-investing.html.

36. World Economic Forum, "Diversity, Equity and Inclusion 4.0."

37. World Economic Forum, "Diversity, Equity and Inclusion 4.0," 2.

38. World Economic Forum, "Diversity, Equity and Inclusion 4.0," 7.

39. World Economic Forum, "Diversity, Equity and Inclusion 4.0," 7 [reference to a figure in the document removed].

40. World Economic Forum, "Diversity, Equity and Inclusion 4.0," 9, 12.

41. World Economic Forum, "Diversity, Equity and Inclusion 4.0," 12.

42. World Economic Forum, "Diversity, Equity and Inclusion 4.0," 12.

43. World Economic Forum, "Diversity, Equity and Inclusion 4.0," 9.

44. E.g., see World Economic Forum, "Global Technology Governance: A Multistakeholder Approach," World Economic Forum in collaboration with Thunderbird School of Global Management and Arizona State University, October 2019, www3.weforum.org/docs/WEF_Global_Technology_Governance.pdf.

45. See also Rod Dreher, "Capitalism, Woke and Watchful," in *Live Not by Lies* (New York: Penguin Publishing Group, 2022), 69–94.

46. Dreher, *Live Not by Lies*, xiii (ebook version).

COLOSSIANS 2:8

SEE TO IT THAT NO ONE TAKES YOU CAPTIVE BY PHILOSOPHY AND EMPTY DECEIT, ACCORDING TO HUMAN TRADITION, ACCORDING TO THE ELEMENTAL SPIRITS OF THE WORLD, AND NOT ACCORDING TO CHRIST.

CHAPTER 2

NEW BATTLES, OLD WAR

GOD'S WORD VERSUS MARXISM

Can you guess which author penned the following words?

> Our heart, reason, intelligence, [and] history all summon us with loud and convincing voice to the knowledge that union with [Christ] is absolutely necessary, that without Him we would be unable to fulfill our purpose, that without Him we would be rejected by God, and that only He can redeem us.[1]

A. CHARLES SPURGEON

B. CHARLES DARWIN

C. WILLIAM WILBERFORCE

D. ALDOUS HUXLEY

E. KARL MARX

As you might have suspected, the answer would surprise many people. These words came from an essay which a certain teenager wrote shortly before leaving home for a secular university.[2] Descended from Jewish rabbis, raised in a nominally Christian household, and baptized a Protestant, this teenager had displayed a "fairly clear and well grounded" knowledge of Christianity.[3] But over the course of his university studies, he was taken "captive by philosophy and empty deceit, according to human tradition . . . and not according to Christ" (Colossians 2:8).

By the time he graduated, this student had thoroughly rejected belief in God. Instead, he eventually devised a worldview of his own founded on atheism. His writings sowed ideas that would lead millions of people to their death over the following centuries. That's right—the teenager who once knew that **only Jesus can redeem humanity** was none other than Karl Marx.[4]

KARL MARX WAS A GERMAN PHILOSOPHER WHO LIVED FROM 1818–1883.

Karl Marx, a German philosopher who lived from 1818–1883, isn't the first person to fall for lies that lead to death. Across history, humans have bought into the same destructive deceptions. Four of these lies, which began in the garden of Eden, recur throughout countless false teachings. New teachings based on old lies represent new battles in an old war—the ancient, futile conflict of man's word against God's Word.

Today's Marxist messages are no exception. To see how this is the case, let's look at how Marxism compares to God's Word. We'll find that God's Word alone offers the answer to humanity's problems, which Marxism fails to solve. We'll also discover that Marxism represents a false gospel grounded in lies as old as Eden.

Just what **are** these lies?

As with so many questions, the answer begins in Genesis.

FOUR ANCIENT LIES

Genesis records that when God created Adam and Eve, he gave them one boundary: "You may surely eat of every tree of the garden, but of the tree of the knowledge of good and evil you shall not eat, for in the day that you eat of it you shall surely die" (Genesis 2:16–17). But then the whisper of a fourfold lie slithered off a serpent's tongue.

The deception began with the serpent's opening words to Eve: "Did God actually say, 'You shall not eat of any tree in the garden'?" (Genesis 3:1). This question implied that God's Word is not completely true, which is the first of four hallmark lies in false teachings throughout history.

LIE #1 GOD'S WORD IS NOT COMPLETELY TRUE.

LIE #2 TRUTH IS ULTIMATELY UP TO HUMANS.

LIE #3 YOU CAN BE "LIKE GOD."

LIE #4 JESUS IS LESS THAN SCRIPTURE SAYS HE IS.[5]

When we think about it, the last three lies follow from Lie #1. If God's Word is not completely true (Lie #1), then humans must be the final authority for deciding what is true (Lie #2). The messages we're judging as true or false might have come from human ideas, from human interpretations of science, from nonhuman entities, or even from artificial intelligence (AI). Either way, we buy into Lie #2 when we make ourselves the ultimate standard for truth instead of God's Word.

The third lie comes into play because if humans can take God's place as the authority for truth (Lie #2), then we can be "like God" (Lie #3). The serpent's following words to Eve fit this pattern perfectly: "You will not surely die. For God knows that when you eat of it your eyes will be opened, and you will be like God, knowing good and evil" (Genesis 3:4–5).

And what about Lie #4? Scripture reveals the truth about who Jesus is right from its earliest books, as Jesus himself taught.[6] If God's Word is not completely true (Lie #1), then Scripture's teachings about Jesus are not necessarily reliable. In that case, Jesus might be less than Scripture attests (Lie #4).

THESE LIES HAVE SURFACED IN COUNTLESS FALSE BELIEF SYSTEMS ACROSS CULTURES, SPACE, AND HISTORY.

Together, these lies have surfaced in countless false belief systems across cultures, space, and history. Their shapes can shift, and their styles change. But at the core, they are the same ancient deception first sold to humanity in Eden. And ever since Eden, the lies we humans cling to, believing that they will buy our divinity, serve only to destroy us. Humans cannot win a war against God. We can only defeat ourselves. But that doesn't seem to stop us from trying.

Marxism reflects one of these destructive attempts to set human thinking above God's Word. To see how, we'll need to unpack some major differences between a biblical world-view and a Marxist worldview. First, a quick refresher on the concept of worldview is in order.

A WAR OF WORLDVIEWS

Like a pair of glasses through which we interpret reality, a worldview is the set of big-picture beliefs we use to explain the world around us. These beliefs shape how we answer major questions.

- How did the universe originate?
- How can we know right from wrong?
- What does it mean to be human?
- What happens when we die?

Our answers to these and similar questions help shape our everyday decisions, behaviors, and interactions. For example, whether we view all humans as God's image bearers will inform how we treat others—if we're living consistently with our worldviews.

Three quick points about worldviews are worth remembering.

1. ALL WORLDVIEWS START WITH FAITH IN SOMETHING

Worldviews begin with presuppositions—statements we can't necessarily prove are true but must assume are true as starting points for our thinking. A biblical worldview starts with the presupposition that God exists and has revealed himself through Scripture. God's Word, right from its first verse, is the authority for truth. But all other worldviews, in one way or another, assume that human thinking, experience, and perception—man's word—is the authority.

2. THERE ARE ONLY TWO WORLDVIEWS

Because our highest authority can be either God's Word or human reasoning, we can interpret reality through

THE 7 C'S OF HISTORY

1. CREATION Genesis reveals that God made the universe in six days—the kind of day with an evening and morning (Genesis 1:1–31; Exodus 20:11). On the sixth day, God created Adam and Eve in his image. God made them male and female, established the institution of marriage between a man and a wife (Genesis 1:27, 2:24; Matthew 19:4–6), and gave humans dominion over the earth (Genesis 1:26–27). Having completed creation, God saw everything he had made as "very good" (Genesis 1:31).

2. CORRUPTION Sadly, creation didn't stay "very good" because Adam and Eve rebelled against God in the first act of human sin (Genesis 3:6–19). Sin severs humans from their Life-Giver, resulting in spiritual and physical death (Genesis 2:17; Romans 6:23). Because Adam and Eve were the first human parents and had been given charge over the earth, sin's corruption affected not only Adam and Eve but also all humanity and all physical creation (Romans 5:12, 8:19–21).

3. CATASTROPHE When our sin-filled planet grew unbearably corrupt, God reset the world with a global flood (Genesis 6:5–13). But he graciously provided instructions for Noah, his family, and representatives from every kind of air-breathing land animal to survive in the ark (Genesis 6:14–21). After the flood, God promised, "While the earth remains, seedtime and harvest, cold and heat, summer and winter, day and night, shall not cease" (Genesis 8:22).

4. CONFUSION God commissioned Noah's family to "multiply and fill the earth" (Genesis 9:1). But Noah's descendants instead settled down to build a tower toward heaven and make a name for themselves (Genesis 11:2–4). When God thwarted that scheme by giving humanity different languages, humans dispersed and became different people groups (Genesis 11:7–9). But Scripture does not teach that different human races exist because God made "from one blood every nation of men" (Acts 17:26, NKJV).

5-6. CHRIST AND THE CROSS Graciously, God did not leave humans without hope. Jesus, the Son of God, came to earth in human flesh (John 1:1–18). As fully God, fully man, and fully sinless, Jesus alone could pay sin's spiritual and physical death penalty on behalf of Adam's descendants who put their faith in him (Hebrews 10:4–23). Dying on the cross and rising again, Jesus became the only way to eternal life for whoever believes in him (1 Corinthians 15:1–49; Acts 4:12, 18:28–39).

7. CONSUMMATION Having defeated the power of sin and death, Jesus will abolish death forever when he creates a new heaven and earth (Revelation 21:1–4). Those who trusted in Christ's saving work on their behalf will live eternally in God's renewed creation, while those who did not will be forever separated from the God who died to offer life (John 3:36; Revelation 21:5–8).

only one of two kinds of worldview glasses: God's Word or man's word. No neutral ground exists between them, for as Jesus said in Matthew 12:30, "Whoever is not with me is against me." So the question isn't about whether a person **has** faith but about what that faith rests in: fallible human thinking or our infallible Creator's Word.[7]

3. WE ALL HAVE THE SAME EVIDENCE

No matter which pair of glasses we look through, we all view the same real world. We see the same humans, same cities, and same fossil layers. We observe the same facts in the present. But we interpret these facts differently based on our lenses: God's Word or man's word.

With these basics in mind, we can look at a biblical worldview to compare its sound doctrine with Marxism, the way examining real currency helps us recognize counterfeit bills.

A BIBLICAL WORLDVIEW

Building the deep familiarity with God's Word that we need in order to spot false teaching is a lifelong exercise. For now, we can glimpse a "thousand-foot overview" of Scripture by using a framework Answers in Genesis calls the 7 C's of History. (Even if these 7 C's are for review, they're great to remember when sharing the whole message of the gospel with others.)

Together, these 7 C's outline the big picture of a biblical worldview, which serves as the foundation for Christian thinking, living, and decision-making. The 7 C's cover topics that also show how all the major doctrines in Scripture—the value of human life, the meaning of marriage, the origin of death and suffering, and the reason we need Jesus as Savior—tie back to Genesis 1–11.[8]

That's why an uncompromised commitment to the authority of God's Word from these first chapters onward is so vital. Without this commitment, we won't have a consistent biblical foundation from which to answer issues that arise when society bases its thinking on faulty worldviews. One of these worldviews is Marxism, which teaches a very different history—with very different practical implications—from God's Word.

THESE 7 C'S OUTLINE THE BIG PICTURE OF A BIBLICAL WORLDVIEW, WHICH SERVES AS THE FOUNDATION FOR CHRISTIAN THINKING.

So what are the basics of a Marxist worldview?

THE "GOSPEL" ACCORDING TO MARX

As we glimpsed a little earlier, Karl Marx rejected God's Word as the foundation for his thinking and developed his own religion instead.[9] Pinning down the details of Marx's beliefs is hardly straightforward. Different writers interpret him in different ways, certain elements of his thinking and terminology shifted throughout his life, and his works were "incomplete and inconsistent."[10]

Entire careers have been devoted to debating the nuances of Marx's statements. This chapter will by no means offer an exhaustive discussion but rather an introduction to a few core basics of Marx's worldview.[11] For starters, here's a sample of Marx's thinking about some key worldview questions.

Q: DOES GOD EXIST?

A: "NO."

Marx became a vocal atheist at university, with atheism providing the basis for Marx's later thinking.[12] Peter Schuller, philosophy professor emeritus for Miami University, argued that "Marx's atheism is an essential premise of his whole theory."[13] Some other scholars suggest that Marx's approach to atheism eventually became more nuanced but still without a return to belief in God.[14]

Q: WHERE DID HUMANS COME FROM?

A: "NATURAL PROCESSES."

Marx developed the basics of his philosophy before Charles Darwin released the book *On the Origin of Species*. In this book, Darwin popularized the idea that all living things evolved from lower life-forms.[15] When Darwin's book arrived, Marx latched onto evolutionary ideas as supposedly scientific justification for his thinking.[16] But Marx had already rejected God as humanity's Creator long before.

Q: WHAT DOES IT MEAN TO BE HUMAN?

A: "TO BE ACTIVE CREATORS OF OUR WORLD AND OURSELVES."

Marx believed humans are creators who constantly shape nature according to our own needs, dreams, and desires.[17] When we are free to do so in harmony with others, thought Marx, we most fully express our humanity.[18] He believed that as we shape our world and societies, our world and societies shape **us**[19] to the point that by creating our world, we create ourselves.[20]

Q: WHAT IS THE MAIN THEME OF HISTORY?

A: "CONFLICT BETWEEN OPPRESSOR AND OPPRESSING CLASSES."

Living in the aftermath of the Industrial Revolution, Marx realized that business owners frequently exploited their employees. Workers—including children—tended to toil, live, and die under horrendous conditions for little pay, while business owners turned a tidy profit.[21] Marx viewed all history as the story of struggle between classes, culminating in the tension he saw between Europe's wealthy class (**the bourgeoisie**[22]) and working class (**the proletariat**).[23]

Q: WHAT IS HUMANITY'S CORE PROBLEM?

A: "OUR SOCIOECONOMIC CONDITIONS."

In Marx's view of history, the rise of labor practices and private property ownership created social division, inequalities, and exploitation.[24] The resulting socioeconomic conditions enslaved workers to oppressive business owners—a situation which Marx believed alienated the masses from being able to fully express their humanity.[25] External conditions of society, not internal conditions of the human heart, are the root of the world's brokenness according to Marx.

Q: WHAT IS HUMANITY'S HOPE?

A: "REVOLUTION."

Marx believed the current economic system, capitalism, is inherently unstable. He thought this system would collapse as workers awaken to their exploited status, band together, and overthrow their oppressors by whatever means necessary.[26] A new communist world order would (in theory) result, where institutions of family, church, and state would be no more.[27] With this vision in mind, Marx and his colleague Friedrich Engels called for the workers of the world to unite and achieve "the forcible overthrow of all existing social conditions."[28]

Just what did Marx hope this revolution would accomplish? First, the means of producing consumer goods would no longer be private property. Instead, the working class would take over factories, farms, and other "means of production," making these assets the collective property of "The People."[29] The working class would also usurp the government to set up a (supposedly temporary) dictatorship.[30] Along the way, thought Marx, workers could justifiably achieve their goals by means of violence.[31]

However, Marx recognized that this dictatorship phase of "crude communism" is hardly ideal.[32] He thought that "higher" stages of communism would emerge as people learned to put the old system of private property behind them.[33] Meanwhile, institutions including family, church, and state—all of which Marxism tends to view as pillars of an oppressive socioeconomic system—would supposedly vanish.[34] Marx said in one of his earlier manuscripts,

> Religion, family, state, law, morality, science, art, etc., are only particular modes of production and fall

> under its general law. The positive transcendence of private property as the appropriation of human life, is therefore the positive transcendence of all estrangement—that is to say, the return of man from religion, family, state, etc., to his human, i.e., social, existence.[35]

In other words, Marx believed the end of private property—and with it, religion, family, and state—would let humanity finally reach its full potential.[36] No longer would social divisions persist. No longer would families be the focal point for raising and educating children.[37] No longer would individuals work and live for themselves. Rather, every person would find their life, purpose, and identity in functioning as a collective human entity meant to serve as its own "god."

Bingo! Humanity's core problem solved.

Right?

Not so fast.

REAL PROBLEMS, WRONG SOLUTIONS

It's no secret that multiple nations tried to apply variations of Marx's ideas throughout the twentieth century—with consistently disastrous results. The revolution Marx had thought inevitable never played out according to plan. Neither did systems of "crude communism" take flight beyond the level of dictatorships.

Of the many possible reasons Marx's predictions failed, two important factors were Marx's (1) mistaken socioeconomic assumptions and (2) faulty worldview beliefs. Regarding the first set of mistakes, Marx seemed to incorrectly assume history **must** progress along a certain path set by socioeconomic conditions.[38] He ignored that many problems with Industrial Revolution capitalism are not necessarily built into **all** free market systems.[39] And he overestimated how motivated **real** people would be to contribute to a collectivist society without directly getting much back for themselves.[40]

But even more significant was Marx's shaky worldview foundation. Rejecting God's Word left Marx with a wrong view of humanity's nature, core problem, and redemptive hope. He mistakenly looked at real Industrial Revolution-era problems through the lens of this faulty worldview and proposed the wrong solutions.

REJECTING GOD'S WORD LEFT MARX WITH A WRONG VIEW OF HUMANITY'S NATURE.

Ultimately, Marx's solutions could not work because they neglected the fact that the root problem behind greed, alienation, and exploitation is not capitalism, private property, or labor—but **sin**. And sinful humans cannot save themselves, much less by sinful means. Even if fallen humans tried committing revolution anyway to establish a "dictatorship of the proletariat,"[41] how likely would they relinquish their powers in hopes of achieving utopia? As Dr. Joe Boot rightly remarked, "Because man is a sinner, these utopian schemes must always be dystopian in their outcomes."[42]

Since the revolution that Marx had expected never unfolded the way he predicted (and certainly never created utopia), later thinkers began to revise Marx's ideas and apply them in new ways.

Enter neo-Marxism.

NEO-MARXISM: THE GHOST OF MARX RETURNS

Neo-Marxism makes the same types of foundational mistakes as Marx did. Neo-Marxist thinkers may recognize problems with Marx's **economic** assumptions. But they hang onto faulty **worldview** assumptions, believing that humanity's core problem and redemptive hope lie somewhere other than what God's Word reveals.[43]

Marx believed humanity's problem lies in oppression between **economic** groups, but neo-Marxist movements believe the problem is oppression between **cultural** groups. While the Bible condemns oppressive **actions** against vulnerable groups, including orphans, widows, and the poor (Jeremiah 22:3–5; Isaiah 1:17, 10:1–3; Zechariah 7:10; Malachi 3:5), neo-Marxist movements view oppression not primarily as an **action** but as an **identity**.

MARX BELIEVED HUMANITY'S PROBLEM LIES IN OPPRESSION.

According to such views, someone is an oppressor not because they commit oppressive **deeds** but because they belong to one or more **groups** considered oppressive, such as European Christian males. Oppressed groups must, by this thinking, awaken to their oppressed status and stage a cultural revolution. These neo-Marxist ideas lie at the roots of influential teachings we see spreading through society today,[44] including gender ideologies, certain types of climate change activism,[45] and critical theories.

Just what are critical theories, anyway? As we'll unpack more in chapter 5, critical theories are modes of thinking that **critique** society in hopes of **revolutionizing** society. Inspired by neo-Marxist thinking, critical theories divide society into oppressive vs. oppressed groups.

Oppressive groups, according to critical theories, include men, Europeans, colonialists, heterosexuals, able-bodied people, and Christians. People who do not identify with such groups are considered **oppressed**. By this thinking, oppressive groups hold all the real power in society while subjugating other groups. Critical theories view the institutions that make up society—like schools, government, church, and family—as systems that help keep the oppressors in power. So critical theories teach that oppressed groups need to revolutionize culture by taking power back from the oppressors. This reversal of power is deemed "social justice."[46]

As Dr. Voddie Baucham describes in his book *Fault Lines*, such critical theories, like Marxism itself, teach a false gospel.[47] Unlike the biblical gospel, which recognizes how guilt for sin spread to all humans through Adam, critical theories teach that **being guilty** is primarily a matter of **belonging to an oppressive identity group**. The critical theory "gospel" offers no real hope of salvation for people labeled as oppressors. Instead, critical theories simply call such people to a works-based system of reparations which—like the animal sacrifices of the Old Testament—can never fully atone.

Ultimately, both Marxism and neo-Marxism offer an entirely different "gospel" from the message of Scripture as portrayed through the 7 C's. Table 1 summarizes just a few of these major differences.

TABLE 1: SUMMARY OF FIVE KEY WORLDVIEW DIFFERENCES BETWEEN GOD'S WORD AND MARXISM

WORLDVIEW	BIBLICAL VIEW	MARXIST (OR NEO-MARXIST) VIEW
Human origins	God created humans in his image.	Humans arose through natural processes.
Human nature	Humans are primarily creatures.	Humans are primarily creators.
Human marriage and family	God ordained marriage between a husband and wife as part of his very good design for creation and the basis for raising and discipling children.	Marriage and family are pillars of an oppressive social system and need to be disrupted or abolished.[48]
Humanity's core problem	The problem comes down to sin.	The problem comes down to economic or cultural conditions.
Humanity's hope of redemption.	Salvation is found only in Jesus.	Salvation is found only through revolution.

FAULTY FOUNDATIONS

Because the false gospels of Marxism and neo-Marxism begin from a faulty worldview foundation, they can never deliver the liberation, justice, and salvation they promise.

And when we think about it, they also have to **borrow principles** from the same biblical worldview they reject. Here are just a few of the biblical concepts borrowed by atheistic thinkers, including Marx.

TRUTH

A biblical worldview affirms the existence of a holy God, whose character is the source of objective truth. God created an orderly universe, designed humans with faculties for knowledge and reasoning, and reveals absolute truth through his Word. This biblical worldview gives us a foundation for truth, knowledge, and scientific reasoning.

But atheism rejects God as the source of truth. **If** objective truth exists, we can't know what it is without relying on our perceptions, feelings, or reasoning. Atheism tells us these things are products of chemicals reacting in lumps of tissue that evolved by unguided processes for no transcendent purpose. Why should unguided, meaningless processes result in reliable perceptions, feelings, and reasoning? We can't search out whether human perceptions, feelings, and reasoning are reliable without relying on human perceptions, feelings, and reasoning. We end up in a vicious cycle of uncertainty.[49] Ultimately, an atheistic worldview can't give us a foundation for objective truth, certainty, or knowledge.

LOGIC

A biblical worldview teaches that our unchanging, logical God designed a logical universe and created us in his image as logical beings. Logic has a philosophical foundation in a biblical worldview but, as Dr. Jason Lisle explains, not in atheistic worldviews.[50] For example, immaterial laws of logic could not exist in a strictly material universe. And if the laws of logic were only agreed-upon human conventions or artifacts of our individual brains, then those laws wouldn't be universally true and unchanging. In other words, reality wouldn't necessarily be logical everywhere and at all times.

MORALITY

Without a foundation for absolute truth, atheistic worldviews lack a foundation for absolute morality.[51] If moral standards are by-products of evolution, cultural constructs, or matters of opinion, then morality isn't rooted in the character of one triune God. Instead, ideas about right and wrong stem from the minds of many humans.

History repeatedly reveals the practical problems with humans assuming we have the "right" to define our own moral standards.[52] Theoretical problems abound as well because secular worldviews provide no consistent basis for defining words like "good" or "bad." We could try saying that "wrong" actions are "immoral" because they cause "harm," which yields "negative" effects. But that would just be another way of claiming "bad actions are bad because they're bad." We wouldn't have foundationally explained what "harm" is, **why** it's wrong, whether or why those standards may change, and who decides these things.

HISTORY REPEATEDLY REVEALS THE PRACTICAL PROBLEMS.

Such challenges inspired the late Yale law professor Dr. Arthur Leff to observe, "There is discontent verging on despair whenever some theorist tries to develop a system in which 'found' ethical or legal propositions are to be treated as binding, but for which there is no supernatural [*sic*] grounding."[53] In other words, trying to ground objective morality without God is logistically impossible.

HUMAN VALUE

With no foundation for truth and morality, there can be no foundation for justice or human rights. If humanity is just a by-product of natural evolution, then we're all accidents with no ultimate purpose but surviving and no ultimate purpose for survival. In this view, no human life has objective, lasting value or meaning. "Human rights" are just a kind of "animal right." We can also define these rights in ways that treat some humans as less valuable than others. This kind of reasoning has contributed to some of recent history's worst atrocities.[54]

A biblical worldview, however, affirms that every human life has objective, lasting value and meaning. God created humans in his image, loves us, died for us, and seeks relationship with us. By providing a foundation for human value and morality, God's Word shows us why actions that harm, exploit, or devalue humans are fundamentally wrong. The Bible gives us a consistent basis for human rights.[55]

ACTIONS THAT HARM, EXPLOIT, OR DEVALUE HUMANS ARE FUNDAMENTALLY WRONG. THE BIBLE GIVES US A CONSISTENT BASIS FOR HUMAN RIGHTS.

Altogether, a biblical worldview—not an atheistic one—supplies a solid foundation for the principles of truth, logic, knowledge, scientific reasoning, morality, and the value of human life. Arguments that borrow these concepts to argue against the Bible rely on a kind of self-defeating logic known as the stolen concept fallacy. (Notably, these stolen concepts also refer to things that are **immaterial** and can't truly exist in **materialistic** worldviews, which say that everything boils down to physical matter.)

None of this implies that only people with a biblical worldview can **exercise** these principles. For example, many secularists practice excellent observational science,[56] behave in moral ways, and defend the value of human life. The point is, doing so requires borrowing principles from God's Word. In the same way, many advocates for Marxism may strive to live morally, fight oppression, and seek justice out of a genuine desire to help others. But doing so from a secular foundation requires heavily borrowing from a biblical worldview. And efforts to fit these borrowed biblical ideas into a Marxist worldview inevitably require **redefining** what key words like **morality**, **oppression**, and **justice** mean.[57]

NEW "GOSPELS," OLD LIES

In the end, many of the "social justice" themes championed in today's culture represent issues being exploited for neo-Marxist agendas based on a false worldview. These agendas may sound compatible with the gospel at first glance because they borrow biblical concepts like **justice**. However, not only do Marx-informed movements redefine these concepts, but the atheism on which Marx based his thinking also can't provide a foundation for them in the first place. So Marxism borrows wording from Scripture to teach a contradictory "gospel," embracing Lie #1 that God's Word is not completely true.

THIS MARXIST "GOSPEL" IDOLIZES HUMANS AS THEIR OWN CREATORS.

This Marxist "gospel" idolizes humans as their own creators, saviors, and authorities for truth. So Marxism pawns Lies #2 and #3 by saying that "truth is up to humans" and that we can be "like God." In promoting these ideas, Marx taught a false view of humanity's nature, core problem, and redemptive hope. Marx insisted this hope resides in **economic** revolution—a theme that later neo-Marxists reframed in terms of **cultural** revolution. By teaching that the world's redemption lies somewhere other than in Christ, Marxism endorses Lie #4, which claims that Jesus is less than who Scripture attests—humanity's only Savior. In promoting these lies, Marx tragically rejected the truth he once knew as a teenager—that Jesus alone can redeem us.

Just like the first people in Eden, people today who embrace deception find only self-destruction. History flows red with examples of such destruction, highlighting the consequences Marxism reaps by approaching real problems from a faulty worldview foundation.

Fast-forward to today, and we see new forms of Marxism rising from the same faulty worldview, engendering new battles in the old war of man's word versus God's Word. But Christians navigating these battles today can learn vital lessons from stories of previous skirmishes in the same war throughout Western history. Those stories begin in the next chapter.[58]

ENDNOTES

1. Citation available in the final footnote of this chapter.

2. Robert Payne, "Three Essays," in *The Unknown Marx: Documents Concerning Karl Marx*, trans. ed. Robert Payne (New York: New York University Press, 1971), 34.

3. Gareth Jones, *Karl Marx: Greatness and Illusion* (Cambridge: The Belknap Press of Harvard University Press, 2016), 9–38.

4. For details on Marx's descent into unbiblical philosophies, see "Karl Marx: What Christians Need to Know About Him," Answers in Genesis, June 23, 2023, AnswersInGenesis.org/blogs/patricia-engler/2023/06/23/karl-marx-what-christians-need-to-know.

5. Scripture attests that Jesus is God, the only and all-sufficient sacrifice for sin, as he himself declared: "I am the way, and the truth, and the life. No one comes to the Father except through me" (John 14:6).

6. Jesus told the Jews of his time, "If you believed Moses, you would believe me; for he wrote of me. But if you do not believe his writings, how will you believe my words?" (John 5:46–47). Luke 24:27 records how Jesus spoke to disciples on the road to Emmaus: "Beginning with Moses and all the Prophets, he interpreted to them in all the Scriptures the things concerning himself."

7. See Ken Ham, *Divided Nation: Cultures in Chaos and a Conflicted Church* (Green Forest, AR: Master Books, 2021). Faith does not require blindly believing a presupposition without solid reasons. A valid presupposition will lead to statements that conflict with neither themselves nor with observable reality. A biblical worldview passes both tests. But as we'll see later in this chapter, worldviews that deny God do not. And more importantly, God's Word stands above man's word as the best basis for faith because God, being self-existent, eternal, and all-knowing, can legitimately attest to the truth of his own Word.

8. For more information, see Ken Ham, *Divided Nation: Cultures in Chaos and a Conflicted Church* (Green Forest, AR: Master Books, 2021), and AnswersInGenesis.org/genesis.

9. The religious nature of Marxism has been discussed in secular scholarly literature, e.g., Murray Rothbard, "Karl Marx: Communist as Religious Eschatologist," *The Review of Austrian Economics: Volume 4* (1990): 123–179.

10. A sign at the Karl Marx House museum in Trier declares that the term *Marxism* "contributes to the misconception that Marx has left a closed doctrine after his death. . . . On the contrary: Marx's critique and analysis of the capitalist society is comprehensive but incomplete and inconsistent. Also, because many of his texts remain[ed] unpublished for a long time, different persons, parties, and movements [tried] to close the gaps. In doing so, they create[d] new 'Marxisms.'"

11. A more unpacked overview of who Marx was and what he believed is available in my blog post, "Karl Marx: What Christians Need to Know About Him," Answers in Genesis, June 23, 2023, AnswersInGenesis.org/blogs/patricia-engler/2023/06/23/karl-marx-what-christians-need-to-know.

12. For more on the importance of atheism in Marx's thinking, see Peter Schuller, "Karl Marx's Atheism," *Science & Society* 39, no. 3 (1975): 331–345. While Marxism is often associated with materialism (the belief that nothing exists except for physical reality), it has been argued that "Marx is more accurately described as a naturalist" because he did not necessarily think that human consciousness can be reduced to matter. (Philip Kain, "Marx's Theory of Ideas," *History and Theory* 20, no. 4 [1981]: 372.)

13. Schuller, "Karl Marx's Atheism," 331.

14. E.g., Charles Devellennes, "Marx and Atheism," in *Marxism, Religion and Ideology*, eds. David Bates, Iain MacKenzie, and Sean Sayers (New York: Routledge, 2016).

15. For information on why the idea that all life-forms evolved from common ancestors cannot fit with a biblical worldview and undermines the gospel, see Ken Ham, "Couldn't God Have Used Evolution?" in *The New Answers Book 1*, ed. Ken Ham (Green Forest, AR: Master Books, 2006), available at AnswersInGenesis.org/theistic-evolution/god-and-evolution/couldnt-god-have-used-evolution.

16. For instance, Marx wrote, "Darwin's book is very important and serves me as a basis in natural science for the class struggle in history. . . . Despite all [Darwinism's] deficiencies, not only is the death-blow dealt here for the first time to 'teleology' [the idea that natural things and creatures were created for a purpose] in the natural sciences but their rational meaning is empirically explained." (Karl Marx, in a letter to Ferdinand Lassalle, dated January 16, 1861, available in *Karl Marx and Friedrich Engels Correspondence 1846–1895: A Selection with Commentary and Notes*, trans. Dona Torr [London: Lawrence & Wishart, 1936], 125.) See also Jerry Bergman, "The Darwinian Foundation of Communism," originally published in *Journal of Creation* 15, no. 1 (April 2001): 89–95, available at AnswersInGenesis.org/charles-darwin/racism/the-darwinian-foundation-of-communism.

17. Marx was already articulating these themes in his early writings, saying, "The entire history of the world is nothing but the creation of man through human labor." (Karl Marx, "Private Property and Communism," in *Economic and Philosophic Manuscripts of 1844*, trans. Martin Milligan [New York: International Publishers, 1964], 145.) See also Karl Marx, "Estranged Labour," in *Economic and Philosophic Manuscripts*, 113–114, and Karl Marx, *Capital: A Critique of Political Economy vol. 1*, ed. Friedrich Engels, trans. Samuel Moore and Edward Aveling, revised according to 4th German ed. by Ernst Untermann (Chicago: Charles H. Kerr and Co., 1906), 197–198.

18. See Marx, *Economic and Philosophic Manuscripts*, 114–115.

19. See Karl Marx and Friedrich Engels, *The German Ideology* (Moscow: Progress Publishers, 1976), 62; Karl Marx and Friedrich Engels, *The Holy Family, or Critique of Critical Criticism* (Moscow: Progress Publishers, 1975 [from third printing in 1980]), 162.

20. See Marx, *Capital*, 198. Notably, a biblical worldview affirms that humans are *creative* as image bearers of God, but not *creators* anywhere close to the sense in which God is. See "Are We Co-Creators with God?" Answers in Genesis, April 18, 2023, AnswersInGenesis.org/god/are-we-co-creators-with-god.

21. Friedrich Engels, *The Conditions of the Working Class in England in 1844*, trans. Florence Kelley Wischnewetzky (London: Swan Sonnenschein & Co., 1892).

22. The term *bourgeoisie* referred to the upper-middle class in France, mainly lawyers and state officials, who revolted against the nobility in the French Revolution. However, despite the way *bourgeoisie* later became synonymous with *capitalists*, the French Revolution was not a conflict between lower classes and capitalists, as capitalism had not yet developed in France. (See George Comninel, *Alienation and Emancipation in the Work of Karl Marx* [New York: Palgrave Macmillan, 2019], 165–173.)

23. See Karl Marx and Friedrich Engels, *Manifesto of the Communist Party*, ed. Friedrich Engels, trans. Samuel Moore (Chicago: Charles H. Kerr & Company, 1910), 12, 28–29.

24. See Marx, "Estranged Labour," in *Economic and Philosophic Manuscripts*, 106–119; Marx and Engels, *The German Ideology*, 37–44, 71–84.

25. Marx, "Estranged Labour," in *Economic and Philosophic Manuscripts*, 106–119.

26. See Marx and Engels, *The Holy Family*, 46–47; Marx and Engels, *Manifesto*, 28–29, 58.

27. E.g., see Marx and Engels, *Manifesto*, 36; Karl Marx, "A Contribution to the Critique of Hegel's Philosophy of Right," in *Karl Marx and Friedrich Engels on Religion* (New York: Schocken Books, 1964), 41–42; see also Richard Weikart, "Marx, Engels, and the Abolition of the Family," *History of European Ideas* 18, no. 5 (1994): 657–672; David Myers, "Marx, Atheism and Revolutionary Action," *Canadian Journal of Philosophy* 11, no. 2 (1981): 309–331. (Some argue that it was Engels, not Marx, who primarily predicted the state's disappearance after communism. See Solomon Bloom, "The 'Withering Away' of the State," *Journal of the History of Ideas* [1946]: 113–121.)

28. Marx and Engels, *Manifesto*, 58.

29. Marx and Engels, *Manifesto*, 40–42; Karl Marx, "Private Property and Communism," in *Economic and Philosophic Manuscripts*, 134–135.

30. Marx and Engels, *Manifesto*, 134–135.

31. For example, Marx and Engels spoke of the "phases of the development of the proletariat" as culminating with "the violent overthrow of the bourgeoisie" (Marx and Engels, *Manifesto* [Chicago: Charles H. Kerr & Company, 1910], 28). While writing critically of the killings during clashes between revolutionaries and government forces in the 1848 Hungarian Revolution, Marx also concluded that the only way to shorten the duration of such bloodshed was via "revolutionary terror" (Karl Marx, "The Victory of the Counter-Revolution in Vienna," *Neue Rheinische Zeitung* no. 136, November 1848, marxists.org/archive/marx/works/1848/11/06.htm.).

32. Karl Marx, "Private Property and Communism," in *Economic and Philosophic Manuscripts*, 132–135.

33. Karl Marx, *Economic and Philosophic Manuscripts*, 135.

34. See footnote 29 above.

35. Karl Marx, "Private Property and Communism," in *Economic and Philosophic Manuscripts* (New York: International Publishers, 1964), 136.

36. But Scripture fully supports private property ownership (Genesis 23:17–20; Exodus 22:5–14; Deuteronomy 19:14, 27:17; Ezekiel 46:18) and penalizes those who wish to take private property away from the rightful owner.

37. Marx and Engel's opposition to parental education of children is clear in *Manifesto*, 36; see also Richard Weikart, "Marx, Engels, and the Abolition of the Family," 657–672.

38. For instance, Marx wrote that private property automatically seals its own fate by producing a revolutionary working class. "Indeed private property drives itself in its economic movement towards its own dissolution . . . inasmuch as it produces the proletariat. . . . The proletariat executes the sentence that private property pronounces on itself by producing the proletariat, just as it executes the sentence that wage-labour pronounces on itself by producing wealth for others and poverty for itself" (Marx and Engels, *The Holy Family*, 46). However, some argue that Marx and Engels held a more dynamic view of the relationships between social and economic factors than an "orthodox" interpretation of Marx as an economic determinist portrays (Wayne Au, "Against Economic Determinism: Revisiting the Roots of Neo-Marxism in Critical Educational Theory," *Journal for Critical Education Policy Studies* 4, no. 2 [2006]: 11–35).

39. For example, the Industrial Revolution contributed to initial heightened inequalities (Niall Ferguson, "The Essence of Marxism," Hoover Institution, March 20, 2020, hoover.org/research/essence-marxism); factory conditions often *were* deplorable (Engels, *The Conditions of the Working Class*), and the exploitation of workers, including children, tragically continues around the world in the name of "capitalism." But as this chapter emphasizes, such exploitation stems from sin. Capitalist systems—like any system, structure, or tool—can be misused for sinful purposes. Biblically, we expect such temptations *would* be prone to occur in societies that elevate the love of money, which fuels greed, idolatry, and "all kinds of evils" (1 Timothy 6:10). Scripture

condemns such evils (e.g., Ezekiel 16:48–50; Revelation 18:2–8). But neither money itself nor capitalism itself is evil. As fair-trade initiatives and other ethical consumption strategies attest, free market practices need not be exploitative. In fact, a biblical worldview provides the basis for decrying and combating exploitation, as Industrial Revolution-era Christian factory reformers understood. God's Word presupposes institutions like free trade and private property but provides guidelines to guard against covetousness, self-seeking, and oppression (e.g., Exodus 20:10–17, 21:33–22:15; Numbers 27:8; Proverbs 20:23, 23:10–11; 2 Corinthians 9:6–7; 1 Timothy 6:17–19; Hebrews 13:5). More information is available in this book's "Answering Common Objections" section.

40. Tibor Machan, "The Right to Private Property," Hoover Institution, October 1, 2002, hoover.org/research/right-private-property.

41. This phrase was popularized by Marx's friend Joseph Weydemeyer. See Hal Draper, "Joseph Weydemeyer's 'Dictatorship of the Proletariat,'" *Labor History* 3, no. 2 (1962): 208–213, doi.org/10.1080/00236566208583899.

42. Joe Boot, "The Makings of the Utopian Power State," Ezra Institute, September 2, 2020, ezrainstitute.com/resource-library/articles/the-makings-of-the-utopian-power-state.

43. That's not to say that people who hold to Marxist ideas cannot at the same time have saving faith in Jesus; the point is that Marxism as a whole teaches a different gospel than Scripture, so a person cannot embrace a *consistent, holistic* biblical worldview and a *consistent, holistic* Marxist worldview at the same time.

44. Owen Strachan, *Christianity and Wokeness* (Washington, DC: Salem Books, 2020); Voddie Baucham, *Fault Lines* (Washington, DC: Salem Books, 2021).

45. See Jackie Smith, "Counter-Hegemonic Networks and the Transformation of Global Climate Politics: Rethinking Movement-State Relations," *Global Discourse* 4, no. 2–3 (2014): 120–138; Charles Reitz, *Ecology and Revolution: Herbert Marcuse and the Challenge of a New World System Today* (Routledge, 2018). For a biblical understanding of environmental stewardship, see AnswersInGenesis.org/environmental-science.

46. The neo-Marxist definition of *justice* differs significantly from a biblical understanding of justice, as chapter 5 will describe. A biblical view of justice emphasizes *actions and attitudes over identity* (Ezekiel 18:20; Colossians 3:25) and insists upon impartiality, righteous legal judgments, honest dealings, and the defense of the needy (e.g., Leviticus 19:15; Psalm 82:3; Proverbs 11:1, 31:9; Isaiah 1:17; Jeremiah 22:3; Amos 5:15). See Erwin Lutzer, *We Will Not Be Silenced: Responding Courageously to Our Culture's Assault on Christianity* (Eugene: Harvest House Publishers, 2020), 78–81. See also "Answering Common Objections."

47. Voddie Baucham, *Fault Lines*. (See chapter 4, "A New Religion.")

48. Notably, movements rooted in Marxism may sometimes still support family values when it is strategic to do so. For instance, after trying to destabilize the family as a pillar of pre-communist society, the Soviet Union later tried to restabilize aspects of family life to strengthen society again under communism. (N. S. Timasheff, "The Family, the School and the Church: The Pillars of Society Shaken and Re-Enforced," in *The Stalinist Dictatorship*, ed. Chris Ward [London: Arnold, and New York: Oxford University Press, 1998], 303–308.) Still, the initial or eventual breakdown of the family remains a stated theme within Marxist and other early socialist movements (see Weikart, "Marx, Engels, and the Abolition of the Family").

49. See Calvin Smith, "Atheism: The Weakest of Worldviews," Answers in Genesis, July 20, 2020, AnswersInGenesis.org/blogs/calvin-smith/2020/07/20/atheism-the-weakest-of-worldviews.

50. Jason Lisle, "Atheism: An Irrational Worldview," Answers in Genesis, October 10, 2007, AnswersInGenesis.org/world-religions/atheism/atheism-an-irrational-worldview.

51. A more in-depth breakdown of why this is the case is available in "Is There a Secular Foundation for Morality?" Answers in Genesis, July 14, 2023, AnswersInGenesis.org/morality/there-secular-foundation-morality.

52. We'll see some examples of this in the next chapter.

53. Arthur Leff, "Unspeakable Ethics, Unnatural Law," *Duke Law Journal* 1979, no. 6 (1979): 1229, 1232.

54. See Jerry Bergman, *How Darwinism Corrodes Morality* (Kitchener, ON: Joshua Press, 2017).

55. More information is available in my article, "God's Image as the Foundation for Human Rights," Answers in Genesis, January 25, 2023, AnswersInGenesis.org/sanctity-of-life/gods-image-as-the-foundation-for-human-rights.

56. That is, the kind of science that involves measuring, describing, and experimenting on things we can see in the present. See "What Is Science?" in Roger Patterson, *Evolution Exposed: Biology* (Hebron, KY: Answers in Genesis, 2006), available at AnswersInGenesis.org/what-is-science/what-is-science.

57. If truth is up to humans, then so is language. Logical inconsistencies will result, but without a foundation for logic, that's a moot point.

58. Reference for this chapter's opening quotation: Karl Marx, "On the Union of the Faithful with Christ According to John XV, 1–14, Described in Its Ground and Essence, in Its Unconditional Necessity and in Its Effects," in *The Unknown Marx: Documents Concerning Karl Marx*, trans. and ed. Robert Payne (New York: New York University Press, 1971), 41.

HEBREWS 10:23

LET US HOLD FAST THE CONFESSION OF OUR HOPE WITHOUT WAVERING, FOR HE WHO PROMISED IS FAITHFUL.

CHAPTER 3

ROME, ROUSSEAU & REVOLUTION

PATTERNS OF PERSECUTION, COMPROMISE, AND CONSEQUENCES

Behind the stone walls that stretched skyward from the pavement where I stood, countless life stories had ended. Those walls had once resounded with the roar of crowds, the clash of steel, and the shouts of gladiators. But the battles fought here in Rome's Colosseum were only shadows of the real warfare in this city. The greater conflict lay in the age-old war of worldviews, with humans waging their futile—and disastrous—war against God's Word.

As the birthplace of Western civilization, Rome offers a strategic vantage point for understanding the worldview war behind the neo-Marxist ideas storming Western culture today. That's why I'd chosen Rome as the original starting place for my journey to trace the history and consequences of Marxism. Along with many other destinations, two later stops would include the Swiss island home of an exiled "Enlightenment" philosopher and the city of Paris—the epicenter of the French Revolution.

Why these locations? Because ancient Rome, the Enlightenment, and the French Revolution mark three eras in Western history that offer warnings Christians today can't afford to ignore. In all these eras, the worldview battle of man's word versus God's Word played out in ways that remain incredibly relevant to our own times. Let's trace patterns of persecution, compromise, and cultural consequences in these eras, which present important lessons for navigating our own neo-Marxist culture.

WELCOME TO ROME

Follow the flocks of tourists through Rome's labyrinthine streets, and you'll find a mammoth monument to paganism: the Pantheon. Given that **pan** means "all" and **theos** refers to divinity, you might guess the Pantheon once housed a smorgasbord of idols. You'd be right. From the "god of cattle worms"[1] to the "goddess of grain mildew,"[2] the Romans worshipped a myriad of mythic deities. But no idols, not even those hewn from the toughest stone, can provide a solid worldview foundation on which to build a culture. As the famous Christian scholar Francis Shaeffer pointed out,

> Like the Greeks, the Romans had no infinite god. This being so, they had no sufficient reference point intellectually; that is, they did not have anything big enough or permanent enough to which to relate either their thinking or their living. Consequently, their value system was not strong enough to bear the strains of life, either individual or political. All their

> gods put together could not give them a sufficient base for life, morals, values, and final decisions.[3]

As a result, Rome increasingly turned to the worship of livelier idols: emperors. A period called the Great Persecution began as one such emperor, Diocletian, decreed edicts that placed increasing pressure on Christians.[4] By considering the process Diocletian used, we can recognize similar patterns of persecution in other past—and present—societies.

First, Diocletian dismissed soldiers and palace officials who refused to sacrifice to Roman deities. Next, he ordered the removal of Christian texts and church buildings, prohibited Christians from holding services, and restricted Christians' legal rights. He then issued an edict that spelled imprisonment for clergy members, adding another edict which granted clergy freedom **if** they offered Roman sacrifices. Meanwhile, Diocletian's government found ways to scapegoat Christians for local crises, such as "failed sacrifices" or palace fires. Finally, in AD 304, a decree gave Christians an ultimatum: offer sacrifices or endure punishments including torture, imprisonment, and death.[5]

> **FINALLY, IN AD 304, A DECREE GAVE CHRISTIANS AN ULTIMATUM.**

Thousands of believers refused to compromise with the Roman government's unbiblical demands—and faced horrific deaths. But remember, the Christians could have avoided these fates. All they had to do was comply with their culture, blending a Roman worldview with Christianity by adding the worship of local deities to their worship of Jesus. But that would have meant obeying man's word above God's Word, which says, "You shall have no other gods before me" (Exodus 20:3). Where culture and

Scripture disagreed, many believers in Rome followed God's Word on pain of death.

FROM CHRISTIANIZED TO COMPROMISED

After Diocletian and his co-emperor resigned, one of the new emperors, Constantine, granted religious freedom with the Edict of Milan in AD 313.[6] Rome's Christianization soon began, with the church staying central to European civil and political life long after the Roman Empire declined. But as the centuries progressed, three related veins of compromise corroded the worldview foundation beneath Western culture's Christianized veneer.[7]

1. COMPROMISE ON BIBLICAL AUTHORITY

Instead of accepting God's Word as their final authority, many Christians began viewing human-made teachings and church traditions from **outside** the Bible as equal to Scripture. (Part of this problem stemmed from the fact that most Christians could not access God's Word for themselves. Today's Western Christians don't share this limitation, thanks to courageous believers including John Wycliffe and William Tyndale, who translated Scripture in opposition to human decrees.)

2. COMPROMISE ON BIBLICAL DOCTRINE

Tolerating the syncretism of man's word with God's Word opened the door for Christians to import unbiblical teachings into their beliefs. For instance, people increasingly viewed salvation as a reward for human efforts rather than accepting the Bible's revelation that salvation is God's gift of grace through Jesus Christ alone (Ephesians 2:8–9).

3. COMPROMISE WITH PAGAN PHILOSOPHY

Along the way, many mainstream believers began incorporating secular teachings into their Christianity. For example, ideas by the Greek philosopher Aristotle became so influential that church officials "warned against the theological use of Aristotle" repeatedly throughout the 1200s.[8] Even so, the Dutch theologian Desiderius Erasmus (1469–1536) lamented in 1514 that Aristotle had "contaminated" contemporary theology.[9]

Realizing that Western culture's mainstream religion had drifted alarmingly far from God's Word, Reformers like Martin Luther (1483–1546) urged Christians back to a biblical foundation. But in the years between Aquinas and Luther, a rekindling of Europeans' interest in pagan Greece and Rome sparked a revival of classical philosophy. This "revival" became known as the Renaissance, from the French word for **rebirth**.

Renaissance thinkers, following the teachings of Aristotle, thought humans could construct their own meaningful "big picture" of reality by reasoning about the pieces of the world they could perceive rather than by starting with God as the authority for truth and meaning.[10] This thinking helped ignite the "Enlightenment," a period from the late 1600s to mid-1700s when rejecting God's Word in favor of human reasoning became as fashionable as tricorn hats and powdered wigs. Contrary to its cheery name, the Enlightenment led Western culture further into the darkness of destructive philosophies.

THE WORSHIP OF FEELINGS

While most Enlightenment philosophers viewed human reasoning as the authority for truth, the Swiss-born thinker

Jean Jacques Rousseau (1712–1778) had other ideas. Instead of deifying **reason**, Rousseau enthroned **feelings** as the authority.[11] By suggesting that our feelings define who we are, Rousseau launched what one scholar called the "Modern Cult of Sincerity."[12] We can think of this Cult of Sincerity as being a human-centered religion that says the highest good is being "true to yourself."

Rousseau's religion sets feelings in place of God as the foundation for reality, definer of our identities, and source of society's moral norms.[13] So Rousseau's thinking stands behind today's movements that say people's feelings determine their true selves and that others who don't affirm these identities deserve punishment. To resist affirming another person's self-identity is to break a cultural blasphemy law, committing heresy against the doctrine that **feelings are God**.

But that's not the only way Rousseau's thinking still reverberates. We can trace Rousseau's Cult of Sincerity all throughout popular messages that say, "You do you," "Follow your heart," or "Just be yourself." Rousseau clearly expressed such messages through the voice of a (decidedly unbiblical[14]) vicar in his novel *Emile*. "I need only consult myself with regard to what I wish to do," said the vicar, adding, "what I feel to be right is right, what I feel to be wrong is wrong. . . . Our first duty is towards ourself."[15]

WHAT I FEEL TO BE RIGHT IS RIGHT, WHAT I FEEL TO BE WRONG IS WRONG. . . . OUR FIRST DUTY IS TOWARDS OURSELF.

Sound familiar?

For even further déjà vu, here are a few other Rousseau quotes that reflect our culture's current thinking.

- "We should be ourselves at all times instead of struggling against nature."[16]
- "In weighing up so carefully what I owed to others, have I paid enough attention to what I owed myself? If one must act justly towards others, one must act truthfully towards oneself."[17]
- "When man is content to be himself he is strong indeed."[18]
- "The highest enjoyment is that of being contented with ourselves."[19]

These ideas could easily flicker across the nearest social media feed. Yet they're lines from a Swiss philosopher over 200 years ago. Rousseau's doctrines clearly contradict the Bible's revelation[20] that "the heart is deceitful above all things, and desperately sick" (Jeremiah 17:9). But they've become deeply ingrained in contemporary culture. Because Rousseau's thinking saturates society today, it's worth stepping back in time to see what else Rousseau was up to.

FALSE DOCTRINES, FAULTY SOLUTIONS

Head to Switzerland's Lake Biel, hop a ferry to St. Peter's Island, rewind history to 1765, and you'll find Jean Jacques Rousseau pacing the quarters of his exile home. He recently fled here because of troubles that boiled over from his controversial writings. But on a deeper worldview level, Rousseau's troubles started much earlier.

Although Rousseau identified as a Catholic or Protestant at different times in his life, his worldview remained far from biblical. His writings instead reflect a kind of deism—the belief that a God created the world but does not care about humans, cannot be known by them, and has not revealed truth through his Word.[21] Rousseau also rejected the Bible's revelation that human corruption stems from **sin**. Rather, he argued in an award-winning essay that **society** corrupts humans.[22]

In this essay and its sequel, Rousseau assumed humans are naturally "innocent and virtuous."[23] He believed that humans originally lived in peaceful simplicity as hunter-gatherers but that life in society brought the division of labor, the rise of private property, and the need for laws and morals.[24] Along the way, thought Rousseau, humans began comparing themselves; competing for power, status, and property; and viewing their self-worth in terms of others' evaluations.[25] Physical differences between people meant that some individuals—the strongest, smartest, or most beautiful—could best succeed, leading to other forms of inequality.[26]

Rousseau believed all these societal factors corrupted humanity's original goodness, causing envy, rivalry, cheating, theft, cruelty, warfare, and other evils.[27] Worse still, people could no longer live comfortably without conforming themselves to society—the very source of vice and inequality in Rousseau's thinking. Individuals began to mask their true selves to fit into a corrupting culture, in which they could never be free.[28] **That**, concluded Rousseau, explains the world's problems. This faulty view of God, truth, humanity, and the source of humans' corruption led Rousseau to propose a faulty solution: the "social contract."[29]

ROUSSEAU BELIEVED ALL THESE SOCIETAL FACTORS CORRUPTED HUMANITY'S ORIGINAL GOODNESS.

THE SOCIAL CONTRACT

Before reading the fine print of the social contract, we need to step back and look at the bigger dilemma Rousseau's worldview created. Remember how Rousseau esteemed feelings, not God, as the authority? As catchy as this "follow your heart" philosophy may sound, it fails at a practical level. Individual feelings can't function as the authority in a world where different people's feelings lead to conflicting truth claims. **Some people's feelings must be more authoritative than others.** In a battle of wills, whose feelings should win?

For Rousseau, the answer lay in determining the "General Will," a collective consensus based not on what most people actually **want** so much as on what's supposedly **good for** them.[30] Rousseau thought the only way humans could live together while still having freedom to be "true to themselves" was to paradoxically **give up** their individual freedom and submit to this General Will.[31] The result would be a type of totalitarian state[32] governed by "the people"—or at least, by the people considered qualified to participate.[33]

CITIZENS WOULD ALSO BE REQUIRED TO RELINQUISH PRIVATE OWNERSHIP . . .

The General Will would become the final authority for truth, to the point that people who oppose the General Will must be punished by exile or death.[34] Citizens would also be required to relinquish private ownership of whatever property the General Will demanded of them.[35] In these respects, Rousseau believed that a system foreshadowing what would later be known as **communism** could cure humanity's ills.[36]

Rousseau didn't advocate for reshaping society this way through violent revolution but rather through a long process of education.[37] Still, revolutionaries who sought a quicker path to "curing inequalities" championed Rousseau's ideas during the French Revolution. These revolutionaries drove parts of Rousseau's teachings to their logical conclusions in ways that carried thousands of people to their deaths.[38] To see how the French Revolution offers vital warnings for Christians today, let's start by looking at the worldview climate in which it arose.

THE COMPROMISE BEFORE THE STORM

Before the time of Christ, Rome had conquered the land that would later become France, leaving the region officially Roman Catholic after the empire's Christianization. But the compromise that ran rampant into the Renaissance infected France's church circles in at least three ways.

1. BLENDING BIBLICAL AND GREEK WORLDVIEWS

A biblical worldview recognizes the importance of both physical ("earthly") and spiritual ("heavenly") realms.[39] But a branch of Greek philosophy called dualism viewed nonphysical realities as separate from and superior to the material world.[40] As this unbiblical thinking slipped into the church, many Christians began withdrawing from society to focus on solely "spiritual" pursuits.[41] This opened the door for criticism that Christendom had no practical value and needed a secular religion to replace it.[42]

2. VIEWING HUMANS AS THE AUTHORITY FOR TRUTH

Before the Reformation, Christians had increasingly begun to view the church as (more or less) equal to Scripture as the authority for truth—even if teachings by church spokespersons contradicted the Bible.[43] Meanwhile, the French monarchy had grown so enmeshed with the mainstream church that being a French citizen meant identifying with royalty-approved Christendom.[44] Whoever reigned had power to punish—even by banishment or death—people whose convictions didn't match official teachings,[45] which had become untethered from biblical authority. This cleared the way for French Enlightenment philosophers to criticize Christianity as being all about having (and abusing) political power.[46]

3. REFLECTING THE PHARISEES

Leaders who committed such abuses in the name of "religion" resembled the religious rulers whom Jesus rebuked for hypocritically pursuing power, prestige, and possessions while neglecting "the weightier matters of the law: justice and mercy and faithfulness"[47] (Matthew 23:23). Professing Christians who commit wrongdoings or otherwise act hypocritically have no excuse for misrepresenting Christ; however, their sins do not change the truth of God's Word. In fact, the truth of God's Word provides a foundation for criticizing hypocrisy and wrongdoing in the first place. The Enlightenment philosophers' unbiblical views didn't give them a solid basis for criticizing the wrongdoings of professing Christians. Even so, those wrongdoings opened channels for later anti-Christian propaganda.

THEIR SINS DO NOT CHANGE THE TRUTH OF GOD'S WORD.

Ultimately, these three factors boil down to Christians not living out a consistent biblical worldview. A consequence was that France's history grew mottled with bloodshed in the name of religion—just as blood would spill in the name of the Revolution's secular religion. But professing Christians who shed innocent blood were acting inconsistently with their worldview, while the revolutionaries were acting consistently with theirs.[48] To see what consequences unfolded, let's go back to the start of the French Revolution.

THE REVOLUTION BEGINS

The day is May 5, 1789. France is a feudal kingdom, with a royal family reigning over three social tiers called "Estates": the clergy, the nobility, and the commoners. King Louis XVI has summoned a meeting of representatives from all three Estates due to pushback over tax reform proposals. But tensions mount as the Estates disagree on how to count votes. These tensions reach a breaking point when the Third Estate—the commoners—take matters into their own hands by dubbing themselves the National Assembly.

THEN ON AUGUST 26, THE NATIONAL ASSEMBLY RELEASES A DOCUMENT MEANT TO SERVE AS AN IDEOLOGICAL FOUNDATION.

After being locked out of the royal meeting hall on June 20, the National Assembly gathers on the king's tennis courts, vowing not to leave until devising a new national constitution. Then on August 26, the National Assembly (now known as the National Constituent Assembly) releases a document meant to serve as an ideological foundation for the budding revolutionary government: The Declaration of the Rights of Man.[49]

THE DECLARATION OF THE RIGHTS OF MAN

This declaration showcases a striking effort to ground justice, freedom, and equality in human ideas rather than in God's Word. The document begins:

> The representatives of the French people, organized as a National Assembly, believing that the ignorance, neglect, or contempt of the rights of man are the sole cause of public calamities and of the corruption of governments, have determined to set forth in a solemn declaration the natural, unalienable, and sacred rights of man.[50]

We can already see the Assembly didn't begin from the foundation of Scripture. Specifically, they blamed humanity's core problem on ignoring the "rights of man" rather than on sinning against God. The trouble is that God's Word establishes the **basis** for the human rights, which the Assembly presupposed. The Assembly did appeal to a kind of deism by proclaiming man's rights "under the auspices of the Supreme Being."[51] But a nebulous "Supreme Being" doesn't reveal clear moral standards through Scripture. Humans must determine those standards themselves. The resulting standards might **sound** compelling but can appeal to no foundation higher than fallible human reasoning to define, defend, and demand moral "goodness."

A NEBULOUS "SUPREME BEING" DOESN'T REVEAL CLEAR MORAL STANDARDS.

Take, for instance, this crucial line from the Declaration: "Liberty consists in the freedom to do everything which injures no one else; hence the exercise of the natural rights of each man has no limits except those which assure to the other members of the society the enjoyment of the same rights. These limits can only be determined by law."[52] This might look reasonable at first glance. But as chapter 2 mentioned, rejecting God's Word leaves society with no moral authority higher than capricious human calculation, opinion, and rhetoric. Consequently, humans can redefine **bad** in ways that justify guillotining thousands of people, despite theoretically being opposed to harm and injury. Redefining language reflects human attempts to redefine truth—and with it, morality, ethics, and justice.

When a collection of humans (like the National Assembly) makes itself the authority for truth in this way, the outcome is totalitarianism. To enforce their own power, totalitarian states must subjugate—or eliminate—anyone and anything that holds to a higher authority, including God's Word. The result is the kind of dechristianization that unfolded during the French Revolution.

HALLMARKS OF DECHRISTIANIZATION

Whether looking at the French Revolution or later totalitarian regimes, we find that dechristianization programs often involve recurring patterns of steps that serve as a warning today. (We saw some of these patterns earlier when examining Christian persecution in Rome.) Such steps don't necessarily unfold in a set order; they might happen simultaneously or cyclically with different levels of (usually increasing) intensity. Here are just three of these steps.

1. REQUIRE TOTAL ALLEGIANCE

As part of dechristianization, new policies begin commanding the church to bow to the state's authority above God's authority. Officially, the state may maintain a policy of religious freedom or tolerance. However, this tolerance only applies so far as Christians ultimately submit to the state. Where Scripture conflicts with the state, Christians are told to compromise God's Word to accommodate the unbiblical culture. In response, regional Christendom tends to divide into an "official church," which complies with the regime, and an "unofficial church," which operates under the radar.

2. REMOVE CHRISTIAN INFLUENCE

To show that the state, not God, is considered the final authority, totalitarian regimes increasingly begin to suppress, marginalize, and villainize the church. Christian leaders, especially within the unofficial church, are strategic targets in the early phases. But eventually, no Christian is immune. Visible signals of Christian influence disappear as churches close, crosses vanish, and services cease. Meanwhile, popular culture paints Christianity as outdated or dangerous. To speed up, justify, and rally public support for more extreme dechristianization, the regime begins to paint biblical Christians as "enemies of the state" and to scapegoat Christians for local crises.[53]

3. REPLACE CHRISTIANITY WITH AN ALTERNATE WORLDVIEW

As spiritual beings, humans need an outlet for worship. Regime leaders, philosophers, or celebrities embodying the regime's ideals may become objects of idolatry in lieu of Christian worship, while the totalitarian system itself plays the role of "God." Meanwhile, people may turn to non-Christian forms of spirituality that blend with—or revolve around—the state religion.

So how did these steps play out during the French Revolution?

A CAMPAIGN TO ERASE CHRISTIANITY

As an early hint that the Revolution would require total allegiance, the Declaration of the Rights of Man stated, "No one shall be disquieted on account of his opinions, including his religious views, provided their manifestation does not disturb the public order established by law."[54] The trouble was that the Declaration defined law not as objective morality grounded in God's Word[55] but as "the expression of the general will."[56] If the people's will changed, so would the law. This meant religious freedom existed on paper so long as the state remained the authority for truth and for determining the boundaries of that freedom.[57] Within a few years, this facade of religious tolerance would crumble, unmasking a war against Christianity.

The mask fell slowly at first. A few months after an August 1789 decree to abolish tithing, the Assembly decided to simplify France's financial troubles by taking over church-owned land.[58] The next summer, the Revolution's demand for total allegiance intensified through legislation known as "The Civil Constitution of the Clergy."[59] As historian Noah Shusterman described it, "The Civil Constitution was the Constituent Assembly's attempt to reshape the church, to make it part of the Revolution—and, in the process, strengthen the government's authority over the church."[60]

THE CIVIL CONSTITUTION OF THE CLERGY = LEGISLATION DURING THE FRENCH REVOLUTION CREATED TO STRENGTHEN THE GOVERNMENT'S AUTHORITY OVER THE CHURCH

So many clergy pushed back against the Constitution that, in November 1790, the Assembly issued an ultimatum: clergy could either sign the Constitution or lose their positions and pensions.[61] About 45% of clergymen refused to sign, dividing the church into official ("Constitutional") and underground ("refractory") branches.[62]

With the lines drawn, the removal of Christian influence gathered momentum. In August 1792, the Assembly ordered refractory clergy to either leave France or be forcibly exiled to Guiana.[63] Incidents of brutality against nuns had already begun, unhindered by the National Guard, by spring of 1791.[64] Then in 1793–1794, the mask fell away entirely during the Reign of Terror.

BRUTALITY AGAINST NUNS HAD ALREADY BEGUN.

No longer could clergy dodge persecution by being "Constitutional." **All** priests faced the ultimatum of resignation or imprisonment—or worse.[65] The darkness only deepened after the Law of Suspects in September 1793 decreed the arrest of "enemies of liberty," including anyone who hadn't been granted a *certificat de civisme*—certificate of good citizenship.[66] People couldn't travel or conduct public business without these certificates, which could be refused to anyone who wasn't considered sufficiently zealous for the Republic.[67]

That same autumn, the new Republican calendar arrived to try erasing Christianity from time itself, replacing the seven-day week with a ten-day one less clearly linked to Genesis.[68] A wholesale destruction of visible references to Christianity ensued. Crosses came down from buildings.[69] Sacred books went up in smoke.[70] The revolutionaries changed the names of streets, towns, or other sites that referenced Christianity.[71] Meanwhile, synagogues and church buildings from every denomination were closed to be demolished, repurposed, or converted into "Temples of the Worship of Reason."[72]

The "Worship of Reason" clearly signaled many revolutionaries' agenda to replace Christianity with other worldviews. An even subtler sign had already appeared with a June 1792 decree that each commune (township) erect an "altar of the fatherland."[73] As a darkly ironic illustration of the problems with worshipping reason, liberty, and virtue instead of God who is the source of these gifts, the leaders of the Cult of Reason were themselves guillotined in the spring of 1794.[74] Maximilien Robespierre (1758–1794), an infamous figurehead of the Reign of Terror and an ardent admirer of Rousseau, replaced the Cult of Reason with a more Rousseauean "Cult of the Supreme Being."[75] Less than two months after inaugurating the cult, however, Robespierre himself faced the guillotine.[76]

THE CULT OF REASON WERE THEMSELVES GUILLOTINED IN THE SPRING OF 1794.

LOOKING BACK ON THE REVOLUTION

Ultimately, the French Revolution illustrates how attempts to achieve freedom, justice, and morality on the foundation of man's word ultimately backfire. Describing the cost of human life involved, historian Timothy Tackett reported:

> We will never know the precise death toll. One careful count of all those executed through the judicial process yielded a total of just under 17,000. But such figures do not include executions without trial or deaths during incarceration—and given the miserable conditions in many of the prisons, a substantial number succumbed

> before they could appear before a tribunal. A total of at least 40,000 deaths seems not unlikely. All classes, moreover, were touched by the executions: over a fourth of the victims were peasants, and nearly a third were artisans or workers. Only 8.5 percent were nobles and 6.5 percent were clergymen.[77]

These statistics show how horribly "solutions" can go awry when people try solving real problems (in this case, of France's feudal system) from a faulty worldview foundation. All that's not to say the Revolution didn't produce any useful effects. For instance, revolutionary governments implemented measures to make education accessible, aid the needy, and abolish slavery in the French colonies.[78] Scholars have also commented at length on the Revolution's role in advancing modern democracies.[79] But similar ends have been accomplished in other places without such violent, totalitarian means—often thanks to the influence of a biblical worldview.[80] The fact that the revolutionaries' worldviews lacked this biblical foundation could not remain hidden, however noble some of their intentions.

Despite the Revolution's flawed foundation and fatal fruits, Marx would later champion the French Revolution as a victory that brought civilization one step closer to the revolution of the working class.[81] He called this event "the most colossal revolution that history has ever known."[82] Even today, various secular voices admire the Revolution's humanistic ambitions.[83]

MARX WOULD LATER CHAMPION THE FRENCH REVOLUTION AS A VICTORY.

This admiration highlights a recurring refrain among people who, like Rousseau, Marx, and secular humanists today, hope a works-based salvation plan of being "good without a God" will liberate humanity. When confronted with the disastrous results of regimes that enacted such plans, the hopeful tend to stay optimistic. They conclude that these regimes' founders had the right ideas but simply didn't (or couldn't) apply those ideas the right way. However, studying history should remind us that **there is no right way to build society on a faulty foundation.** When fallen, finite humans try to function as the authority for truth, goodness, and human rights, the results are consistently **dysfunctional**.

A FOUR-WAY WARNING

In the end, a journey through Rome, the Enlightenment, and the French Revolution offers at least four warnings Christians today must not ignore.

First, the Great Persecution in Rome reminds us that violence against Christians doesn't necessarily start overnight. Instead, it often arises through a series of steps that undermine Christians' rights and ask Christians to compromise God's Word to accommodate the culture.

The French Revolution stands as a similar warning about how dechristianization happens. With human reasoning as its foundation instead of God's Word, a society that initially embraced freedom, equality, and tolerance came to demand total allegiance, remove Christian influence, and replace Christianity with other worldviews. By understanding these processes, we can better recognize and respond to similar patterns today.

A SIMILAR WARNING ABOUT HOW DECHRISTIANIZATION HAPPENS

Second, the way that Christians' inconsistency before the Revolution added fuel to the later dechristianization agenda warns us to live out an uncompromised biblical worldview. Otherwise, we risk standing with the hypocrites of whom Paul said, "The name of God is blasphemed among the Gentiles because of you" (Romans 2:24).

Third, the worldview battle leading up to the Revolution warns us how a culture's **ideas** come to shape its **realities**—not always for the better. We must pay careful attention to who is discipling our culture's young people because the ideas instilled in them today will form the philosophical basis of society tomorrow. And right now, many young people (including in the church) get most of their discipleship from the destructive Marxist-Rousseauean messages of secular culture.

Fourth, the Revolution warns us of the consequences that unfold when a well-intentioned society tries to be "good without God." The Declaration of the Rights of Man sounded wonderful in theory but quickly showed its flawed foundation once in practice. Without God's Word as the basis for morality, the revolutionaries could redefine **being good** to mean violently exterminating those who disagreed with them.

Each of these warnings reminds us to stand on God's Word without compromise, just like the Christians who remained faithful during the Great Persecution in Rome. But history still harbors more insights that apply to understanding culture today. So let's pick up the story after the French Revolution. We'll see how other thinkers before Karl Marx influenced Western culture, anticipated today's attack on the family, and even revealed dark spirituality behind globalist socialism. **You might want to buckle in—it's going to be a wild journey!**

EACH OF THESE WARNINGS REMINDS US TO STAND ON GOD'S WORD WITHOUT COMPROMISE.

ENDNOTES

1. "Verminus," as mentioned by Lawrence Richardson, *A New Topographical Dictionary of Ancient Rome* (Baltimore: John Hopkins University Press, 1992), 411.

2. "Robigo," as mentioned by Christian Smith, "The Religion of Archaic Rome," *A Companion to Roman Religion*, ed. Jörg Rüpke (Malden, MA: Blackwell Publishing, 2007), 37.

3. Francis Shaeffer, *How Should We Then Live?* (Old Tappan, NJ: Fleming H. Revel, 1976), 21. (Note that Francis Shaeffer unfortunately adopted a compromised view on the age of the earth, although his philosophical analysis of Western culture remains extremely relevant. For more information, see Calvin Smith, "A Tale of Two Prophets," Answers in Genesis, October 19, 2020, AnswersInGenesis.org/blogs/calvin-smith/2020/10/19/a-tale-of-2-prophets.)

4. Hartmut Leppin, "Old Religions Transformed: Religions and Religious Policy from Decius to Constantine," *A Companion to Roman Religion*, ed. Jörg Rüpke (Malden, MA: Blackwell Publishing, 2007), 103.

5. You can read an eyewitness account of the rise of the Great Persecution, and what happened during it, in Eusebius of Caesarea's (c. AD 260–339) manuscript *Martyrs of Palestine*, with several English translations available online. (Note that much of the content, understandably, contains graphic descriptions of violence.)

6. Leppin, "Old Religions Transformed," 104.

7. Shaeffer, *How Should We Then Live?* 56.

8. See Gilles Emery and Matthew Levering, eds., *Aristotle in Aquinas's Theology* (Oxford: Oxford University Press, 2015), vii.

9. Desiderius Erasmus, "Erasmus' Letter to Martin Dorp (1514)," in *The Praise of Folly*, trans. Clarence Miller (New Haven: Yale University Press, 1979), 155. For more on how classical philosophy became incorporated into the mainstream Western church, see Dr. Danny Faulkner, *The Expanse of the Heavens: Where Creation and Astronomy Intersect* (Green Forest, AR: Master Books, 2017), 48–52, available at AnswersInGenesis.org/store/product/expanse-heaven.

10. See Shaeffer, *How Should We Then Live?* 51–56. This human-centered approach might seem reasonable at first glance, but deprives humans of a foundation for reason in the first place. See Dr. Jason Lisle, *The Ultimate Proof of Creation* (Green Forest, AR: Master Books, 2009).

11. According to Dr. Arthur Melzer in *The Harvard Review of Philosophy*, "For Rousseau, the true self is not the rational self. We are not our intellect, our mind, but our feelings. The ground of our being is the sentiment of existence, which is a sentiment, a feeling: 'to exist, for us, is to feel [*sentir*]'" (Arthur Melzer, "Rousseau and the Modern Cult of Sincerity," *The Harvard Review of Philosophy* 5, no. 1 [1995]: 4–21).

12. Melzer, "Rousseau and the Modern Cult of Sincerity."

13. Critical theorist Alessandro Ferrara wrote, "Among the modern philosophers who have shaped the world we inhabit, Rousseau is the one to whom we owe the idea that identity can be a source of normativity (moral and political) and that an identity's potential for playing such a role rests on its capacity for being authentic" (Alessandro Ferrara, "Rousseau and Critical Theory: An Excerpt from Alessandro Ferrara's Latest Book," *Public Seminar*, November 8, 2017, publicseminar.org/2017/11/rousseau-and-critical-theory). In other words, the idea that political and moral standards should align not with God's Word, but with the identities that people believe to reflect their authentic selves, traces straight back to Rousseau.

14. For instance, the vicar espouses belief in an unknowable "Supreme Being" rather than the God of Scripture, suggests that all religions are equal (in contrast with John 14:6), and rejects the biblical doctrine of hell. See Rousseau, *Emile* [1762] (New York: Barnes and Noble, 2005), 316–363.

15. Rousseau, *Emile*, 330.

16. Rousseau, *Emile*, 418.

17. Jean-Jacques Rousseau, *Reveries of the Solitary Walker* [1782] (New York: Penguin Books, 1984), 80.

18. Rousseau, *Emile*, 55.

19. Rousseau, *Profession of Faith of a Savoyard Vicar* [1762] (New York: Eckler, 1889), 44.

20. Notably, the Bible gives us the foundation for contentment in whom God made us; however, our satisfaction rests ultimately in Jesus—not in ourselves. Also, God's Word doesn't suggest we *shouldn't* care about ourselves at all. Scripture says we must love our neighbors as *ourselves* (Matthew 12:31) without putting our own interests ahead of others (1 Corinthians 10:24; Philippians 4:2). That said, the Bible clearly condemns self-centeredness (James 3:14; Philippians 2:2–4) and warns against those who are "lovers of self" (2 Timothy 3:2). Seeking truth and morality within ourselves rather than in God's Word also clearly conflicts with a biblical view.

21. For instance, Rousseau's vicar character in *Emile* states, "I believe, therefore, that the world is governed by a wise and powerful will; I see it or rather I feel it, and it is a great thing to know this. But has this same world always existed, or has it been created? Is there one source of all things? Are there two or many? What is their nature? I know not; and what concern is it of mine?" (316–317).

22. Jean-Jacques Rousseau, "A Discourse on the Moral Effects of the Arts and Sciences," in *Social Contract and Discourses*, trans. G. D. H. Cole (London: Dent; New York: Dutton, 1913), 129–154.

23. Rousseau, *Social Contract and Discourses*, 145.

24. See Rousseau, *Social Contract and Discourses*, 214–223.

25. See Rousseau, *Social Contract and Discourses*, 218–219, 232–238.

26. Rousseau, *Social Contract and Discourses*, 145, 207–215, 236–238.

27. Rousseau, *Social Contract and Discourses*, 149, 152, 218–219.

28. For further commentary, see Melzer, "Rousseau and the Modern Cult" and Carl Trueman, *The Rise and Triumph of the Modern Self: Cultural Amnesia, Expressive Individualism, and the Road to Sexual Revolution* (Wheaton, IL: Crossway, 2020).

29. Rousseau, "The Social Compact," in *Social Contract and Discourses*, 5–123. More information on the Social Contract and its implications is available in "Rousseau's Social Contract: How a False Doctrine Inspired Totalitarianism," Answers in Genesis, September 16, 2022, AnswersInGenesis.org/blogs/patricia-engler/rousseau-social-contract-totalitarianism.

30. Rousseau, *Social Contract and Discourses*, 34. (The question of who decides what's "good" for the majority of people is another problem, as the last chapter noted.)

31. Rousseau, *Social Contract and Discourses*, 14–16.

32. For more on Rousseau's role in the theoretical development of modern totalitarianism, see Robert Nisbet, "Rousseau and Totalitarianism," *The Journal of Politics* 5, no. 2 (1943): 93–114.

33. On this note, C. H. Lincoln comments, "It is assumed that Rousseau intended all men, of whatever grade, to possess an equal influence in the state. Nothing could be more false. So long as there is a difference in individual capacity, our author [Rousseau] distinctly says the lower grades should not be considered part of the state, but he does not hesitate to affirm that these classes should be prepared for citizenship as soon as possible, and when qualified should be admitted to full rights" (C. H. Lincoln, "Rousseau and the French Revolution," *The Annals of the American Academy of Political and Social Science* 10, no. 1 [1897]: 54–72). In other words, only those considered "qualified" should be given a voice in the General Will. But who decides what sort of people count as qualified and on what grounds?

34. Rousseau, *Social Contract and Discourses*, 25, 31.

35. Rousseau, *Social Contract and Discourses*, 19–22.

36. Lucio Colletti, a Western Marxist and former member of the Italian Communist Party, detailed the connection between Rousseau and communism in his book, *From Rousseau to Lenin: Studies in Ideology and Society*, trans. John Merrington and Judith White (New York: New Left Books, 1972). Colletti notes, "Rousseau sees this 'socialization' essentially in moral and political terms, not yet in economic [terms]" that extend to "the socialization of property"; however, Colletti suggests that Rousseau's historical context prevented him from "thinking concretely of a solution of that kind" (174).

37. Lincoln, "Rousseau and the French Revolution," 54–72.

38. Lincoln, "Rousseau and the French Revolution"; see also Gordon McNeil, "The Cult of Rousseau and the French Revolution," *Journal of the History of Ideas* 6, no. 2 (1945): 197–212. While Rousseau's political ideas in *The Social Contract* had not been widely read before the Revolution and therefore did not necessarily play a significant public role in causing the Revolution, they were rediscovered, popularized, and ideologically weaponized *during* the Revolution. (Other political parties, including those who opposed the Revolution, cited Rousseau in support of their causes as well; however, Rousseau's teachings matched the revolutionary agenda so well that revolutionaries soon created a virtual cult—complete with iconography and hymns—around Rousseau and the Social Contract.) See Gordon McNeil (1945).

39. For instance, the Bible affirms that Jesus created, sustains, stepped into, has authority over, and will one day restore all physical creation. Meanwhile, biblical Christianity entails following Jesus in every aspect of physical life, serving others as he did (John 13:1–17; Philippians 2:3–11).

40. Dr. Joe Boot discusses dualism and its impact on Christian thinking in "The Root of Jesse: Unifying and Renewing a Divided Life," Ezra Institute, January 5, 2021, ezrainstitute.com/resource-library/articles/the-root-of-jesse-unifying-and-renewing-a-divided-life/. You can learn more from Dr. Boot in the *Creation, Cross, and Culture* video series available on Answers in Genesis–Canada's YouTube channel and Answers TV. See also Abraham Bos, "'Aristotelian' and 'Platonic' Dualism in Hellenistic and Early Christian Philosophy and in Gnosticism," *Vigiliae Christianae* 56, no. 3 (2002): 273–291. It's worth noting that the church has been battling gnosticism since the first century. See Henry Longueville Mansel, *The Gnostic Heresies of the First and Second Centuries*, ed. J. B. Lightfoot (London: John Murray, 1875).

41. Boot, "The Root of Jesse." Please note that pursuing spiritual disciplines and staying set apart from the world's ungodliness are biblically imperative (Scripture references below). But *withdrawing from earthly society* in the dualistically minded sense meant "going out of the world" (compare to 1 Corinthians 5:9–11) rather than remaining "in the world" (John 17:14–18) while being set apart from its ungodliness, as Scripture mandates (James 1:17, 4:4; 1 John 2:15–17).

42. E.g., Baron Paul-Henri d'Holbach, an atheistic *philosophe*, opined, "Nature tells man in society to cherish glory, to labour to render himself estimable, to be active, courageous, and industrious: religion tells him to be humble, abject, pusillanimous, to live in obscurity, to occupy himself with prayers, with meditations, and with ceremonies; it says to him, be useful to thyself, and do nothing for others" (*The System of Nature*, trans. H. D. Robinson, vols. 1 and 2 [Boston: J. P. Mendum, 1889], 280.)

43. See "The Reformation," in Schaeffer, *How Should We Then Live?* 79–105.

44. Dale Van Kley, "The Religious Origins of the French Revolution, 1560–1790," in *The Origins of the French Revolution*, ed. Peter Campbell (New York: Palgrave MacMillan, 2006), 165.

45. A history of these times is documented in John Southerden Burn's (remarkably titled) book, The History of the French, Walloon, Dutch and Other Foreign Protestant Refugees Settled in England from the Reign of Henry VIII to the Revocation of the Edict of Nantes: With Notices of Their Trade and Commerce, Copious Extracts from the Registers, Lists of the Early Settlers, Ministers, &c., and an Appendix Containing Copies of the Charter of Edward VI, &c (London: Longman, Brown, Green, and Longmans, 1846).

46. Some of Rousseau's statements to this effect are documented in Arthur Melzer, "The Origin of the Counter-Enlightenment: Rousseau and the New Religion of Sincerity," *American Political Science Review* 90, no. 2 (1996): 344–360. Melzer points out that Rousseau also criticized other Enlightenment intellectuals for making themselves absolute authorities for truth—the same mistake they criticized official church leaders of making—by viewing themselves as nature's "supreme interpreters" (348).

47. As a reminder from chapter 2, the biblical concept of justice does not align with later neo-Marxist representations of justice.

48. While the revolutionaries weren't always acting consistently with some of the key ideals they espoused (as we'll soon see), they nonetheless acted consistently with their secular worldviews, which did not provide a stable foundation for those ideals. For a related topic, see Bodie Hodge, "Isn't the God of the Old Testament Harsh, Brutal, and Downright Evil?" in *The New Answers Book 3* (Green Forest, AR: Master Books, 2010).

49. National Assembly of France, "Declaration of the Rights of Man," August 26, 1789, accessed May 2024 from the Yale Law School Lillian Goldman Law Library, avalon.law.yale.edu/18th_century/rightsof.asp.

50. National Assembly of France, "Declaration."

51. National Assembly of France, "Declaration."

52. National Assembly of France, "Declaration," Article 4.

53. We'll see more examples of this strategy in chapter 8.

54. National Assembly of France, "Declaration," Article 10.

55. That's clearly not to suggest that the Bible provides guidelines for all civic laws, like zoning regulations or traffic rules. The issue here is whether the foundation for the existence of laws—and for the standards we use to determine, evaluate, and understand those laws—is objective morality rooted in God's character or subjective morality rooted in human perception.

56. National Assembly of France, "Declaration," Article 6.

57. Notably, Rousseau had suggested a similar model of "religious tolerance" years earlier. (Rousseau, *Social Contract and Discourses*, 122.)

58. Noah Shusterman, *The French Revolution: Faith, Desire, and Politics* (New York: Routledge, 2014), 65.

59. Nigel Aston, *Christianity and Revolutionary Europe, 1750–1830* (Cambridge: Cambridge University Press, 2002), 189–193.

60. Shusterman, *The French Revolution*, 65.

61. Aston, *Christianity and Revolutionary Europe*, 190.

62. Aston, *Christianity and Revolutionary Europe*, 191.

63. Aston, *Christianity and Revolutionary Europe*, 200.

64. Aston, *Christianity and Revolutionary Europe*, 200.

65. Aston, *Christianity and Revolutionary Europe*, 213.

66. Décret qui ordonne l'arrestation des Gens suspects," Article II, September 17, 1793, in Louis Rondonneau, *Code Militaire: Recueil Méthodique Des Décrets Relatifs Aux Troupes de Ligne Et À La Gendarmerie Nationale*, vol. 4 (Paris: Printing House of the Depot of Laws, "Year II of the Republic"), 278–280, accessed May 2024 from gallica.bnf.fr, translation confirmed using deepl.com/en/translator.

67. See David Andress, *The Terror: Civil War in the French Revolution* [2005] (London: Abacus, 2006), 211–212.

68. Emmet Kennedy, *A Cultural History of the French Revolution* (London: Yale University Press, 1989), 345–353.

69. Simon Schama, "The French Revolution Did Not Transform French Society," in *The French Revolution*, ed. Laura Egendorf (San Diego: Greenhaven Press, 2004), 148.

70. Timothy Tackett, *The Coming of Terror in the French Revolution* (London: Belknap Press of Harvard University Press, 2015), 316.

71. Tackett, *The Coming of Terror*, 316.

72. Aston, *Christianity and Revolutionary Europe*, 213.

73. Aston, *Christianity and Revolutionary Europe*, 192.

74. See Louis Thiers, *The History of the French Revolution* 1789–1800, trans. Frederick Shoberl, vol. 3 (London: Richard Bentley and Son, 1895), 336–346.

75. Charles A. Gliozzo, "The Philosophes and Religion: Intellectual Origins of the Dechristianization Movement in the French Revolution," *Church History* 40, no. 3 (1971): 277; McNeil, "The Cult of Rousseau," 2006. Also see Shusterman, *The French Revolution*, 223.

76. Shusterman, The French Revolution, 223–231. It's only fair to note that, despite his penchants for terror and tyranny, Robespierre strategically opposed the excesses of the dechristianization movement and had presented a speech on December 6, 1793, calling for the observation of religious freedom, as supposedly guaranteed by the Declaration of the Rights of Man. However, David Andress observes this measure "did little to stem the tide of local activism" (Andress, The Terror, 242–243). See also Tackett, The Coming of Terror, 317. Robespierre's December 6 speech is reprinted in *Archives Parlementaires de 1787 à 1860*, vol. 80 (Paris: Librairie Administrative de P. Dupont), 712–713, available at SearchWorks.stanford.edu.

77. Tackett, *The Coming of Terror*, 330.

78. A book excerpt reprinted on the website for the socialist *Jacobin* magazine, named after the foremost political club behind the French Revolution's Reign of Terror, pointed out that "after much controversy, they [the revolutionary leaders] voted to abolish slavery and to grant full rights to people of all races, but only after they were faced with history's largest slave uprising, the beginning of a 'Haitian Revolution' that ended in 1804 with the creation of the first independent black nation in the Americas." Originally, the author notes, the revolutionary leaders had been in alliance with the French colonial slave owners, despite the opening line in The Declaration of the Rights of Man that "Men are born and remain free and equal in rights" (Jeremy Popkin, "The French Revolution Was the Beginning of the Modern World," *Jacobin*, October 5, 2021, jacobin.com/2021/10/french-revolution-history-slave-revolt-haitian-revolution-popular-welfare). Again, this contradiction highlights how revolutionaries frequently acted inconsistently with the ideals of the revolution but consistently with their unbiblical worldview. Because this worldview had no ultimate foundation for morality or the equal value of every human life, laws for or against slavery were changeable matters of human opinion. In contrast, professing Christians who advocated for slavery were acting inconsistently with a holistic biblical worldview, which provides an unchanging foundation for protesting human rights abuses. For more information, see Bodie Hodge and Paul Taylor, "Doesn't the Bible Support Slavery?" in *The New Answers Book 3* (Green Forest, AR: Master Books, 2010). See also Tackett, *The Coming of Terror*, 313.

79. Melvin Edelstein, *The French Revolution and the Birth of Electoral Democracy* (London: Routledge, 2016).

80. In England, for instance, the spread of the Protestant Reformation provided an important backdrop for transitioning the government to a parliamentary democracy under a constitutional (rather than absolute) monarchy. (That's certainly not to imply the motives behind the rise of English Protestantism and the "Glorious Revolution" were primarily biblical or that the professing Christians involved in this revolution [and especially its aftermath] always acted consistently with a biblical worldview. However, it remains clear that the changes that ushered in England's more democratic government would not have happened as they did without the context of the Reformation. Several analyses of the Reformation's complex contribution to political development in Europe are summarized in Becker, Sascha O., Steven Pfaff, and Jared Rubin, "Causes and Consequences of the Protestant Reformation," *Explorations in Economic History* 62 [2016]: 1–25.) Meanwhile, Christians acted consistently with their worldviews to help reform factories, prisons, hospitals, and orphanages; make education accessible for the needy; and abolish the British slave trade. Such results were possible because God's Word provides a consistent foundation for doing good, condemning evil, and renouncing hypocrisy.

81. If anything, Marx thought the revolutionary spirit in France didn't go far enough because he believed that it mainly benefited the middle class rather than stirring the working class to their own greater revolution. See *Karl Marx and Fredrich Engels, The Holy Family*, trans. R. Dixon (Moscow: Foreign Language Publishing House, 1956), 110.

82. Karl Marx and Friedrich Engels, *The German Ideology* (Moscow: Progress Publishers, 1976), 208.

83. For instance, a recent web article published by the American Humanist Association, whose motto is "good without a God," stated that "for humanists, the French Revolution marks the beginning of a new age of enlightenment, freedom, and rational thought" (Julia Shapiro, "Storming of the Cults: A Revolutionary Remembrance," thehumanist.com, July 14, 2020, thehumanist.com/commentary/storming-of-the-cults-a-revolutionary-remembrance).

1 JOHN 4:1

BELOVED, DO NOT BELIEVE EVERY SPIRIT, BUT TEST THE SPIRITS TO SEE WHETHER THEY ARE FROM GOD, FOR MANY FALSE PROPHETS HAVE GONE OUT INTO THE WORLD.

CHAPTER 4

POETS, PRINTERS & POLTERGEISTS

THE DARK SPIRITUAL ROOTS OF GLOBALIST SOCIALISM

How familiar do these ideas sound?

"Society needs a total restructuring toward globalist socialism."

"People would be happier if they shared everything instead of owning anything."

"Marriage is unnaturally restrictive."

"Humans are basically good but behave badly when they lose touch with who they really are inside."

"People should be free to love whomever they want, however they want."

"The nuclear family is a source of injustice."

"Socialism is the solution for humanity's problems."

"Men are oppressors."

These types of messages inundate our culture in everything, from movies to bumper stickers to social media posts. So it might come as a shock to learn that all these ideas hatched in the writings of radical poets and socialists nearly 200 years ago. In fact, some of these thinkers advocated for types of communism even before Marx.

Here's another plot twist: many of the ideas listed above appear in a document that one nineteenth-century communist claimed had been endorsed by séance spirits.[1] Even back in the 1800s, these spirits reportedly wished to reconstruct global society by the means this communist had been advocating.[2] The goal, according to the spirits, was to bring humanity together inclusively as "one brotherhood and one family."[3]

THESE SPIRITS REPORTEDLY WISHED TO RECONSTRUCT GLOBAL SOCIETY.

Clearly, today's messages pushing for a form of globalist socialism are nothing new. Neither are agendas that promote this societal reset by attacking the marriage and family institutions God established in Genesis. To understand the long history—and dark spirituality—behind these messages, let's unearth some crucial realities about three movements in the 1700–1800s. These movements helped pave the way for certain aspects of Marxism or related ideas influencing culture today: Romanticism, utopian socialism, and Theosophy.

THE NOT-SO-ROMANTIC POETS

What's so romantic about Romanticism? Not much, it turns out. "Romance" here doesn't refer to the rom-com sense of the word but to a movement among certain artists, writers, and thinkers in eighteenth- and nineteenth-century Europe. With a focus on praising nature, emotion, beauty, and the human individual, this movement emphasized the worship of creation rather than the Creator

(Romans 1:25). Within this movement, two provocative poets are especially worth highlighting for how they anticipated the "sexual humanism"[4] influencing culture today: William Blake and Percy Bysshe Shelley.[5]

WILLIAM BLAKE (1757–1827)

Hail a horse-drawn cab outside Westminster Abbey in eighteenth-century London, journey less than two miles northwest to 27 Broad Street, and you'll find the print shop of Parker and Blake. Inside, William Blake leans over a copper engraving plate, crafting the metal into a template for illustrating the latest manuscript of a politically radical publisher.[6] But the ink stains on Blake's fingers aren't only from his printing and engraving profession. He's also a writer. And what he writes is unbiblical.

Despite growing up in a family of Christian nonconformists,[7] Blake turned from God's Word as the ultimate authority and invented his own form of spirituality. For instance, instead of accepting the Bible's core salvation doctrines that humans are fallen and only Jesus can save us, Blake wrote that "men are admitted into Heaven . . . because they have cultivated their understandings."[8] In fact, Blake endorsed that age-old lie we saw in chapter 2, "You can be like God." He believed "men forgot that all deities reside in the human breast"[9] and was quoted by an acquaintance as blasphemously declaring that "[Jesus] is the only God . . . and so am I, and so are you."[10]

BLASPHEMOUSLY DECLARING THAT "[JESUS] IS THE ONLY GOD . . . AND SO AM I, AND SO ARE YOU."

Having rejected God's Word, Blake also famously shunned a biblical view of sexuality founded in Genesis, which Jesus cited when questioned about marriage

(Matthew 19:3–9). Spurning the truth in Scripture, Blake criticized purity as an unnatural stricture associated with "pale religious lechery."[11] The church, according to Blake, functions as an oppressive force suppressing sexual "freedom."[12]

In Blake, we see the early themes of sexual revolution that later movements would leverage to destabilize society by undermining family.[13] The marriage and family institutions God ordained in Genesis serve as pillars of civil stability. And it's no secret that an efficient way to demolish a building is to weaken its pillars (more on **that** in chapter 6).

AN EFFICIENT WAY TO DEMOLISH A BUILDING IS TO WEAKEN ITS PILLARS.

Not everyone agrees about the extent to which Blake personally pursued this destabilization. Historian E. P. Thomson states, "Blake was not a hurrah-revolutionary, as he is sometimes represented, nor was he a premature practitioner of Marxist dialectic."[14] Even so, Blake has been claimed as a figure of socialism. An entry on Marxists.org states:

> Blake was a political radical for his times, being a democrat, a republican, a supporter of the American Revolution and the French Revolution, a free thinker, a critic of industrial capitalism, a fierce opponent of slavery,[15] empire and imperialism, a champion of free love and women's rights, and committed to a proto form of Anarchism and of Socialism. . . . Blake was a left-wing radical and is still respected today within the British Left and the British Radical movement.[16]

Another entry on Marxists.org notes that both Blake and Marx structured their thinking around a vision for the future transformation of humanity—a vision later picked up by today's transhumanists:[17]

> There is no need to repeat: Marx is not Blake. But while "Marxism" merely sought some changes in economic structure, Marx was concerned with "self-alteration" [Selbstveränderung], "the alteration of men on a mass scale." This question of self-alteration—the aspect which Marx has in common with Blake—is not an aspect but the whole point of Marx.[18]

PERCY BYSSHE SHELLEY (1792–1822)

Blake's fellow Romantic poet, Percy Bysshe Shelley, anticipated certain elements of Marxist thinking even more. For instance, both Shelley and Marx remarked that the social systems of their days needed to be overthrown.[19] Even so, not all scholars interpret Shelley as a forerunner of Marxism so much as a voice for anarchism.[20]

Whatever the strength of his links with Marxism, Shelley clearly stood alongside Blake in the path toward today's "sexual humanism." Just like today's messages about sexuality are symptoms of our society abandoning a biblical foundation, Shelley's views about sexuality arose from his rejection of God's Word.

SHELLEY DABBLED IN THE OCCULT AS A YOUNGSTER.

Instead of sticking with Scripture, Shelley dabbled in the occult as a youngster before becoming a vocal atheist.[21] Although Charles Darwin hadn't yet popularized evolutionary thinking, Shelley read the evolutionary writings of Darwin's grandfather[22] and promoted ideas which have been called "evolutionary pantheism."[23] Karl Marx's daughter and her common-law partner even praised Shelley for possessing "a certain conception of evolution long before it had been enunciated in clear language by Darwin, or had even entered seriously into the region of scientific possibilities."[24]

From his unbiblical worldview foundation, Shelley advocated for "free love," calling purity "a monkish and evangelical superstition."[25] And like Blake, he viewed Christianity as a storm cloud of oppression hovering over society in general and sexuality in particular.[26]

In a helpful analysis of these themes in Shelley's writings, Carl Trueman explains how Shelley believed that a key to political liberation was to "free" humanity from marriage.[27] Shelley viewed marriage as a restrictive, unnatural, and inauthentic institution that thwarted human happiness.[28] Like Marx, he thought that inequality and oppression resulted from society's economic system, which kept its stability thanks to marriage.[29] Because marriage rests on the biblical doctrines founded in Genesis, "freeing" society would require rejecting God's Word.

Shelley promoted the idea that freedom, justice, and authenticity demanded the erosion of marriage and "religion"—themes we see in contemporary culture. And like today's culture harnesses popular media to convey these themes to the public, Shelley harnessed poetry as a weapon of social transformation.[30]

TODAY'S ATTACKS ON FAMILY, MARRIAGE, AND RELIGION IN THE NAMES OF FREEDOM, JUSTICE, AND AUTHENTICITY ARE NOTHING NEW.

Altogether, these eighteenth-century poets remind us that today's attacks on family, marriage, and religion in the names of freedom, justice, and authenticity are nothing new. Rather, such attacks echo the ancient lies that God's Word is not completely true and that humans can become "like God" as their own authorities. We see these attacks again, with the spiritual darkness behind them even further unmasked, in another movement among early nineteenth-century thinkers: the utopian socialists.

THE UTOPIAN SOCIALISTS

"Utopian socialists" like Charles Fourier (1772–1837) and Robert Owen (1771–1858) believed a reorganized form of society would redeem humanity from its core problems. In theory, this societal reset would usher in a utopia—a type of heaven on earth.[31] The utopian socialists recognized the world as a broken place filled with poverty, abuse, and suffering. But they attributed this brokenness not to human sinfulness, as Genesis reveals, but to "arbitrary deviations from the 'eternal principles' of 'natural law,' justice, and reason."[32]

> **IN THEORY, THIS SOCIETAL RESET WOULD USHER IN A UTOPIA.**

These deviations supposedly included marriage, which the utopian socialists viewed as an "unnatural" institution that restricted free sexual expression. By this thinking, marriage is an oppressive system that suppresses happiness, authenticity, and productivity.[33] Clearly, these ideas run opposite to a biblical worldview. Jesus, for example, quoted Genesis when questioned about marriage, stating that "he who created them from the beginning made them male and female, and said, 'Therefore a man shall leave his father and his mother and hold fast to his wife, and the two shall become one flesh'" (Matthew 19:4–5).

According to a biblical worldview, departures from this God-ordained institution are the real unnatural deviations. But Satan, the father of lies (John 8:44), loves to switch labels, calling evil "good," good "evil," freedom "chains," and chains "freedom."

The utopian socialists bought and sold such lies without restriction. Fourier and Owen both devised new schemes for society, which, if humans adopted them correctly, promised freedom, peace, and harmony.[34] But first, the current social systems would have to be abandoned—a feat that would require overturning the pillars of present civilization.

What are these pillars? In answer, Friedrich Engels (1820–1895), who coauthored *The Manifesto of the Communist Party* with Marx, observed, "Three great obstacles seemed to [Owen] especially to block the path to social reform: private property, religion, [and] the present form of marriage."[35] Marx and Engels believed these institutions would dissolve after a communist revolution. However, Fourier and Owen thought the very act of "redeeming" humanity through socialism would require abolishing the family.[36]

THE UTOPIAN SOCIALISTS BOUGHT AND SOLD SUCH LIES WITHOUT RESTRICTION.

Marx and Engels criticized utopian socialism for lacking the supposed rigor of their own "scientific socialism," which they thought was better grounded in historical analyses.[37] Even so, as one philosophy professor has remarked, "Marx and Engels explicitly and repeatedly stated that they owed a great debt to the utopian socialists, who, according to Engels, are to be 'reckoned among the most significant minds of all time.'"[38]

CONNECTIONS TO TODAY'S CRITICAL THEORIES

If Marxism owes such a debt to utopian socialists, then it's no surprise to find themes from their thinking in today's neo-Marxian-informed "critical theories." As chapter 2 mentioned, these theories view societies in terms of oppressed and oppressing classes. Oppressed groups, according to critical theories, must awaken to their oppression, stage a cultural revolution, and overthrow their oppressors (stereotypically, Christian European males) to create a more equitable world.

These ideas are nothing new. For instance, Fourier anticipated a theme of later Marxian feminists by calling men the "oppressing sex" and revering women who "resisted the oppressive system necessitated by the bond of marriage."[39] Fourier stated, "It is women who suffer most from civilization; it was up to them to attack it."[40] However, he blamed women for not sufficiently awakening to the need to revolt against civilization.[41] If these ideas sound familiar, it may come as no surprise that Fourier has been credited with coining the term **feminist**.[42]

A THREE-PART STRATEGY

Further unsurprisingly, three strategies that utopian socialists proposed for overturning their own societies reflect patterns we find unfolding today (more on **that** in part two):

- Undermine marriage and family
- Target young people, especially through the education system
- Subvert the church and state, making these institutions agents of revolution rather than guardians of the status quo

We've already seen how the utopian socialists wished to undermine family and marriage. But what role would the institutions of education, church, and state play?

In answer, historian Richard Weikart explains that both Owen and Fourier "vigorously touted the superiority of the communal education of children and the removal of children from parental control and influence."[43] Feminist political scientist Leslie Goldstein adds that in Fourier's proposed socialist society, "Education was to begin by age two, and to be handled by skilled experts (rather than haphazardly qualified parents), at community expense, for all, regardless of economic status or gender."[44]

In other words, Fourier understood that the key to controlling society is to control the youth who represent society's future decision-makers. For Fourier's plan to succeed, the job of discipling youth must belong not to the family or church but to the state.

THE KEY TO CONTROLLING SOCIETY IS TO CONTROL THE YOUTH.

Furthermore, the state and church themselves must be recruited to become agents of the socialist agenda. Robert Owen believed these institutions, as the current "powers that be," must be persuaded to help install a new system of global socialism. In a pamphlet entitled *The Future of the Human Race*, Owen admonished,

> Therefore, convince the authorities of the world in Church and State that there is another mode of human existence than the present, and one now easily attainable . . . in which they . . . shall enjoy greater advantages and happiness . . . than it is possible they can attain amidst any circumstances which men can devise under the existing false and irrational system.[45]

Written in 1854, Owen's pamphlet strikingly illustrates the way lies from bygone centuries are resurging in today's culture—and the dark spirituality behind these lies. Let's look closer at this telling document.

THE FUTURE OF THE HUMAN RACE

Reflecting strategies one and two above, Owen's pamphlet predicted that humanity would attain a state of pure happiness "when law-made marriages shall be abandoned."[46] In this state, according to Owen,

> Children can be relieved from the evil effects of false and unnatural parental associations, from the evils of family training and education, and from being made family-selfish, and unjust to all other families. It is only thus that a true equality, according to age and personal qualities, can be attained. It is only thus that men and women can be trained and educated from birth to become truly good, wise, and happy, and that the human race can become superior citizens of the world, and be united to form one cordial brotherhood.[47]

Basically, Owen believed the overthrow of marriage, family, and education by parents would be required for achieving a new globalist era founded on his version of socialism. Owen also envisioned this era as being "free" from private property, which he thought served no purpose except to grant power and privilege to oppressors.[48] Instead, he claimed, "Under a rationally arranged system of public property, each one will feel himself to be sovereign of the world, with all its immeasurably increased advantages . . . ever open to his use and enjoyment."[49] In other words, Owen thought that in the new global socialist system enabled by the overthrow of marriage, "you'll own nothing. And you'll be happy."[50]

DARK SPIRITUAL CONNECTIONS

How did Owen believe this global system would come about? Here's where some interesting history comes in. Back in 1817, Owen had publicly professed atheism.[51] But by the time he wrote *The Future of the Human Race*, Owen had converted to spiritism—the occult. In fact, Owen devoted a lengthy portion of this pamphlet to describing communications from "spirits," who advised him on how to distribute the document.[52]

Owen believed that establishing the envisioned new global system would require assistance from these spirits. He wrote, "The wisdom of refined, good, and superior spirits, could alone suggest to mortals this new view of society—this high order of our future existence—this final redemption of the human race, from ignorance, sin, and misery."[53] According to Owen, this spirit-assisted socialist "redemption" was now within reach if governments could "compel everyone in [the] future to become good, wise, and united" by means of "the most pleasant unperceived force."[54] Owen also claimed the spirits told him not to worry if others rejected his message because the spirits would gradually compel humanity "to believe in this new mode of re-creating the character of man, and of re-constructing society over the world."[55]

ACCORDING TO OWEN, THIS SPIRIT-ASSISTED SOCIALIST "REDEMPTION" WAS NOW WITHIN REACH IF GOVERNMENTS COULD "COMPEL EVERYONE IN [THE] FUTURE TO BECOME GOOD."

Strikingly, Owen further remarked, "It is most gratifying to observe how uniformly they [the spirits] discountenance all divisions of class, sect, colour, or country. Their object is to permanently benefit all of humankind equally, without reference to divisions of any kind."[56] Again, the parallels between this message and today's culture are hard to miss. While the restoration of human unity is a biblical theme (Galatians 3:28; Revelation 7:9), God's Word clearly communicates that this reconciliation comes through Jesus, on his terms.

Attempts to establish "equality," "inclusivity," and "harmony" in a fallen world on human terms contrary to God's Word can never produce utopia—quite the opposite. Experimental societies that attempted to enact utopian socialism throughout America and Europe consistently failed, reaping frustration instead of satisfaction.[57] Satan, as we saw earlier, loves switching labels.

TESTING THE SPIRITS

How do we know Owen's poltergeist "friends" were satanic? Although Owen believed he was communicating with the spirits of deceased "superior men and women,"[58] Scripture clearly forbids such dabbling as an abomination to God (Deuteronomy 18:10–12). The Bible also exhorts believers,

> Beloved, do not believe every spirit, but test the spirits to see whether they are from God, for many false prophets have gone out into the world. By this you know the Spirit of God: every spirit that confesses that Jesus Christ has come in the flesh is from God, and every spirit that does not confess Jesus is not from God. This is the spirit of the antichrist, which

> you heard was coming and now is in the world already. (1 John 4:1–3)

So did Owen's contacts confess Jesus? Not at all—in fact, they blasphemously told Owen to begin his pamphlet by calling Jesus "an inspired medium" rather than the Son of God.[59] Biblically, Owen was fraternizing with spirits who were against Christ—demonic forces.

According to Owen, these forces fully endorsed the teachings he had spent his life propagating. He wrote, "The spirits . . . [have] come to advise me as to further proceedings for the benefit of the human race, and to encourage me in the continuance of the measures which I have been impelled and deeply impressed to pursue from my youth upward."[60] He later reiterated, "The principles and practices herein advocated, are those which from my youth upward until now, without ceasing, I have endeavoured to place before the human race for its everlasting adoption."[61]

"THE SPIRITS . . . [HAVE] COME TO ADVISE ME..."

The measures, practices, and principles Owen had spent his life promoting centered on communism. *The Future of the Human Race* reveals that a pioneering socialist—whom Engels called one of history's most eminent minds[62]—associated his political views with a globalist agenda endorsed by "spirits."

Interesting.

But not surprising. Any system, from any political stance, which attempts to overthrow the institutions of marriage and family that God ordained in Genesis cannot be of Christ.[63] And as chapter 2 mentioned, Jesus said, "Whoever is not with me is against me" (Matthew 12:30).

Neutrality is not an option. Whether in nineteenth-century utopian socialist writings or twenty-first-century culture, any system of thinking that contradicts God's Word is against Jesus—in a word, **antichrist**.

THEOSOPHY

Another anti-Christian movement connected at the deepest roots with certain ideas rampant today is Theosophy. Founded in the late 1800s by a small group of people, including a woman named Helena Blavatsky (1831–1891), Theosophy is a type of occult religion. Aspects of this religion seem linked to Hermeticism—a set of unbiblical spiritual ideas supposedly based on writings by a combined Greek and Egyptian deity.[64]

Blavatsky claimed her teachings were not her own but came from supposedly highly evolved, reincarnated "masters of wisdom" with whom she spoke—sometimes in person, sometimes through means including dreams.[65] Like Owen's poltergeists, these "masters" taught that Jesus was merely one of them. So based on God's Word (1 John 4:1–3), Blavatsky's masters qualify as antichrist beings.

BLAVATSKY CLAIMED HER TEACHINGS WERE NOT HER OWN BUT CAME FROM SUPPOSEDLY HIGHLY EVOLVED, REINCARNATED "MASTERS OF WISDOM" WITH WHOM SHE SPOKE.

How did Blavatsky's ideas gain traction in the West, where she helped to popularize yoga and other Eastern spiritual practices?[66] Part of the answer is that Blavatsky lived when old-earth interpretations of geology and Darwin's ideas about evolution were shaking many Westerners' trust in Scripture. In response, Blavatsky "outlined an occult cosmology which embraced both a [millions-of-years old] geological time scale and an evolutionary view of development."[67] She taught that an impersonal deity called "the Absolute" pervaded the universe.[68] Life forms, thought Blavatsky, evolve through a series of progressively higher entities until being absorbed back into "divinity."[69] By blending Eastern mysticism and Hermeticism with evolution and long ages, Blavatsky marketed a false doctrine that let people feel "spiritual" without giving up beliefs in human interpretations of science.

The philosopher Friedrich Hegel—who significantly influenced Marx's thinking—taught a related idea linked to Hermeticism.[70] Hegel believed that ideas drive history and that the material world is part of a (capital-*I*) Idea in the process of coming to grips with itself as being "the Absolute."[71] Marx would later turn Hegel's thinking around by teaching that **material realities** give rise to processes that—sometimes **by way of** ideas—drive history.[72] Even so, Hegel's impact on Marx means we shouldn't be surprised to find traces of Hegel's Hermeticism-influenced thinking in Marxist ideas about humans as self-creators.[73]

> **CONNECTIONS BETWEEN MYSTICISM, SOCIALISM, AND EVOLUTIONARY IDEAS GO MUCH DEEPER.**

But the connections between mysticism, socialism, and evolutionary ideas go much deeper. To see how, let's look briefly at the ideas of two other women involved in Theosophy: Annie Besant and Alice Bailey.

ANNIE BESANT (1847–1933)

Annie Besant, who became president of the occult Theosophical Society[74] and edited the Society's *Lucifer* magazine,[75] was a committed evolutionist, social Darwinist, and eugenicist.[76] She, like Blavatsky, taught that Eastern spiritual practices including yoga would "quicken" individuals' evolution to let them become "like God."[77]

Besant believed biological evolution serves as a model for social evolution,[78] with society evolving toward a "new Republic of Man."[79] One pair of scholars wrote:

> In 1908, Besant began lecturing on the imminent appearance of a master known as the World-Teacher . . . who would present a teaching that would lead to the establishment of the New Civilization. The New Civilization would develop as a new human type was evolved, which possessed a faculty by which universal unity would be perceived.[80]

Echoing the call for inclusiveness that Owen's "spirits" championed, Besant appreciated that the Theosophical Society wanted to "found a Universal Brotherhood without distinction of race or creed."[81] Whether this new era should dawn "in peace or in revolution," Besant felt convinced that one way or another, socialism would triumph. She declared that "all the mighty, silent forces of evolution make for Socialism, for the establishment of the Brotherhood of Man."[82]

Practicing what she preached, Besant dedicated a chapter of her autobiography to describing her activism as a vocal socialist.[83] She joined a group of socialists known as the Fabian Society, where she "worked hard . . . as a speaker and lecturer" and "won recruits for the army of propagandists from the younger of the educated middle class."[84] Summarizing her convictions, Besant declared, "I am a socialist because I believe in Evolution."[85]

ALICE BAILEY (1880–1949)

Another woman drawn into the Theosophical Society was Alice Bailey. What was her spiritual imprint on the West? One group of religious professors noted, "The terms *New Age* and *Age of Aquarius* were probably first used by Alice Bailey . . . who broke away from the Theosophical Society and said that her writings were dictated to her by Masters."[86] (In Bailey's case, the "master" behind many of her writings was an entity called the Tibetan, aka Djwhal Khul.[87])

Bailey, like Marx, adopted an evolutionary worldview featuring humans as self-creators.[88] She stated, "We are laying the foundation for the emergence of a new species of human being—a more highly evolved unit within the human family."[89]

Although not a Marxist herself, Bailey endorsed certain ideas in line with Marx's vision for communism. She spoke against forms of communism based on totalitarian dictatorships but assured humanity that "true Communism (in the spiritual sense of the term) will take the place of the present wickedness."[90] Despite recognizing the "mistakes and cruelty" of Russia's communist dictatorship, Bailey believed that behind them lay "great ideals."[91] For instance, she thought these ideals included "the supply of the need of all, the beauty of mutual service, and the divinity of constructive work."[92]

ALTHOUGH NOT A MARXIST HERSELF, BAILEY ENDORSED CERTAIN IDEAS IN LINE WITH MARX'S VISION FOR COMMUNISM.

Reflecting these ideals, Bailey believed Western individualism would give way to a more collective-focused mentality in a new era she called the "Age of Aquarius." She wrote, "This coming age will be as predominantly the age of group interplay, group idealism and group consciousness. . . . Selfishness, as we now understand it, will gradually disappear, for the will of the individual will voluntarily be blended into the group will."[93]

Bailey believed progress toward this new age was the plan of a "planetary Hierarchy,"[94] a group of entities we can biblically recognize as demonic. The Hierarchy's plan, wrote Bailey, involved bringing together a globalized Fellowship of Religions, a World Federation of Nations[95] and a "new state of awareness."[96] She thought these outcomes would happen through developments in science, psychology, and education.[97] In a book dictated by the Tibetan, Bailey stated,

THE HIERARCHY'S PLAN INVOLVED BRINGING TOGETHER A GLOBALIZED FELLOWSHIP OF RELIGIONS.

> The old established rhythms, inherent in the old forms of religion, politics and of the social order, must give place to newer ideals, to the synthetic understanding, and to the new order. The laws and modes of procedure which are characteristic of the New Age must supersede the old, and these will, in time, institute the new social order and a more inclusive regime.[98]

If these ideas from Bailey's Tibetan sound uncannily like those of Owen's contacts, the similarities only continue. Like Owen, Bailey believed family life produces selfishness and that education outside the family must teach children to live more collectivistically. She wrote:

> Families (under any category and bracket) present a united front to the world; parents defend their own children and position and situation, right or wrong; family pride, tradition, pedigree are overemphasised, leading to the different barriers which today separate man from man, family from family and group from group. . . . However, under the coming world order, educators will prepare the young people in school and college for participation in an active and consciously realised group life.[99]

Now for a few more plot twists. Alice Bailey founded an organization called Lucis Trust, which describes on its website how Bailey and her husband started a publishing house known as "Lucifer Publishing Company."[100] The website says the name changed to Lucis Publishing Company in 1924 because Christians "mistakenly identified Lucifer with Satan" instead of an "angel who brought light to the world."[101] (Remember that 2 Corinthians 11:14 says, "Even Satan disguises himself as an angel of light."[102])

BAILEY AND HER HUSBAND STARTED A PUBLISHING HOUSE KNOWN AS "LUCIFER PUBLISHING COMPANY."

The website goes on to mention an organization the Lucis Trust established called "World Goodwill." The website also comments that for many years, the Lucis Trust's headquarters was near the United Nations. A 1999 newsletter from World Goodwill goes further, explaining, "World Goodwill is recognised by the United Nations as a Non-Governmental Organisation and is represented at regular briefing sessions at UN Headquarters. The Lucis Trust is on the Roster of the United Nations Economic and Social Council."[103]

Even more concerning, the newsletter lists several organizations under a section titled *Transition Activities*, stating, "Throughout the period of transition into a new world order of unity, peace and right relations, many groups of people of goodwill are emerging whose activities are characteristic of the new group of world servers. The following organisations and activities may be of interest."[104] Among the entities listed are UNESCO, the United Nations University for Peace, and the World Core Curriculum developed by the United Nation's former Assistant Secretary-General, Robert Muller.[105]

More concerning still is Muller's preface to the teachers' manual for his World Core Curriculum. In it, Muller wrote, "The underlying philosophy upon which The Robert Muller School is based will be found in the teachings set forth in the books of Alice A. Bailey by the Tibetan teacher, Djwhal Khul and the teachings of M. Morya as given in the Agni Yoga Series Books."[106] Muller's efforts including the curriculum won him the 1989 UNESCO Prize for Peace Education.[107] In other words, the world's largest education organization endorses a program founded on teachings by an occult spiritual entity.

THE WORLD'S LARGEST EDUCATION ORGANIZATION ENDORSES A PROGRAM FOUNDED ON TEACHINGS BY AN OCCULTIC SPIRITUAL ENTITY.

A SATANIC AGENDA UNMASKED

Ultimately, the writings of Romantic poets, utopian socialists, and occult Theosophists offer far deeper insight into today's culture than we may have bargained on unearthing. These writings together illustrate how attempts to reinvent civilization by overturning family, targeting youth, and subverting the church and state are nothing new. Rather, they are centuries-old strategies that multiple voices had been promoting even before Marx and Engels declared that a "spectre of Communism" was haunting Europe.[108] Given Owen's claim that these strategies were central to a global agenda endorsed by spirits, "spectre" may have been a more accurate description than Marx and Engels realized.

That's not to say nothing good came from early socialists' projects. For instance, Owen helped reform factory conditions and Blake opposed legalized slavery.[109] But these individuals sought to fix the world's brokenness from the wrong foundation, leading—as Owen's failed experimental socialist communities illustrated—to faulty solutions. Only God's Word offers a flawless foundation for understanding and addressing the world's brokenness.[110] The Bible not only provides a solid basis for human value, morality, and justice but also points to Jesus. Jesus Christ alone offers the hope, peace, and abundant life the Romantics, utopian socialists, and Theosophists sought.

THESE INDIVIDUALS SOUGHT TO FIX THE WORLD'S BROKENNESS.

Unfortunately, key aspects of poltergeist-approved ideas, which point people to seek redemption apart from Jesus, have taken the world by storm, thanks to neo-Marxism. Let's look closer at how this happened so we can better understand what to do about it.

ENDNOTES

1. Robert Owen, *The Future of the Human Race; Or, A Great, Glorious and Peaceful Revolution Near at Hand, to Be Effected Through the Agency of Departed Spirits of Good and Superior Men and Women* (London: Effingham Wilson, 1854). We'll look at this document in more detail shortly.

2. Owen, *The Future of the Human Race*, 15.

3. Owen, *The Future of the Human Race*, 15.

4. See Bodie Hodge, "The Religion of Sexual Humanism," Answers in Genesis, July 15, 2023, AnswersInGenesis.org/culture/religion-sexual-humanism.

5. For more on these and other Romantic poets and their connections to culture today, see Carl Trueman, *The Rise and Triumph of the Modern Self* (Wheaton, IL: Crossway, 2020), 129–161.

6. See Jeffrey Barclay Mertz, "A Visionary Among the Radicals: William Blake and the Circle of Joseph Johnson, 1790–95," (PhD dissertation, University of Oxford, 2010).

7. That is, a church movement which did not conform to the official Church of England. See Keri Davies, "The Lost Moravian History of William Blake's Family: Snapshots from the Archive," *Literature Compass* 3, no. 6 (2006): 1297–1319, doi.org/10.1111/j.1741-4113.2006.00370.x.

8. William Blake, "A Vision of the Last Judgement" (1810), in *The Complete Writings of William Blake, with Variant Readings*, ed. Geoffrey Keynes (Oxford: Oxford University Press, 1996), 615.

9. William Blake, "The Marriage of Heaven and Hell (circa 1790–93)," in *The Complete Writings of William Blake* (1996), 153.

10. William Blake, quoted by Henry Crabb Robinson in G. E. Bentley, *Blake Records* (Oxford: Clarendon Press, 1969).

11. Blake, "The Marriage of Heaven and Hell," 160; and William Blake, "America," in *The Complete Writings of William Blake* (1996), 199.

12. E.g., William Blake, "The Garden of Love," in *The Complete Writings of William Blake* (1996), 163. See also Carl Trueman, *The Rise and Triumph of the Modern Self*, 155–158. The irony of "free" sexuality is that the promised freedom comes with the chains of snares described in Proverbs 7. Meanwhile, biblical sexual purity brings the genuine flourishing described elsewhere in Scripture (e.g., Song of Solomon and 1 Corinthians 7). Such irony is hardly surprising because Satan is "the father of lies" (John 8:44) and switches the labels on things.

13. An example is the neo-Marxian radical feminist movement, which has been especially vocal about the abolition of family and marriage. In a book promoting these themes, radical feminist Shulamith Firestone wrote, "Feminism, when it truly achieves its goals, will crack through the most basic structures of our society" (Shulamith Firestone, *The Dialectic of Sex: The Case for Feminist Revolution* [New York: William Morrow, 1970], 43; see also pages 232–274).

14. E. P. Thomson, *Witness Against the Beast: William Blake and the Moral Law* (New York: The New Press, 1993), 58. *Dialectic* refers here to Marx's way of viewing the world in terms of interactions between material conditions and human activity. These interactions produce the cycle that Marx believed drove history, in which basic human needs give rise to socioeconomic conditions that cause oppression, which creates the need for

revolution, creating new socioeconomic conditions, creating new oppression, creating the need for another revolution, and so on.

15. This is an example of how Marxists may critique real problems (in this case, slavery) but from the wrong worldview foundation. We saw in chapter two that the wrong worldview does not provide the foundation for morality and human value required for recognizing slavery as a problem.

16. Marxists.org, "Blake, William (1757–1827)," Marxists Internet Archive Encyclopedia of Marxism, marxists.org, accessed May 16, 2024, marxists.org/glossary/people/b/l.htm.

17. Transhumanism is a movement that hopes to use technology to achieve higher levels of human evolution and, possibly, even a version of "divinity." More information is available in "Thinking Biblically About Transhumanist Technologies," Answers in Genesis, January 11, 2023, AnswersInGenesis.org/human-evolution/thinking-biblically-about-transhumanist-technologies.

18. Cyril Smith, "Marx and the Fourfold Vision of William Blake," Marxists.org, accessed May 16, 2024, marxists.org/reference/archive/smith-cyril/works/articles/blake.htm.

19. By way of specific examples, Marx and Engels declared that communism required "the forcible overthrow of all existing social conditions" (Karl Marx and Friedrich Engels, *Manifesto of the Communist Party* [1848], ed. Friedrich Engels, trans. Samuel Moore [Chicago: Charles H. Kerr & Company, 1910], 58), while Shelley stated, "The system of society as it exists at present must be overthrown from the foundations with all its superstructure of maxims and of forms before we shall find anything but disappointment in our intercourse with any but a few select spirits" (Percy Bysshe Shelley, in a letter to Leigh Hunt dated May 1, 1820, available in Roger Ingpen, *The Letters of Percy Bysshe Shelley*, vol. 2 [London: G. Bell and Sons, 1914], 777).

20. See Paul A. Cantor, "Shelley's Radicalism: The Poet as Economist," in *Literature and the Economics of Liberty: Spontaneous Order in Culture*, eds. Paul A. Cantor and Stephen Cox (Auburn, AL: Ludwig von Mises Institute, 2009), 225–261.

21. Richard Holmes, Shelley: *The Pursuit* (London: Flamingo, 1995), 16–25, 50.

22. See Holmes, *Shelley*, 75.

23. Pantheism is the idea that God is in all things, in the sense that everything is part of God. While Shelley rejected belief in God, Shelley has been interpreted as viewing nature itself (or some "spiritual" element of nature) as an eternal, life-giving force which exists in all natural things and which drives evolution. See Edward and Eleanor Marx-Aveling, "Shelley and Socialism." See also Petru Golban, "Nature as a Mode of Existence: Dualism, Escapism, Pantheism and Co-Authorship in English Romantic Poetry," *Ankara Anadolu ve Rumeli Araştırmaları Dergisi* 2, no. 3: 89–110.

24. Edward and Eleanor Marx-Aveling, "Shelley and Socialism," transcribed by Ted Crawford, marxists.org, accessed May 16, 2024, To-Day (April 1888), 103–116, marxists.org/archive/eleanor-marx/1888/04/shelley-socialism.htm.

25. Percy Bysshe Shelley, *Queen Mab* (London: R. Carlile, 1822), 112.

26. Examples of these themes are clear in Shelley's profoundly blasphemous poem *Queen Mab*, as Carl Trueman explains (Carl Trueman, *The Rise and Triumph of the Modern Self*, 144–158).

27. Trueman, *The Rise and Triumph*, 144–158.

28. See Percy Bysshe Shelley, "Against Legal Marriage," in *Shelley on Love: An Anthology*, ed. Richard Holmes (Berkley: University of California Press, 1980), 45–48; see also Trueman, *The Rise and Triumph*, 148–149.

29. Trueman, *The Rise and Triumph*, 152.

30. For more on Shelley's strategy of wielding poetry as an instrument of revolution, see Truman, *The Rise and Triumph*, 144–148.

31. For a more nuanced explanation, see Roger Paden, "Marx's Critique of the Utopian Socialists," *Utopian Studies* 13, no. 2 (2002): 67–91. Another famous utopian socialist often listed with Fourier and Owen was Henri St. Simon.

32. Morris Hillquit, *History of Socialism in the United States*, 5th ed. (New York: Funk and Wagnalls, 1910), 18.

33. For example, Fourier praised women who "resisted the oppressive system necessitated by the bond of marriage" (Charles Fourier, in *The Utopian Vision of Charles Fourier: Selected Texts on Work, Love, and Passionate Attraction*, eds. Jonathan Beecher and Richard Beinvenu [Boston: Beacon Press, 1971], 176). Historian Richard Weikart notes, "Fourier advocated the replacement of monogamous marriage with a system allowing much greater latitude for sexual passions, since he believed that monogamy was an institution contrary to human nature and was thus an impediment to human happiness" (Richard Weikart, "Marx, Engels, and the Abolition of the Family," *History of European Ideas* 18, no. 5 [1994]: 657–672).

34. Paden, *"Marx's Critique of the Utopian Socialists."*

35. Friedrich Engels, "Socialism: Utopian and Scientific," in *Karl Marx and Friedrich Engels*: Selected Works, vol. 3, ed. Institute of Marxist-Leninism (Moscow: Progress Publishers, 1973), 125.

36. Weikart, "Marx, Engels, and the Abolition of the Family."

37. Paden, "Marx's Critique of the Utopian Socialists."

38. Paden, "Marx's Critique of the Utopian Socialists."

39. Charles Fourier, *The Utopian Vision of Charles Fourier*, 175–176.

40. Fourier, *The Utopian Vision*, 177.

41. Fourier, *The Utopian Vision*, 177.

42. In French, *féministe*. See Leslie Goldstein, "Early Feminist Themes in French Utopian Socialism: The St.-Simonians and Fourier," *Journal of the History of Ideas* 43, no. 1 (1982): 92.

43. Weikart, "Marx, Engels, and the Abolition of the Family," 665.

44. Goldstein, "Early Feminist Themes," 98.

45. Owen, *The Future of the Human Race*, 13.

46. Owen, *The Future of the Human Race*, 6.

47. Owen, *The Future of the Human Race*, 6.

48. For instance, Owen wrote, "The object aimed at by private property is to give to the individuals possessing more of it than others, privileges not to be attained by their less wealthy neighbours; and to give them power to oppress those who are less wealthy" (Owen, *The Future of the Human Race*, 6).

49. Owen, *The Future of the Human Race*, 7.

50. As mentioned in chapter 1, this is the famous statement found in a video posted on social media by the World Economic Forum (@wef), Twitter, April 9, 2018, twitter.com/wef/status/983378870819794945. (For another angle of commentary on this statement, see also Reuters, "Fact Check: The World Economic Forum Does Not Have a Stated Goal to Have People Own Nothing by 2030," Reuters, February 25, 2021, reuters.com/article/uk-factcheck-wef-idUSKBN2AP2T0.)

51. Richard William Leopold, *Robert Dale Owen: A Biography* (Cambridge: Harvard University Press, 1940), 8.

52. Owen, *The Future of the Human Race*, 19–50.

53. Owen, *The Future of the Human Race*, 12.

54. Owen, *The Future of the Human Race*, 17.

55. Owen, *The Future of the Human Race*, 15–16.

56. Owen, *The Future of the Human Race*, 15.

57. See Paden, "Marx's Critique of the Utopian Socialists." A more detailed look at various experimental communities is also available in Hillquit, *History of Socialism in the United States*.

58. The full title of Owen's pamphlet was *The Future of the Human Race; Or, A Great, Glorious and Peaceful Revolution Near at Hand, to Be Effected Through the Agency of Departed Spirits of Good and Superior Men and Women.*

59. Owen, *The Future of the Human Race*, 29 (see also the cover page).

60. Owen, *The Future of the Human Race*, 15.

61. Owen, *The Future of the Human Race*, 31.

62. Friedrich Engels, *The Peasant War in Germany* (Moscow: Foreign Language Publishing House, 1956; originally written in German in 1850), 33.

63. This does not logically imply that all systems that *do* uphold the *biblical* institution of marriage are necessarily biblical, but it is logically the case that systems that *attack* these biblical institutions are necessarily *unbiblical*.

64. Erin Prophet, "Hermetic Influences on the Evolutionary System of Helena Blavatsky's Theosophy," *Gnosis: Journal of Gnostic Studies* 3, no. 1 (2018): 84–111.

65. Sylvia Cranston, *HPB: The Extraordinary Life and Influence of Helena Blavatsky, Founder of the Modern Theosophical Movement* (New York: G. P. Putman's Sons, 1993), xix.

66. Mark Singleton, *Yoga Body: The Origins of Modern Posture Practice* (Oxford: Oxford University Press, 2010), 44. Curiously, the occultist Blavatsky spoke against hatha yoga (yoga involving posture and breathing practices, which ended up becoming most popular in the West) as being for a person who is, in Singleton's paraphrasing, "a common, ignorant sorcerer . . . who converses with the devil" (Singleton, Yoga Body, 77). However, Blavatsky more broadly extolled capital-Y Yoga as "union with Brahma [the Hindu creator deity] exoterically" (Helen Blavatsky, *The Secret Doctrine: The Synthesis of Science, Religion, and Philosophy, Vol. II: Anthropogenesis* [London: Theosophical Publishing Company, 1888], 115).

67. Mark Bevir, "The West Turns Eastward: Madame Blavatsky and the Transformation of the Occult Tradition," *Journal of the American Academy of Religion* 62, no. 3 (1994): 747–767.

68. Henry Ridgely Evans, "Madame Blavatsky," *The Monist* (1904): 387–408.

69. Bevir, "The West Turns Eastward."

70. Glen Magee, *Hegel and The Hermetic Tradition* (Ithaca, NY: Cornell University, 2001).

71. While Hegel's philosophy is typically opaque at best, a nonacademic summary of his core beliefs is available in Paul Strathern, *The Essential Hegel* (London: Virgin Books, 2003), 14–20. Notably, "idealists" like Hegel didn't believe that the material world doesn't exist or isn't real, just that it isn't *everything or ultimate*. See Jeremy Dunham, Iain Hamilton, and Sean Watson, *Idealism: The History of a Philosophy* (Durham, England: Acumen, 2011), 4–13, 144–152. Further insights into Hegel's view of history and his influence on Marx are available in Isaiah Berlin, *Karl Marx: His Life and Environment* (London: Oxford University Press, 1963), 46–61.

72. This concept was the basis of Marx's hypothesis about history, known as "historical materialism." The book *The German Ideology*, comprised of manuscripts not published until well after Marx's and Engels' deaths, has been called the "first and most comprehensive statement of historical materialism" despite not "expressing the final opinions of Marx and Engels" regarding economic history (R. Pascal, "Introduction," in Karl Marx and Friedrich Engels' *The German Ideology* [New York: International Publishers, 1947], ix–xv).

73. E.g., Cyril Smith stated, "Marx takes the side of the heretics and Hermetics, of course. Like them, he knows that humanity is collectively self-creating. The heretical-Hermetic-Hegelian tradition grasped human creative activity only encased in a divine package. Marx, focusing attention on material labour, could allow God to fade away into history, and open the path to universal human emancipation, the unity of subjectivity and objectively free social practice." Cyril Smith, "Marx, Hegel, the Enlightenment and Magic," 2001, marxists.org, accessed May 16, 2024, marxists.org/reference/archive/smith-cyril/works/articles/magic.htm.

74. Annie Besant, "The Wider Outlook," in H. P. Blavatsky, H. S. Olcott, Dr. Annie Besant, and C. Jinarajadasa, *The Theosophical Society: The First Fifty Years*, ed. Basil Howell (London: The Theosophical Publishing House Ltd., 1925), 53.

75. A page from the magazine naming Besant as its editor is included among the final pages of Annie Besant, *Essays on Socialism*.

76. Mark Singleton, "Yoga, Eugenics, and Spiritual Darwinism in the Early Twentieth Century," *International Journal of Hindu Studies* 11, no. 2 (2007): 125–146.

77. For instance, she wrote, "That which we know as Yoga is the method by which evolution is quickened in the individual, and all the powers of the Self, up to the threshold of divinity, may by it be brought into manifestation in the man of the present. That is why Yoga training was necessary for the ancient scientist; he must develop in himself the three aspects of God, if he were to understand them as manifested in the universe around him" (Annie Besant, "First Lecture: Ancient and Modern Science," in Four Lectures delivered at the *Twenty-third Anniversary Meeting of the Theosophical Society at Adyar, Madras*, 1898, 2nd ed. [London: Theosophical Publishing Society, 1900], 20).

78. Annie Besant, "The Evolution of Society," 3, in Annie Besant, *Essays on Socialism* (London: Freethought Publishing Company, 1886).

79. Annie Besant, "The Socialist Movement," 22, in Annie Besant, *Essays on Socialism*.

80. Robert Ellwood and Catherine Wessinger, "The Feminism of 'Universal Brotherhood': Women in the Theosophical Movement," *Women's Leadership in Marginal Religions: Explorations Outside the Mainstream* (Chicago: University of Illinois Press, 1993), 78. Ellwood and Wessinger note that Besant promoted the idea that the "physical vehicle of the World-Teacher" was a man named J. Krishnamurti, who lived and died in the twentieth century.

81. Annie Besant, *Annie Besant: An Autobiography*, 2nd ed. (London: T. Fisher Unwin, 1893), 532. Note that while the idea of one human race is based on Scripture, the idea

that the lines can be blurred between biblical Christianity and other "creeds" certainly is not.

82. Annie Besant, "The Socialist Movement," 24, in Annie Besant, *Essays on Socialism*.

83. Annie Besant, "Socialism," in *Annie Besant: An Autobiography*, 299–328.

84. Besant, *Annie Besant*, 311.

85. Annie Besant, "Why I Am a Socialist," in *Essays on Socialism*, 2.

86. Catherine Wessinger, Dell deChant, and William Michael Ashcraft, "Theosophy, New Thought, and New Age Movements," in *Encyclopedia of Women and Religion in North America*, eds. Rosemary Skinner Keller and Rosemary Radford Ruether (Bloomington, IN: Indiana University Press, 2006), 761.

87. Alice Bailey, *The Unfinished Autobiography of Alice Bailey* (New York: Lucis Publishing Co., 1994 [originally 1951]), 162–168, 298–299.

88. She wrote, "In the work of the evolutionary cycle, however, man has to repeat what God has already done. He must himself create, in both the world of consciousness and of life." See Alice Bailey, *Education in the New Age* (New York: Lucis Publishing Co., 1987 [originally 1954]), 32.

89. Bailey, *Education in the New Age*, 14.

90. Alice Bailey, "Five Great Spiritual Events," in *The Rays and the Initiations: A Treatise on the Seven Rays*, vol. 5, (Lucis Trust, 1960), 745, accessed May 28, 2024, lucistrust.org/online_books/rays_and_the_initiations_obooks/appendix1/five_great_spiritual_events.

91. Alice Bailey, "The Present Ray Plan and the Workers," in *Esoteric Psychology: A Treatise on the Seven Rays*, vol. 1 (Lucis Trust, 1962), 174, accessed May 28, 2024.

92. Alice Bailey, "The Present Ray Plan and the Workers," 174.

93. Alice Bailey, "Rule Four," in *The Rays and the Initiations*, 109, lucistrust.org/online_books/rays_and_the_initiations_obooks/part_one_the_fourteen_rules_for_group_initiation/rule_four.

94. E.g., Alice Bailey, "The Present Ray Plan and the Workers," 171.

95. The Federation, although cooperative, is not necessarily a centralized one-world government. (Bailey, "The Present Ray Plan and the Workers," 187.)

96. Alice Bailey, "The Present Ray Plan and the Workers," 177.

97. Alice Bailey, "The Present Ray Plan and the Workers," 177.

98. Alice Bailey, "The World Situation," in Esoteric Philosophy: A Treatise on the Seven Rays, vol. 2 (Lucis Trust, 1942), 631, accessed May 28, 2024, lucistrust.org/online_books/esoteric_psychology_volume_ii/chapter_iii_humanity_today/1_the_world_situation#:~:text=The%20old%20established%20rhythms%2C%20inherent,and%20to%20the%20new%20order.

99. Alice Bailey, *Education in the New Age*, 130.

100. Lucis Trust, "History," accessed May 16, 2024, lucistrust.org/about_us/history.

101. Lucis Trust, "History," accessed May 16, 2024, lucistrust.org/about_us/history.

102. See also Bodie Hodge, "Who Is Satan and Was He Always Called 'Satan'?" Answers in Genesis, March 16, 2010, AnswersInGenesis.org/angels-and-demons/satan/who-is-satan-and-was-he-always-called-satan/; and Troy Lacey, "Lucifer and Sin," Answers in Genesis, July 18, 2008, AnswersInGenesis.org/angels-and-demons/satan/lucifer-and-sin.

103. World Goodwill, *World Goodwill Newsletter: A Quarterly Bulletin Highlighting the Energy of Goodwill in World Affairs*, no. 4 (1999): 8, accessed May 16, 2023, lucistrust.org/content/download/1740/21203/file/1999-4.PDF.

104. World Goodwill, "Transition Activities," *World Goodwill Newsletter*, 6–8.

105. World Goodwill, "Transition Activities," 6.

106. Robert Muller, *World Core Curriculum Manual* (Arlington, TX: Robert Muller School, 1986), preface quoted at openlibrary.org/works/OL16799107W/World_Core_Curriculum_Manual, accessed May 16, 2024. [Parenthetical publishing information for each book reference removed from the quote here for readability.]

107. Robert Muller, "UNESCO Prize 1989 for Peace Education," UNESCO Digital Library, 1990, accessed May 16, 2024, unesdoc.unesco.org/ark:/48223/pf0000122735.

108. Karl Marx and Friedrich Engels, *Manifesto of the Communist Party*, ed. Friedrich Engels, trans. Samuel Moore (Chicago: Charles H. Kerr & Company, 1910 [originally published in 1848]), 11.

109. Joseph Clayton, *Robert Owen: Pioneer of Social Reforms* (London: A. C. Fifield, 1908), 18–26; "Blake, William (1757–1827)," Marxists Internet Archive Encyclopedia of Marxism, marxists.org, accessed May 16, 2024, marxists.org/glossary/people/b/l.htm. It's worth remembering here that secularism, as chapter 2 pointed out, does not provide an ultimate philosophical foundation for the utopian socialists' moral projects. "Is There a Secular Foundation for Morality?" Answers in Genesis, July 14, 2023, AnswersInGenesis.org/morality/there-secular-foundation-morality.

110. Correspondingly, Christians alive during Blake and Owen's lifetimes acted consistently with a biblical worldview to help abolish Britain's official slave trade, make education more accessible for the needy, and reform factories, prisons, hospitals, and orphanages. A few famous examples of such reformers in England include William Wilberforce, Hannah Moore, and Lord Shaftesbury. More information is available in Eric Metaxas, *Amazing Grace: William Wilberforce and the Heroic Campaign to End Slavery* (Grand Rapids, MI: Zondervan, 2007); Eric Metaxas, *Seven Women: And the Secret of Their Greatness* (Nashville: Thomas Nelson, 2015); and David Furse-Roberts, *The Making of a Tory Evangelical: Lord Shaftesbury and the Evolving Character of Victorian Evangelicalism* (Eugene, OR: Wipf and Stock, 2019).

MATTHEW 7:15-16

BEWARE OF FALSE PROPHETS, WHO COME TO YOU IN SHEEP'S CLOTHING BUT INWARDLY ARE RAVENOUS WOLVES. YOU WILL RECOGNIZE THEM BY THEIR FRUITS.

CHAPTER 5

HOW THE WEST BECAME WOKE

THE RISE AND REIGN OF NEO-MARXISM

- "At least 25 Americans were killed during protests and political unrest in 2020."[1]
- "Churches burned to the ground in Canada in 'anti-church hate crime wave.'"[2]
- "Preacher arrested for preaching biblical marriage from Genesis on a London street."[3]
- "New Jersey is the latest state to require schools to offer courses on diversity and unconscious bias."[4]
- "Court rules against employee fired for refusing to attend LGBTQ training session."[5]
- "Proposed Canadian law could see Christians jailed for quoting the Bible."[6]

That's just a snapshot of the types of headlines we're bound to see more often—at least in the places that preserve freedom of the press.[7] The topics in these headlines reflect themes from the neo-Marxist posters I saw on my travels, which pointed to issues including colonialism, the climate crisis, patriarchy, and racism (even though Marx himself expressed blatantly racist statements).[8]

As we saw in chapter 2, neo-Marxist movements approach these issues through a faulty worldview. The result can only be faulty solutions. Even so, the false gospel of neo-Marxism has gained massive momentum, becoming a staple doctrine taught at schools, churches, and society at large. In today's cancel culture, Christians who resist affirming the unbiblical aspects of such teachings face increasing personal, professional, and academic risks.

THE FALSE GOSPEL OF NEO-MARXISM HAS GAINED MASSIVE MOMENTUM.

For all these reasons, Christians must be equipped to recognize and respond to neo-Marxist messages. Let's start by recapping the major tenets of neo-Marxism in today's critical theories. Then we can look at some influential thinkers behind these theories in order to better trace their teachings, strategies, and impacts today.

CRITICAL THEORY 101

Rooted in the Marxist worldview outlined in chapter 2, critical theories are modes of thinking that "question all aspects of the current system of society . . . with the goal of instantiating new social forms."[9] In other words, critical theorists critique society in hopes of igniting a revolution.[10]

Like Marx, critical theorists divide society into **oppressor** vs. **oppressed** groups, with no neutral ground between. We've seen how Marx viewed the wealthy as **oppressors** and workers as **oppressed**. But critical theories extend these labels of "oppressors vs. oppressed" to other social categories, including "men vs. women," "'White' vs.

'Black,'"[11] "heterosexual vs. LGBTQ," "able-bodied vs. disabled," and "colonialists vs. indigenous."

If a person belongs to a group considered oppressive, critical theorists automatically deem that individual guilty of being an oppressor, regardless of the person's outward behavior or inward character.[12] By definition then, critical theories are prejudiced. They pre-judge people as **guilty** based on traits, including gender and skin tone.

How could anyone be an oppressor without intentionally oppressing anyone? To find out how critical theorists might answer, we'll have to think about how critical theories define "justice" and "oppression" in contrast to the biblical view. God's Word portrays **justice** primarily as a matter of righteous actions, attitudes, and personal character. God is a just God who performs just actions. Biblical justice insists upon impartiality, righteousness in legal judgments, honest dealings, and the defense of the needy.[13] Relatedly, Scripture depicts **oppression** in terms of wrong actions committed against other image bearers—especially vulnerable groups, including widows, orphans, and the poor.[14]

CRITICAL THEORIES =
MODES OF THINKING THAT "QUESTION ALL ASPECTS OF THE CURRENT SYSTEM OF SOCIETY . . . WITH THE GOAL OF INSTANTIATING NEW SOCIAL FORMS."

In contrast, critical theories portray justice and oppression primarily in terms of **identity** and **power**. According to critical theories, people with certain identifying traits (for instance, Christian European males) hold all the relevant power in society. The resulting power imbalance splits society into **domineering** and **dominated** groups—the **oppressors** and the **oppressed**.

Critical theorists believe that social institutions, including churches, schools, families, and governments, keep oppressors in power. These systems, which cause **disparities**, **inequalities**, and **injustices**, are embedded within society.[15] (Remember that critical theories define concepts like **equality** and **justice** far differently than a traditional, biblical understanding of these words.[16]) This is the idea of **systemic oppression**.

THIS IS THE IDEA OF SYSTEMIC OPPRESSION.

By this thinking, even a blonde two-year-old boy toddling along with a teddy bear would count as an oppressor. The teddy-toting toddler may never have hurt a soul, but because he's an able-bodied European male, critical theorists would say he's benefiting from a social system that gives him power over others. Therefore he's guilty of being an oppressor.

Critical theorists believe that the more oppressive groups you identify with, the more you benefit from a society that privileges oppressors and the more oppressive you personally are. On the flip side, the more **oppressed** groups you identify with, the more injustices you experience and the more oppressed you personally are. This is the idea of **intersectionality**. Critical theorists conclude that people need to agree that systemic oppression is happening (in other words, to become "woke") and struggle for social transformation (revolution) by transferring power to oppressed identities.

As Dr. Owen Strachan points out, Christians must not confuse such "wokeness" with righteous stances stemming from a biblical worldview.[17] These stances include:

- Hating evils, including ethnic prejudice,[18] exploitation, and violence.
- Recognizing past and present patterns of abuse and partiality and "wanting to leave such evil behind."[19]
- Seeking unity, peace, and justice as presented in the Bible.
- Being troubled about past instances where Christians have acted unbiblically in these regards.

Where patterns of unbiblical partiality exist—whether in healthcare, education, corporations, or elsewhere—God's Word provides a basis for addressing them. But critical theories go far beyond a biblical view by prejudging people as "bad" or "good" based on their identities regardless of their actions. Instead of recognizing sin as the ultimate problem, critical theorists view **certain identity groups** as the problem. A person who belongs to a group considered **oppressed** can effectively do no evil, while a person who belongs to a group considered **oppressive** cannot help being evil.

CRITICAL THEORISTS VIEW CERTAIN IDENTITY GROUPS AS THE PROBLEM.

Critical theorists unbiblically see morality in terms of "good" and "bad" identities, forgetting that, as Soviet dissident Aleksandr Solzhenitsyn pointed out, "The line separating good and evil passes not through states, nor between classes, nor between political parties either—but right through every human heart—and through all human hearts."[20] As Romans 3:23 says, "All have sinned and fall short of the glory of God." It's not our demographics that make us bad or good; every human needs Jesus. The gospel offers hope because Jesus alone addresses the problem of the sinful human heart.

Along with embracing unbiblical views of morality, oppression, and justice, critical theories assume a faulty view of truth. Rather than acknowledging truth as rooted in God's character, the philosophy behind critical theories "[rejects] all claims to absolute truth."[21] Critical theories instead claim that "what is true is whatever fosters social change in the direction of a rational [i.e., a revolutionized] society."[22] In practice, these theories make the inner feelings and "lived experiences" of oppressed identity groups the authority for truth. No questions allowed.

WHERE DID THESE UNBIBLICAL IDEAS ORIGINATE?

Dr. Voddie Baucham and Dr. Owen Strachan have shown how critical theories have gained massive traction not only in secular society but also in evangelical churches.[23] Where did these unbiblical ideas originate, and how did they become so popular? In other words, how did the West become woke? To find out, let's rewind through history to meet some of the key thinkers behind today's neo-Marxist messages.

ANTONIO GRAMSCI (1891–1937)

To answer that question, we must first travel to the town of Turi in Southern Italy. Ask for directions to the *Carcere di Turi*, and you'll find the prison where, nearly a hundred years ago, a certain political prisoner spent hours writing. His name? **Antonio Gramsci, former leader of the Communist Party of Italy.**

Gramsci wished for the communist workers' revolution, which Marx had thought inevitable. That revolution hadn't happened as Marx predicted, and Gramsci believed he knew why. Even if the workers tried to revolt, Gramsci reasoned, they couldn't succeed because the **ideas** which kept the current system in place were too ingrained in culture. Before a **political** revolution could happen, society needed a **cultural** revolution.[24]

> **BEFORE A POLITICAL REVOLUTION COULD HAPPEN, SOCIETY NEEDED A CULTURAL REVOLUTION.**

With these ideas, Gramsci became one of the first famous thinkers to apply Marx's ideas of conflict between **economic** groups to conflict between **cultural** groups. To Gramsci, groups with the most mainstream influence in culture have power to dominate marginalized groups. He called this power "cultural hegemony."[25] Hegemonic power, thought Gramsci, lets oppressive groups keep their political control by dominating civil institutions like churches, schools, and law enforcement.[26]

According to Gramsci, this system didn't just oppress the working class. One Gramscian scholar wrote, "In Notebook 25, Gramsci identifies slaves, peasants, religious groups, women, different races, and the proletariat as subaltern [marginalized] social groups."[27] (Already, we can see parallels between Gramsci's teachings and critical theories.[28])

How did Gramsci think oppressed groups could turn the tables? Much like today's critical theorists teach, Gramsci believed these groups needed to awaken to their oppression, organize themselves, and struggle to change their social positions.[29] This struggle, according to Gramsci, would involve oppressed groups setting up a **counter-hegemony** by solidifying their own culture, creating social values, and replacing their oppressors' cultural influence.[30] The key to political revolution lies in capturing the culture.

COUNTER-HEGEMONY = A PROCESS THAT AIMS TO CHALLENGE THE STATUS QUO AND THE LEGITIMACY OF EXISTING POWER STRUCTURES

This cultural transformation would require subverting the institutions of "civil society," including church, media, and schools, which Gramsci viewed as sustaining oppression.[31] Meanwhile, the media[32] and public education[33] could be harnessed to influence a new generation of revolutionaries. (We'll look closer at **how** Gramsci planned to execute these strategies in part two.)

Gramsci's explicit goal was to establish a new religion of Marxist secular humanism.[34] Although an atheist, he recognized that humans need some sort of spirituality—something greater than ourselves to believe in, giving us meaning, morality, and social stability.[35] But Gramsci didn't want this stability for the **current** society, which he believed had to be overthrown. Humanity needed a **new** society with a new religion: Marxism. Gramsci lamented that in Italy, "religion has remained at the level of superstition, but it has not been replaced by a new humanistic and secular morality, because of the impotence of the lay intellectuals."[36] He also wrote that "socialism is precisely the religion that has to kill Christianity."[37]

GRAMSCI'S EXPLICIT GOAL WAS TO ESTABLISH A NEW RELIGION OF MARXIST SECULAR HUMANISM.

Clearly, Gramsci's goals, strategies, and impacts are too significant for Christians to ignore. But Gramsci wasn't alone in applying Marx's ideas to culture. To meet the group responsible for directly translating Marxism into critical theories, let's leave the *Carcere di Turi* and head northwest to Frankfurt, Germany.

THE FRANKFURT SCHOOL

Not every philosophical movement is born under a whale skeleton. But in 1923, a skeletal whale, ichthyosaur, and dinosaur presided over the birth of the Frankfurt Institute for Social Research (the Frankfurt School).[38] Until the institute could move into its headquarters at Frankfurt's Goethe University, a natural history museum had lent the Frankfurt School temporary desk spaces among the skeletons.

So began the group of thinkers famous for developing Critical Theory.[39] A 1999 article in *The Canadian Journal of Sociology* summarized,

> The Frankfurt School was a tight network of independent radical philosophers, economists and sociologists associated with the German Institute for Social Research—essentially a Marxist think tank bankrolled by the radical son of a German millionaire grain merchant. The institute was founded in the early 1920s with the purpose of promoting the development of radical intellectual ideas not controlled by traditional Marxist and social democratic parties or academic disciplines.[40]

Underscoring the Frankfurt School's Marxist nature, historian Martin Jay wrote that the name "Institute for Social Research" had been chosen because "the original idea of calling it the *Institut für Marxismus* (Institute for Marxism) was abandoned as too provocative."[41] Jay also reported that in the dedication speech for the institute's building, the group's original leader declared "his personal allegiance to Marxism" to reaffirm that "Marxism would be the ruling principle" at the institute.[42]

This commitment to Marxism took a subtler turn when Nazism forced the institute to relocate to New York's Columbia University. In those days, said Jay, "careful editing prevented emphasizing the revolutionary implications of their thought."[43] The following years saw institute members accept teaching positions at universities across America and in the UK.[44] Higher education became a quiet but effective engine for distributing the Frankfurt brand of neo-Marxism, which blended ideas from Karl Marx and Sigmund Freud. Before looking closer at these ideas, we'd better check what Freud had been up to.

MARXISM WOULD BE THE RULING PRINCIPLE.

SIGMUND FREUD (1856–1939)

Follow Vienna's scenic streets to the address *Berggasse 19, 1090 Wien*, climb the stairs beyond the building's arch-shaped entrance, and you'll enter the former office, home, and clinic of pioneering psychoanalyst Sigmund Freud. Whether interpreting nightmares, evaluating psychotic episodes, or explaining phobias, Freud chalked up almost every aspect of human behavior to repressed sexual motives.

These motives, thought Freud, existed from infanthood. Carl Trueman wrote, "[The] sexualization of childhood and even infancy . . . owes more to Freud than to any other individual thinker."[45] As the next chapter unpacks, child sexualization plays a strategic—and unspeakably destructive—role in agendas to destabilize society, consistent with a neo-Marxist worldview.

Freud, as an atheist, rejected a biblical worldview. Beginning instead from an evolutionary perspective,[46] Freud constructed his own beliefs around the idea that unconscious processes drive the bulk of human behavior. In Freud's (now largely discredited) thinking, the human mind has three aspects.[47]

1. The **id** looks for gratification by pursuing "animal instincts" (especially sexual ones).
2. The **ego** tries to make sure the id only expresses itself in ways that won't reap disaster.
3. The **superego** works as a moral compass that usually disagrees with the id.[48]

Freud thought that even babies possess an id (and therefore sexuality), with the ego and superego arising later as children learn to live in families and civilization.[49] This thinking led Freud to unbiblically view morality as a human construct. Echoing Rousseau's ideas from chapter 3, Freud thought humans invented morals to get along in society at the cost of having to repress their authentic selves.[50] By welding Freud's thinking with Marxism, the Frankfurt School forged a new philosophical weapon for attacking the biblical institution of family.

FREUD THOUGHT THAT EVEN BABIES POSSESS AN ID (AND THEREFORE SEXUALITY).

THE FRANKFURT ATTACK ON FAMILY

How high did the task of deconstructing family rank on the Frankfurt School's agenda? In answer, feminist scholar Barbara Umrath wrote in the *Berlin Journal of Critical Theory*:

> [A]n early research proposal available at the archives of the Institute for Social Research in Frankfurt makes the case for focusing on a particular social institution: the family. . . . Stressing its role as a nexus of economy, culture, and psyche,[51] the research proposal concludes that the family represents a particularly promising starting point for developing a non-economistic, comprehensive critical social theory.[52]

In other words, critical theory is quite literally founded on a Marxist critique of family. Umrath connects this critique to the institute's "first major research project" under its second leader, Max Horkheimer. The project's name? *Studien über Autorität und Familie*—Studies on Authority and Family.

Horkheimer's first essay for this project treated the nuclear family as "neither 'natural' nor 'eternal.'"[53] Instead, he viewed the family through a Marxist lens as a social construct that grew from men and women adopting different labor roles.[54] The family, by this thinking, functions as a unit of oppression, with men oppressing women, parents oppressing kids, and kids learning to perpetuate oppression.[55]

Adding Freud's ideas to this view, another early member of the institute, Erich Fromm, speculated that fathers oppress wives and children to release unconscious domineering tendencies.[56] Along the way, thought Fromm, sons begin to identify with their patriarchal dads, becoming conditioned to obey the powerful and oppress the powerless.[57] In the Frankfurt School's critique of the family, we glimpse the silhouette of today's critical theories which pin the label "oppressor" on **men** in general and **fathers** in particular.

Aspects of our current culture's messages, which claim that **male** and **female** are social constructs, also appeared in the Frankfurt School. Umrath said that in their quest to blend Marx and Freud, "major Frankfurt School protagonists even went as far as suggesting that the binary character of gender was nothing natural or innate, but rather a product of culture."[58]

Sound familiar?

These aren't the only ways a cocktail of Marxist and Freudian thinking still influences culture. To see more, we'll need to meet one of the Frankfurt School's most famous members: Herbert Marcuse.

HERBERT MARCUSE (1898–1979)

He's been called the "grandfather of the New Left,"[59] America's "most visionary social philosopher,"[60] and "one of the principal architects of critical theory."[61] Marcuse's story, however, began in Berlin. While Nazism rose in Germany, Marcuse joined the Frankfurt School's Swiss office. He emigrated to America in 1934, working at the Frankfurt School's Columbia University headquarters before joining the US Office of War Information and Office of Strategic Services. Marcuse also taught as a professor at American institutions, including Harvard, the University of San Diego, and Columbia University, where he "openly taught Marxism."[62]

Like other Marxists, Marcuse thought modern capitalism inherently oppressed people, preventing them from being free.[63] But what did Marcuse mean by "freedom"? Following Freud's belief that civilization forces people to repress their sexuality,[64] Marcuse understood "freedom" as the absence of "repression."[65] Although God's Word reveals that sexual immorality enslaves its practitioners (e.g., Ecclesiastes 7:26; 1 Corinthians 6:12–18), Marcuse assumed the opposite. Liberty, he suggested, entails licentiousness.[66]

Marcuse believed capitalism had provided the scientific, technological, and material resources to let people be "free" this way—to live primarily for gratifying their ids rather than spending all their time working.[67] But he thought capitalistic societies trick people into wasting these resources on needless consumerism.[68] The result, according to Marcuse, is that people **sustain** the system which oppresses them instead of **revolting against** that system.

MARCUSE ASSUMED THE OPPOSITE. LIBERTY, HE SUGGESTED, ENTAILS LICENTIOUSNESS.

Unlike Marx, Marcuse didn't think this revolution would only involve workers or could only happen at an economic level.[69] The revolution Marcuse sought would require a transformation in humanity itself—a change in human thinking, desires, and even (at least in a figurative sense) biology.[70]

So who would bring about this ultraradical revolution, if not the working class? Marcuse suggested the best agents for opposing capitalism included **youth**, **intellectuals**, **ethnic minorities**, and **the underprivileged**—a group Marcuse called the "ghetto class."[71] He also saw revolutionary potential in environmental movements[72] and the homosexual community, which he perceived as rebelling against society's repressiveness.[73]

Already, we can see how many ways Marcuse's thinking is playing out in society today. But there's more. To sense just how Marcusian our culture has become, we only need to look at Marcuse's views on "tolerance."

AN INTOLERANT TOLERANCE

In his essay "Repressive Tolerance," Marcuse (by all appearances) advocated for a kind of "tolerance" based on **intolerance**.[74] He called for "**intolerance** toward prevailing policies, attitudes, opinions, and the extension of tolerance to policies, attitudes, and opinions which are outlawed or suppressed."[75]

WHO SHOULD DEFINE WHICH OPINIONS DESERVE TOLERANCE?

Who should define which opinions deserve tolerance? Marcuse said this task belonged to "everyone 'in the maturity of his faculties' as a human being, everyone who has learned to think rationally and autonomously."[76] But who decides which people have mature faculties? Marcuse's answer leaves no doubt about his meaning—or his politics. His essay consistently implied that for all practical purposes, being 'rational' and 'mature' meant affirming neo-Marxism.[77] Marcuse clarified: "Liberating tolerance, then, would mean intolerance against movements from the Right and toleration of movements from the Left."[78]

So Marcuse wanted a tolerant society—as long as that tolerance only extended to certain people. (Ironic, right?) By calling for **intolerance** in the name of tolerance, Marcuse's essay serves as a recipe for cancel culture. This becomes even clearer in a passage about democracy.

The passage in his essay argues that, because democracy lets citizens make decisions, people should be able to make decisions that **undermine** democracy—even if allowing these decisions requires "apparently undemocratic means."[79] Wait, *what* kind of means? Marcuse answers, "[These means] would include the withdrawal of toleration of speech and assembly from groups and movements which promote aggressive policies, armament, chauvinism, discrimination on the grounds of race and religion, or which oppose the extension of public services, social security, medical care, etc."[80]

Essentially, Marcuse is arguing for taking away certain basic freedoms from people whose views he considers aggressive, discriminatory, or too conservative.[81] He advocated not only for censorship but also for "precensorship."[82] This precensorship would involve "stopping the words and images" that feed a mindset Marcuse called "false consciousness"—the idea that society is fine as is and can't (or shouldn't) be revolutionized.[83] He wrote,

HE ADVOCATED NOT ONLY FOR CENSORSHIP BUT ALSO FOR "PRECENSORSHIP."

> The whole post-fascist period is one of clear and present danger. Consequently, true pacification requires the withdrawal of tolerance before the deed, at the stage of communication in word, print, and picture. Such extreme suspension of the right of free speech and free assembly is indeed justified only if the whole of society is in extreme danger. I maintain that our society is in such an emergency situation, and that it has become the normal state of affairs.[84]

So Marcuse thought that erasing rights was justifiable because false consciousness endangered society by **preventing** society from being revolutionized. He believed that either civil freedoms for "oppressors" must go, or "oppressed groups" would disappear.[85] But is that true?

Not necessarily. Marcuse relied on a logical mistake called an either/or fallacy, which offers only two options when others might be possible. To Marcuse, society's options were *revolution or bust*.

Where did Marcuse think this revolution could unfold? On the stages of the education system. He suggested we may need "new and rigid restrictions on teachings and practices" in schools[86] and forecast the type of cancel culture we see in education systems—and broader society—today.[87]

To better understand some of the other neo-Marxist trends we're seeing in today's education systems,[88] let's leave Marcuse for now and head to Brazil. There we'll meet a radical educator named Paulo Freire.

PAULO FREIRE (1921–1997)

Born to a middle-class family in the Brazilian city of Recife, Paulo Freire's earliest influences included his Catholic mother and "spiritualist" father, who died when Freire was 13.[89] The family experienced economic hardship afterward, and Freire recognized poverty as a significant problem which caused suffering to others around him.[90] Despite identifying as a Christian, Freire began to view the world's real problems through a faulty lens that combined Marxism with "progressive theology."[91]

One theologian who profoundly influenced Freire was Pierre Teilhard de Chardin,[92] an evolutionary paleontologist and Jesuit priest who became an influential forerunner of the New Age movement.[93] According to Teilhard, a process called "planetization"[94] would drive human evolution to an "Omega Point" of reaching God-like consciousness. (Doesn't that sound suspiciously like Lie #3, "You will be like God," from chapter 2?)

Blending Teilhard's ideas with Marx's, Freire thought humans could apply revolutionary thinking and action "to recreate, to remake, the natural process through which consciousness appeared in the process of [human] evolution."[95] Central to Freire's thinking were the Marxist doctrines that humans are **creators** of themselves and their world,[96] and that only through revolution could people become "fully human."[97] Freire perceived that the key to this revolution, which he viewed as a **continuous** cultural process,[98] lay in education.

ONLY THROUGH REVOLUTION COULD PEOPLE BECOME "FULLY HUMAN."

To Freire, education is **always political** and **never neutral**.[99] He thought education either promotes revolution or it sustains oppression. Education usually sustains oppression, Freire believed, because "oppressor" groups run the public education systems, impose their values on students, and decide what skills to teach—skills like reading, writing, and math.[100] These skills help society function, but Freire thought society needed to be **changed**, not sustained. He believed that education should teach students to question, critique, and ultimately revolutionize society. Freire suggested, for instance, that learning to read and write "is not a matter of memorizing and repeating given syllables, words, and phrases but rather of reflecting critically on the process of reading and writing itself and on the profound significance of language."[101]

In other words, Freire thought students should not just learn to read but learn to **think about reading** through a Marxist lens. Similarly, instead of simply teaching science, teachers might present a historical lack of gender diversity in science-related jobs as a problem which students should reflect on how to change. This method, called "problem-posing," trains students to think like critical theorists.

Freire taught that education should be a democratic dialogue. As one scholar explained, "Students have equal speaking rights [as the teacher] . . . as well as the right to negotiate the curriculum. They are asked to co-develop and evaluate the curriculum."[102] By these and other methods, schools were to function as Marxist discipleship centers.[103]

BY THESE AND OTHER METHODS, SCHOOLS WERE TO FUNCTION AS MARXIST DISCIPLESHIP CENTERS.

In more ways than one, Freire's ideas had a radical impact on education—and on churches. Freire served as a consultant for UNESCO, worked for the World Council of Churches, and "significantly contributed to the thinking of liberation theology."[104] Reflecting Freire's ongoing influence, a study in 2016 identified his book *Pedagogy of the Oppressed* as Google Scholar's third-most cited social science book up to that time.[105]

SEL = SOCIAL AND EMOTIONAL LEARNING

Freire also comes up by name on the United Nation's web page for its curriculum known as Global Citizenship Education for Social and Emotional Learning (SEL).[106] Because of the role certain types of SEL play in taking neo-Marxism to a new generation, it's worth taking a closer look at what SEL is and where it originated.

A CLOSER LOOK AT SEL

There's not exactly a simple definition for SEL. A primary organization promoting SEL, the Collaborative for Academic, Social, and Emotional Learning (CASEL), defines it as

> the process through which all young people and adults acquire and apply the knowledge, skills, and attitudes to develop healthy identities, manage emotions and achieve personal and collective goals, feel and show empathy for others, establish and maintain supportive relationships, and make responsible and caring decisions.[107]

This might sound fantastic at first. But terms like "healthy identities" can be defined in ways that promote unbiblical ideas, including critical theories. In fact, an entire branch of SEL curriculum called *transformative SEL* is dedicated to this purpose. According to CASEL, transformative SEL "honors and makes connections to students' lived experiences and identities," focusing on examining "current and historical events; social norms; prejudices and biases; and how issues of race, class, and culture impact our society."[108] The goal is to provide "opportunities for youth to use their voice and skills to examine inequities and create solutions for social change."[109]

As transformative SEL's focus on critical theories shows, there's more to SEL than happy buzzwords. For instance, remember Alice Bailey, an occultist from the last chapter? One of her ardent fans and followers was New Age proponent John Fetzer, founder of the Fetzer Institute.[110] As an article in the journal *Educational Psychology Review* notes, the Fetzer Institute financed early research for integrating "emotional intelligence" into education, arranged meetings between emotional intelligence researchers and educators, and "assisted with the development of organizations such as the Collaborative for the Advancement of Social and Emotional Learning (CASEL)."[111]

Considering these connections, we shouldn't be surprised to see overlap between SEL and the goals for education, which Bailey and her New Age organization, Lucis Trust, promoted. For example, the 1999 newsletter by World Goodwill (an NGO established by Lucis Trust) stated,

> What is needed is an education which engages the **whole person right from the start**, developing the latent powers of the individual sequentially throughout life, so that these gifts may be freely used in service to the world. An education of this kind would naturally be a powerful way of **building a different kind of society**, one modelled on the principles of freedom, unity, and right relations. (emphasis added)

These statements align significantly with the language of SEL. For instance, a 2020 report from CASEL promotes SEL as "a driver of systems-wide change,"[112] reflecting World Goodwill's desire to build another kind of society. Further echoing the words of World Goodwill, the *Handbook of Social and Emotional Learning* repeatedly refers to educating the "whole child" starting from an early age, not only **during** school but also through after-school programs.[113] (While whole-child education might sound great, the problem is that the whole child does not belong to the state. Parents, not state schools, have the primary responsibility to disciple their whole child—who belongs to God—with a biblical worldview.)

PARENTS HAVE THE PRIMARY RESPONSIBILITY TO DISCIPLE THEIR WHOLE CHILD.

Given these overlaps between SEL, Bailey's organization, and the UN, we can better see why the UN promotes SEL as part of its Freire-influenced curriculum. In case there was any doubt about its basis in neo-Marxist critical theories, the curriculum's web page previously stated:

> The curriculum for Global Citizenship has been [*sic*] designed using the Libre process. The Libre process adopts a "problem-based" approach to education as a tool that enables learners to build critical consciousness to drive "active citizenship" that not only frames their identity, but powers them to critically analyse and understand the systemic, cultural and physical causes and manifestations of exclusion and marginalization.[114]

Say what?

Basically, the UN is saying that they're teaching students to view the world through the lens of systemic oppression. The UN developed this curriculum as part of its Sustainable Development Goals,[115] which the World Economic Forum (WEF) also strives to advance.[116] Accordingly, the WEF released a 2016 report titled *Vision for Education: Fostering Social and Emotional Learning through Technology*, which advocates for SEL "starting at the earliest stages of [childhood] development and continuing through secondary schooling."[117] But the WEF and UN aren't alone in promoting SEL. SEL is gaining traction in Christian education as well.[118] Although not everything called SEL may necessarily promote unbiblical ideas, Christian parents must be vigilant lest their "whole child" be discipled with ideas that contradict Scripture.

SUMMING UP

Young people are being discipled to think like neo-Marxists. These youth will be Western nations' next voters, parents, business managers, politicians, and other decision-makers. The Freirean-style classes popular now—like the college classrooms of Frankfurt School professors in the 20th century—are sowing a destructive worldview that contradicts God's Word. Meanwhile, as Dr. Owen Strachan and Dr. Voddie Baucham have shown, the same unbiblical teachings have taken root in evangelical churches.[119] The West is now thoroughly woke.

The neo-Marxist worldview pervading culture, classrooms, and churches is the secular religion Gramsci envisioned replacing Christianity. This religion leaves no room for tolerating those who make God's Word their authority. For this reason, we're seeing Marcuse's version of one-way "tolerance" playing out in the form of cancel culture. All these factors help explain why we can expect headlines to only show increasing hostility against Christians who stand on God's Word.

But there's good news too. God's truth has not changed, and neither has our calling to live faithfully for Christ. We'll likely never again live in "Christian nations" with the level of freedom many Westerners in recent generations have experienced. But God remains in control. As we seek to stand on his Word, we can respond to our increasingly hostile culture in biblical, practical ways—including by countering neo-Marxism's own strategies.

This requires **knowing** their strategies, which is the focus of part two of this book.

Ready to get started?

ENDNOTES

1. Lois Beckett, "At Least 25 Americans Were Killed During Protests and Political Unrest in 2020," *The Guardian*, October 31, 2020, theguardian.com/world/2020/oct/31/americans-killed-protests-political-unrest-acled.

2. Joshua Comins, "Churches Burned to the Ground in Canada in 'Anti-Church Hate Crime Wave,'" *Fox News*, July 7, 2021, foxnews.com/media/churches-burned-to-the-ground-in-canada-in-anti-church-hate-crime-wave.

3. Emily Wood, "Preacher Arrested for Preaching Biblical Marriage from Genesis on a London Street," The Christian Post, May 4, 2021, christianpost.com/news/preacher-arrested-for-preaching-biblical-marriage-on-uk-street.html.

4. Sahar Akbarzai, "New Jersey Is the Latest State to Require Schools to Offer Courses on Diversity and Unconscious Bias," CNN, April 11, 2021, cnn.com/2021/04/11/us/schools-new-jersey-new-law-unconscious-bias/index.html.

5. Cortney O'Brien, "Court Rules Against Employee Fired for Refusing to Attend LGBTQ Training Session," *Fox News*, March 15, 2023, foxnews.com/media/court-rules-against-employee-fired-refusing-attend-lgbtq-training-session.

6. David Cooke, "Proposed Canadian Law Could See Christians Jailed for Quoting the Bible," *LifeSite News*, February 20, 2024, lifesitenews.com/opinion/proposed-canadian-law-could-see-christians-jailed-for-quoting-the-bible/.

7. Unfortunately, this freedom already appears to be significantly diminished in countries like Canada, where current legislation affects news visibility. See Sen. David Richards, "Liberals' Bill C-11 is 'Censorship Passing as National Inclusion,'" *National Post*, February 3, 2023, nationalpost.com/opinion/sen-david-richards-liberals-bill-c-11-is-censorship-passing-as-national-inclusion. See also, "'Fake News' and the Rise of Censorship: A Biblical Response," Answers in Genesis, July 21, 2021, AnswersInGenesis.org/blogs/patricia-engler/2021/07/21/fake-news-rise-censorship/.

8. In a letter to Engels, for instance, Marx endorsed Pierre Trémaux's evolutionary book (the French title of which translates to *Origin and Transformations of Man and Other Beings*), calling "its historical and political applications far more significant and pregnant than Darwin. . . . [Trémaux] shows that the common [racial label deleted] type is only a degeneration of a far higher one" (Karl Marx, in a letter to Friedrich Engels dated August 7, 1866, available in Karl Marx and Friedrich Engels: Collected Works, Vol. 42 [1864–1868], trans. Christopher Upward and John Peet [New York: International Publishers; Moscow: Progress Publishers, 1987], 305). While a biblical worldview provides the foundation for calling racism evil, such evil ideas are consistent with the evolutionary worldview that Marx embraced. For the connections between evolution and racism, see AnswersInGenesis.org/charles-darwin/racism/, and Ken Ham and Charles Ware, *One Race One Blood: The Biblical Answer to Racism* rev. ed. (Green Forest, AR: Master Books, 2019), AnswersInGenesis.org/store/product/one-race-one-blood-revised-updated/.

9. Dino Franco Felluga, *Critical Theory: The Key Concepts* (London: Routledge, 2015), xxiii, drawing on Max Horkheimer, "Critical and Traditional Theories," in *Selected Essays*, trans. M. J. O'Connell (New York: Herder and Herder, 1972).

10. See also Dr. Voddie Baucham Jr., *Fault Lines: The Social Justice Movement and Evangelicalism's Looming Catastrophe* (Washington, D.C.: Salem, 2021), xiii.

11. As Dr. Charles Ware and Ken Ham discuss in *One Race One Blood*, all human skin tones are different shades of the same color brown from the pigment known as melanin.

12. See Owen Strachan, *Christianity and Wokeness* (Washington, D.C.: Salem, 2021), 11–13.

13. E.g., see Leviticus 19:15; Psalm 82:3; Proverbs 11:1, 31:9; Isaiah 1:17; Jeremiah 22:3; and Amos 5:15.

14. E.g., Jeremiah 22:3–5; Isaiah 1:17, 10:1–3; Zechariah 7:10; Malachi 3:5. Notably, God's Word absolutely calls Christians to help the hungry, needy, exploited, and destitute—widows and orphans, patients and prisoners, strangers and sojourners (see Matthew 25:31–46; Hebrews 13:1–3; James 2:15–16). We must do so, however, without partiality (see 1 Timothy 5:21; Leviticus 19:15; Acts 10:34–35; Romans 2:11; Ephesians 6:9) in the name of Jesus rather than the name of revolutionary social justice. A biblical worldview is what provides us the basis for valuing, defending, and loving others in these ways.

15. Strachan, *Christianity and Wokeness*, 25.

16. For example, as Dr. Erwin Lutzer explains, today's neo-Marxist messages often speak of "equality" as demanding equal *traits* and *outcomes* in ways that don't align with a biblical understanding of equality, which recognizes that humans possess *equal value* as image bearers of God, have *equal responsibility* as image bearers to use our differing God-given gifts, and deserve *equal rights* associated with being an image bearer (e.g., the rights for an innocent human not to be killed or cursed by another image bearer—see Genesis 9:6 and James 3:9; see also "God's Image as the Foundation of Human Rights," Answers in Genesis, January 25, 2023, AnswersInGenesis.org/sanctity-of-life/gods-image-as-the-foundation-for-human-rights). Lutzer also notes that the word *equality* is being "applied to every imaginable social cause" in ways that contradict God's Word—for instance, demanding "reproductive equality" to argue for abortion. See Erwin Lutzer, *We Will Not Be Silenced: Responding Courageously to Our Culture's Assault on Christianity* (Eugene, OR: Harvest House Publishers, 2020), 74–78 (ebook version). Relatedly, for further discussion of the difference between biblical and neo-Marxist definitions of justice, see Lutzer, *We Will Not Be Silenced*, 78–81.

17. Strachan, *Christianity and Wokeness*, 4–6.

18. Scripture affirms that while a variety of people groups descended from Adam, there is only one human race (see Ham and Ware, *One Race One Blood*).

19. Strachan, *Christianity and Wokeness*, 5.

20. Aleksandr Solzhenitsyn, *The Gulag Archipelago 1918–1956*, trans. Thomas Whitney and Harry Willetts, abridged by Edward Ericson (New York: Perennial Classics, 2002 [originally 1973]), 312.

21. Jay, *Dialectical Imagination*, 63.

22. Jay, *Dialectical Imagination*, 63.

23. Baucham, *Fault Lines*; Strachan, *Christianity and Wokeness*.

24. For a summary of Gramsci's thinking in these regards, see Marcus Green, "Gramsci Cannot Speak: Presentations and Interpretations of Gramsci's Concept of the Subaltern," *Rethinking Marxism* 14, no. 3 (2002): 1–24.

25. Gramsci, *Selections from Prison Notebooks*, 258. For more on Gramsci's concept of hegemony, see Jackson Lears, "The Concept of Cultural Hegemony: Problems and Possibilities," *The American Historical Review* 90, no. 3 (1985): 567–593.

26. See Green, "Gramsci Cannot Speak."

27. Green, "Gramsci Cannot Speak."

28. This isn't to say that real oppression (as biblically defined) of various people groups has not been a serious problem throughout history, demanding effective solutions based on a true worldview foundation. But as chapter 2 discusses, God's Word—not Gramsci's Marxism—provides that consistent foundation for both identifying the problem *and*

enacting a solution. Sad examples of Christian hypocrisy in failing to live out a biblical worldview consistently do not undermine this reality.

29. Green, "Gramsci Cannot Speak," 19.

30. E.g., Gramsci wrote, "This revolution also presupposes the formation of a new set of standards, a new psychology, new ways of feeling, thinking and living that must be specific to the working class, that must be created by it, that will become 'dominant' when the working class becomes the dominant class" (Antonio Gramsci, *The Gramsci Reader*, ed. David Forgacs [New York: New York University Press, 2000], 70). See also Green, "Gramsci Cannot Speak."

31. Green, "Gramsci Cannot Speak." See also Rosario Forlenza, "Antonio Gramsci on Religion," *Journal of Classical Sociology* 21, no. 1 (2021): 38–60.

32. For Gramsci's observations on media, popular culture, journalism, and art as hegemonic forces with counter-hegemonic potential (that is, forces that supposedly keep the oppressive system in power but can be applied to transform culture from the inside), see Gramsci, *The Gramsci Reader*, 363–402.

33. For examples related to education, see Gramsci, *Selections from Prison Notebooks*, 35–36. See also Manojan K. P., "Capturing the Gramscian Project in Critical Pedagogy: Towards a Philosophy of Praxis in Education," *Review of Development and Change* 24, no. 1 (2019): 123–145.

34. Forlenza, "Antonio Gramsci on Religion."

35. See Forlenza, "Antonio Gramsci on Religion," and John Fulton, "Religion and Politics in Gramsci: An Introduction," *Sociological Analysis* 48, no. 3 (1987): 197–216.

36. Gramsci, *The Gramsci Reader*, 370.

37. Antonio Gramsci, "Audacia e Fede," in *Sotto la Mole: 1916–1920*, vol. 10 (Turin: Einaudi, 1960), 94, ebook version accessed August 2023 from Google Scholar, translated with Deeple. The full sentence in Italian reads, "Perché tutta questa gente non si è accorta, essa che a proposito, e piú spesso a sproposito, parla di valori spirituali, che il socialismo è precisamente la religione che deve ammazzare il cristianesimo." (Why have all these people not noticed, they who purposefully, and more often than not, speak of spiritual values, that socialism is precisely the religion that has to kill Christianity.)

38. Martin Jay, *The Dialectical Imagination: A History of the Frankfurt School and the Institute of Social Research 1923–1950* (London: Heinemann, 1973), 10.

39. Neil McLaughlin, "Origin Myths in the Social Sciences: Fromm, the Frankfurt School and the Emergence of Critical Theory," *Canadian Journal of Sociology* 24, no. 1 (1999): 109–139. Following a convention in the literature, Critical Theory is capitalized here only when referring to its original formulation by the Frankfurt School. The Stanford Encyclopedia of Philosophy explains, "While Critical Theory is often thought of narrowly as referring to the Frankfurt School that begins with Horkheimer and Adorno and stretches to Marcuse and Habermas, any philosophical approach with similar practical aims could be called a 'critical theory,' including feminism, critical race theory, and some forms of post-colonial criticism. In the following, Critical Theory when capitalized refers only to the Frankfurt School" (James Bohman, "Critical Theory," ed. Edward Zalta, *The Stanford Encyclopedia of Philosophy* [Fall 2023 Edition], accessed July 2024, plato.stanford.edu/archives/fall2023/entries/critical-theory/.)

40. McLaughlin, "Origin Myths in the Social Sciences," 111.

41. Jay, *The Dialectical Imagination*, 8.

42. Jay, *The Dialectical Imagination*, 11.

43. Jay, *The Dialectical Imagination*, 44.

44. E.g., see Jay, *The Dialectical Imagination*, 284.

45. Carl Trueman, *The Rise and Triumph of the Modern Self: Cultural Amnesia, Expressive Individualism, and the Road to Sexual Revolution* (Wheaton, IL: Crossway, 2020), 207.

46. For a detailed look at Darwin's influence on Freud, see Geoffrey Marcaggi and Fabian Guénolé, "Freudarwin: Evolutionary Thinking as a Root of Psychoanalysis," *Frontiers in Psychology* 9, article 892 (June 2018): Google Scholar.

47. Sigmund Freud, *The Ego and the Id*, trans. Joan Riviere (London: Hogarth Press, 1927).

48. This is a simplified explanation; for more information, see Martin Evan Jay, "Toward a General Theory of Sigmund Freud," History & Society, Britannica, britannica.com/biography/Sigmund-Freud/Toward-a-general-theory.

49. Freud, *The Ego and the Id*, 1927.

50. See Sigmund Freud, *Civilization and Its Discontents*, trans. Joan Riviere (London: Hogarth Press, 1930).

51. Psyche refers to the entire mind, including unconscious processes.

52. Barbara Umrath, "Recovering the Gender Dimension of Frankfurt School Critical Theory: A Feminist Analysis," *Berlin Journal of Critical Theory* 6, no. 1 (2022): 92.

53. Umrath, "Recovering the Gender Dimension," 94.

54. Umrath, "Recovering the Gender Dimension," 92–94.

55. See also Trueman, *The Rise and Triumph of the Modern Self*, 232–237, for a discussion of these themes in the writings of Marxian psychoanalyst Wilhelm Reich.

56. See Umrath, "Recovering the Gender Dimension," 104–105.

57. See Umrath, "Recovering the Gender Dimension," 106.

58. Umrath, "Recovering the Gender Dimension," 111.

59. Tom Bourne, "Herbert Marcuse: The Grandfather of the New Left," *Change* 11, no. 6 (1979): 36–37, marcuse.org/herbert/booksabout/70s/Bourne1979MarcuseGrandfatherNewLeft.pdf.

60. Charles Reitz, *Ecology and Revolution: Herbert Marcuse and the Challenge of a New World System Today* (New York: Routledge, 2018), ebook version.

61. Jay, *The Dialectical Imagination*, 28.

62. Douglas Kellner, "Introduction to the 1985 Edition," in Herbert Marcuse, *Soviet Marxism: A Critical Analysis* (New York: Columbia University Press), x.

63. This is a basic theme found throughout Marcuse's core writings, reiterated, for example, in the introduction to his *Essay on Liberation* (1969), available at marxist.org.

64. This theme is clearly seen, for example, in Marcuse's book *Eros and Civilization*. Details on Marcuse's blending of Marx and Freud in this and other books are available in Arnold Farr, "Herbert Marcuse," eds. Edward Zalta and Uri Nodelman, *The Stanford Encyclopedia of Philosophy* (Spring 2024 Edition), plato.stanford.edu/archives/spr2024/entries/marcuse.

65. He stated, "If absence from repression is the archetype of freedom, then civilization is the struggle against this freedom" (Marcuse, *Eros and Civilization: A Philosophical Inquiry into Freud* [Boston: Beacon Press, 1966], 15). Elsewhere, he also defined freedom more generally in terms of self-determination (Herbert Marcuse, "Repressive Tolerance," in *A Critique of Pure Tolerance* [London: Beacon Press, 1965], 86).

66. E.g., Marcuse critiqued advanced capitalism by saying, "The erotic energy of the Life Instincts cannot be freed under the dehumanizing conditions of profitable affluence" (Herbert Marcuse, "Political Preface 1966," in *Eros and Civilization*, xxiii; see also pages 45–50 [but please be advised that Marcuse's writings are understandably not G-rated]). *The Standford Encyclopedia of Philosophy* further clarifies, "For Marcuse, liberation means a freeing up of the pleasure principle [i.e., the quest for gratification of 'basic' instincts, which Freud believed drove the id]." See Farr, "Herbert Marcuse."

67. Marcuse, *Essay on Liberation*.

68. Marcuse, *Essay on Liberation*. Note that the element of truth in Marcuse's critique of materialistic societies offers an example of how Marxism and neo-Marxism look at a real problem—in this case, superfluous consumerism representing the greed, idolatry, discontentment, and exploitation a biblical view condemns—but approaches it from a faulty worldview foundation, engendering faulty solutions.

69. *The Standford Encyclopedia of Philosophy* summarizes Marcuse's view that, in contrast to Marx's sole focus on the working class, "there is a multiplicity of social groups in our society that seek social change for various reasons. There are multiple forms of oppression and repression that make revolution desirable" (Farr, "Herbert Marcuse").

70. Herbert Marcuse, *Essay on Liberation*.

71. He wrote, "This new consciousness and the instinctual rebellion isolate such opposition [to capitalism] from the masses and from the majority of organized labor, the integrated majority, and make for the concentration of radical politics in active minorities, mainly among the young middle-class intelligentsia, and among the ghetto populations." He reiterated, "The ghetto population of the United States constitutes such a [revolutionary] force. Confined to small areas of living and dying, it can be more easily organized and directed." Marcuse then proceeded to link political revolutionary force specifically to ethnic minorities (Marcuse, *Essay on Liberation*).

72. In the words of Marcusian scholar Charles Reitz, who advocated in 2018 for using Marcuse's teachings to build "an alternative world system" based on "ecosocialism," Marcuse "found the environmental movement to be a particularly promising force for social change" (Reitz, *Ecology and Revolution*).

73. Marcuse, *Eros and Civilization*, 45–51. Notably, Marcuse recognized that capitalistic society was embracing sexual licentiousness too. But he interpreted this as the capitalistic "powers that be" letting people have a little freedom in order to keep them even more dependent on the system (Marcuse, *Essay on Liberation*).

74. Marcuse, "Repressive Tolerance," in *A Critique of Pure Tolerance* (Boston: Beacon Press, 1969), 81. Some have tried to defend Marcuse by saying he advocated *for* tolerance and only called for intolerance under certain circumstances—namely, those in which liberal views were being suppressed, preventing "true" tolerance. Marcuse did critique totalitarianism and advocate for what he called "true" tolerance; however, he essentially argued that this version of tolerance required a more socialistic order (e.g., Marcuse, "Repressive Tolerance," 105–109; see also 81–85), demanding *intolerance* toward non-left-leaning views (e.g., 109–111). Marcuse also stated that he believed society *was* facing circumstances that demanded the radical removal of tolerance toward the right (109–111, see also Marcuse's postscript, 117–123).

75. Marcuse, "Repressive Tolerance," in *A Critique of Pure Tolerance*, 81. Emphasis added.

76. Marcuse, "Repressive Tolerance," in *A Critique of Pure Tolerance*, 106.

77. This is despite Marcuse's insistence that the basis for deciding who gets to define what counts as "liberating" or "repressive" is "not a matter of value-preference but of rational criteria" (Marcuse, "Repressive Tolerance," in *A Critique of Pure Tolerance*, 101).

78. Marcuse, "Repressive Tolerance," in A *Critique of Pure Tolerance*, 109.

79. Marcuse, "Repressive Tolerance," in *A Critique of Pure Tolerance*, 100.

80. Marcuse, "Repressive Tolerance," in *A Critique of Pure Tolerance*, 100.

81. Marcuse argued that the original purpose of free speech and assembly was to let people think for themselves contrary to "established authority and opinion" (89–90). But he claimed that people had gotten so used to parroting the establishment that they weren't thinking freely anyway and that leftist views were being suppressed (89–90, 95–97). (Notably, cancel culture tends to suppress *conservative* views today.) But these critiques, even if valid, would not logically guarantee that free speech for the right must be abolished. Neither would the critique that free speech can be used to promote evil ideas (109). A case can be made that the solution to such problems lies not in censoring (or precensoring) "unauthorized" views but in empowering people to become careful thinkers. (See also, "Censorship Is Not the Answer to 'Fake News,'" Answers in Genesis, July 29, 2021, AnswersInGenesis.org/blogs/patricia-engler/2021/07/29/censorship-not-answer-fake-news/.)

82. Marcuse, "Repressive Tolerance," in *A Critique of Pure Tolerance*, 111. Marcuse did not hyphenate the term.

83. Marcuse, "Repressive Tolerance," in *A Critique of Pure Tolerance*, 111.

84. Marcuse, "Repressive Tolerance," in *A Critique of Pure Tolerance*, 109–110.

85. In Marcuse's words, "the small and powerless minorities which struggle against the false consciousness and its beneficiaries must be helped: their continued existence is more important than the preservation of abused rights and liberties which grant constitutional powers to those who oppress these minorities" (Marcuse, "Repressive Tolerance," in *A Critique of Pure Tolerance*, 110).

86. The full sentence reads: "Moreover, the restoration of freedom of thought may necessitate new and rigid restrictions on teachings and practices in the educational institutions which, by their very methods and concepts, serve to enclose the mind within the established universe of discourse and behavior—thereby precluding *a priori* a rational evaluation of the alternatives" (Marcuse, "Repressive Tolerance," in *A Critique of Pure Tolerance*, 100–101). Notably, censoring divergent opinions—and therefore "enclosing the mind within [a new] established universe"—within education was ironically what Marcuse was advocating for himself.

87. E.g., he wrote, "While the reversal of the trend in the educational enterprise at least could conceivably be enforced by the students and teachers themselves, and thus be self-imposed, the systematic withdrawal of tolerance toward regressive and repressive opinions and movements could only be envisaged as results of large-scale pressure which would amount to an upheaval" (Marcuse, "Repressive Tolerance," in *A Critique of Pure Tolerance*, 101).

88. A detailed description (written from a pro-critical theory perspective) of how education has effectively been transformed into an engine for neo-Marxism is available in Isaac Gottesman, *The Critical Turn in Education: From Marxist Critique to Poststructuralist Feminism to Critical Theories of Race* (New York: Routledge, 2016).

89. James Kirylo, *Paulo Freire: The Man from Recife* (New York: Peter Lang, 2011), 3–16.

90. Freire later wrote, "Because I had been born into a Christian family, I never accepted our precarious situation as an expression of God's wishes. On the contrary, I began to understand that something really wrong with the world needed to be fixed" (Paulo

Freire, *Letters to Cristina: Reflections on My Life and Work*, trans. Donald Macedo, Quilda Macedo, and Alexandre Oliveira [New York: Routledge, 1996], 14).

91. E.g., see Nicolò Valenzano, "Marxist and Personalist Influences in Paulo Freire's Pedagogical Anthropology," *Tendencias Pedagógicas* 38 (2021): 68–82.

92. Irwin Leopando, *A Pedagogy of Faith: The Theological Imagination of Paulo Freire* (London: Bloomsbury Academic, 2017), 95–96, 117–133; Michael Matthews, "Knowledge, Action and Power," in *Literacy and Revolution: The Pedagogy of Paulo Freire*, ed. Robert Mackie (New York: Continuum, 1981), 99–100; Nicolò Valenzano, "Marxist and Personalist Influences."

93. David H. Lane, *The Phenomenon of Teilhard: Prophet for a New Age* (Macon, GA: Mercer University Press, 1996).

94. By "planetization," Teilhard de Chardin referred to a transformative collectivization of global humanity and human consciousness (Pierre Teilhard de Chardin, *The Future of Man*, trans. Norman Denny [London: Collins, 1964], 124–139). For examples of statements linking this collectivization to evolution, see Teilhard de Chardin, *The Future of Man*, 257.

95. Paulo Freire, in an interview transcribed in Rex Davis, "Education for Awareness: A Talk with Paulo Friere," *in Literacy and Revolution*, 58.

96. E.g., see Paulo Freire, *The Politics of Education: Culture, Power, and Liberation* (New York: Bergin & Garvey, 1985), 14–15, 128–130.

97. Stanley Aronowitz, "Paulo Freire's Radical Democratic Humanism," in *Paulo Freire: A Critical Encounter*, eds. Peter McLaren and Peter Leonard (New York: Routledge, 1993), 13–17.

98. E.g., Freire, *The Politics of Education*, 89.

99. E.g., Freire, *The Politics of Education*, 125; see also Ira Shor, "Education Is Politics: Paulo Freire's Critical Pedagogy," in *Paulo Freire: A Critical Encounter*, 25–35, and Paula Allman, "Paulo Freire's Contributions to Radical Adult Education," *Studies in the Education of Adults* 26, no. 2 (1994): 144–161.

100. See Shor, "Education Is Politics," in *Paulo Freire: A Critical Encounter*, 25–35.

101. Freire, *The Politics of Education*, 50.

102. Shore, "Education Is Politics," in *Paulo Freire: A Critical Encounter*, 33.

103. See Allman, "Paulo Freire's Contributions to Radical Adult Education," 144–161.

104. Kirylo, *Paulo Freire*, 60–77, 191. Liberation theology is an attempt to blend Marxist ideas with Christianity despite their fundamental worldview differences discussed in chapter 2. Liberation theology was spearheaded by Gustavo Gutierrez, who wrote, "Only a radical break from the status quo, that is, a profound transformation of the private property system, access to power of the exploited class, and a social revolution that would break this dependence [of some countries upon others] would allow for the change to a new society, a socialist society" (Gustavo Gutierrez, *A Theology of Liberation*, trans. Sr. Caridad Inda and John Eagleson [Maryknoll, NY: Orbis, 1973; originally published as *Theologia de la Liberacion, Perspectivas* by CEP, 1971], 26–27). A detailed overview of liberation theology and its influence is available in the partially declassified CIA report, "Liberation Theology: Religion, Reform, and Revolution," General CIA Records, Digital National Security Archive executive standard document number CIA-RDP97R00694R000600050001-9, approved for release November 18, 2011, cia.gov/readingroom/docs/CIA-RDP97R00694R000600050001-9.pdf.

105. Elliott Green, "What Are the Most-Cited Publications in the Social Sciences (According to Google Scholar)?" *Impact of Social Sciences Blog*, May 12, 2016, eprints.lse.ac.uk/66752/.

106. The web page states that the curriculum "adopts Freire's 'problem-posing' approach in the classroom where learning is essentially driven by the learner's inquiry, and is guided through everyday words that have a direct connection to student's [*sic*] lives." ("Global Citizenship Education," UNESCO, accessed July 2024 from mgiep.unesco.org/global-citizenship.)

107. "Fundamentals of SEL," CASEL, accessed July 2024 from casel.org/fundamentals-of-sel/.

108. "Transformative SEL," CASEL, accessed July 2024 from casel.org/fundamentals-of-sel/how-does-sel-support-educational-equity-and-excellence/transformative-sel/.

109. "Transformative SEL," CASEL.

110. See Brian Wilson, *John E. Fetzer and the Quest for the New Age* (Detroit: Wayne State University Press, 2018).

111. John Mayer and Casey Cobb, "Educational Policy on Emotional Intelligence: Does it Make Sense?" *Educational Psychology Review* 12, no. 2 (2000): 163–183 (quote from page 169). Notably, the fact that SEL's development was assisted by a New Age proponent who was influenced by Alice Bailey does not automatically entail that SEL is *itself* New Ageist or is the direct result of Alice Bailey's influence. These connections merely signal that deeper digging may reveal further overlap between Bailey, New Ageism, and SEL—as we'll see below. (Dr. James Lindsay, an atheist, has also discussed connections between SEL and Alice Bailey in his *New Discourses* podcast. Due to some language, listener discretion is advised.)

112. Justina Schlund, Robert Jagers, and Melissa Schlinger, *Advancing Social and Emotional Learning as a Lever for Equity and Excellence* (Chicago: CASEL, 2020), 5, casel.org/casel-gateway-advancing-sel-for-equity-excellence.

113. Joseph Durlak, Celene Domitrovich, Roger Weissberg, and Thomas Gullotta, eds., *Handbook of Social and Emotional Learning: Research and Practice* (New York: Guilford Press, 2015).

114. "Global Citizenship Education," UNESCO, accessed July 2024 from mgiep.unesco.org/global-citizenship. This web page had been updated by this book's first printing in October 2024 and no longer reflects the quoted wording; however, Answers in Genesis retains a copy of the original web page on file. As of October 2024, similar wording could still be found at www.globalcitizenshipfoundation.org/project/globalcitizenship-schools. UNESCO itself also describes the Libre Process in more detail, mentioning Freire, at mgiep.unesco.org/libre-process.

115. "Global Citizenship Education," UNESCO. (The web page refers to "Sustainable Development Goal" using the acronym SDG.) See also "The 17 Goals," United Nations Department of Economic and Social Affairs, accessed July 2024, sdgs.un.org/goals; "Transforming Our World: The 2030 Agenda for Sustainable Development," United Nations, accessed July 2024, sdgs.un.org/2030agenda; and The Global Goals, "Dear G20 Leaders. A Call to Finance Our Future!" accessed July 2024, globalgoals.org/.

116. E.g., see Rebecca Geldard and Stefan Ellerbeck, "How Much Progress Is Being Made on the UN's Sustainable Development Goals?" WEF, September 11, 2023, weforum.org/agenda/2023/09/un-sustainable-development-goals-progress-report/; "Previous Global Future Council on SDG Investment," World Economic Forum, accessed July 2024 from weforum.org/communities/gfc-on-sdg-investment; Steeve MacFeely, "To Keep Track of the SDGs, We Need a Data Revolution," Sustainable Development, World Economic Forum, January 16, 2019, weforum.org/agenda/2019/01/its-time-for-a-data-revolution/.

117. *New Vision for Education: Fostering Social and Emotional Learning through Technology*, World Economic Forum and Boston Consulting Group, March 2016, accessed July 2024, www3.weforum.org/docs/WEF_New_Vision_for_Education.pdf. The report includes a disclaimer that the views expressed are not necessarily those of the WEF.

118. For instance, the premier accreditor of Christian schools has published documents encouraging the use of SEL (e.g., Lynn Swaner, Cindy Dodds, and Matthew Lee, *Leadership for Flourishing Schools: From Research to Practice*, Association for Christian Schools International, 2021, accessed July 2024, acsi.org/docs/default-source/website-publishing/research/fsci-leadership-report-2021.pdf).

119. Baucham, *Fault Lines*, and Strachan, *Christianity and Wokeness*.

COMMON STRATEGIES OF REVOLUTIONARY AGENDAS + REPLACING CHRISTIAN SOCIETIES WITH TOTALITARIAN REGIMES

PART TWO

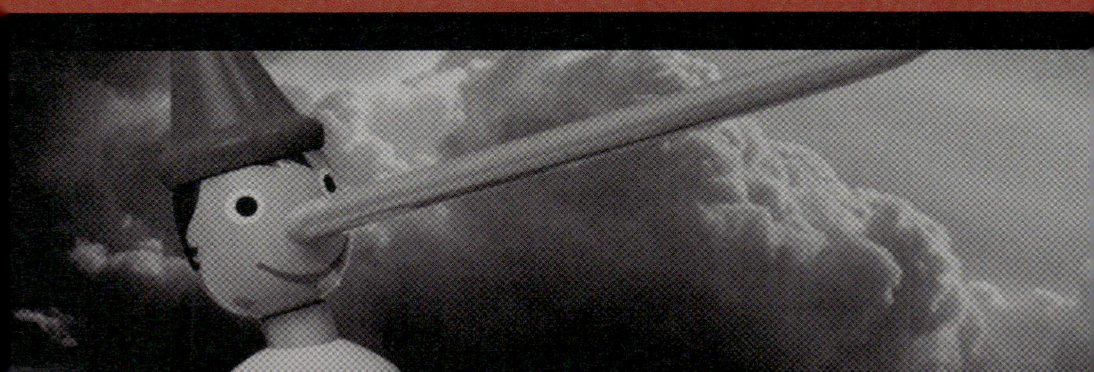

2 THESSALONIANS 2:15

SO THEN, BROTHERS, STAND FIRM AND HOLD TO THE TRADITIONS THAT YOU WERE TAUGHT BY US, EITHER BY OUR SPOKEN WORD OR BY OUR LETTER.

CHAPTER 6

FIRING AT THE FOUNDATIONS

STRATEGIES THAT TARGET CHURCHES, FAMILIES, AND YOUNG PEOPLE

Some plans have a disastrous way of backfiring. Plans that contradict God's designs for humanity are no exception. But Vladimir Lenin, the first leader of the Soviet Union, had neglected that reality in 1917. That's the year the Russian Revolution unfolded, enabling Lenin's followers to bind the iron chains of communism around millions of people.

How did Lenin's followers—a group of Marxists known as the Bolsheviks—revolutionize their world? The answer really matters for at least two reasons. First, understanding the strategies of historical Marxist groups can help us recognize similar processes in our neo-Marxist cultures. Second, learning how the Bolsheviks' strategies backfired reminds us that "ideas have consequences."

We'll look more closely in chapter 8 at how the Bolsheviks rose to power. For now, let's investigate how they destabilized their society's foundations to build a **new** society founded on communism.

WAIT, WHAT FOUNDATIONS?

What sort of "foundations" hold up a society? The **ultimate** foundation for any society consists of its citizens' worldview beliefs.[1] God's Word provides the worldview foundation for human society to function as God intended. And God's Word suggests our Creator established the family, church, and government as basic institutions under his authority.[2] When these institutions function properly, resting on a stable foundation, society itself remains stable. So regimes that want to overthrow a society must undermine these institutions.

In Lenin's case, the events leading up to the Russian Revolution had already left Russia's government in shambles.[3] But to establish total power, the Bolsheviks needed to do more than take over the government. They also needed to disrupt the family, repress the church, and capture Russia's youth. Russian sociologist Nicholas Timasheff summarized,

> [The] pillars of society are the family, the school, and the Church. . . . Hence, for those who are eager to endow a nation with a new culture, a definite program of action follows: they must loosen the family ties; they must destroy or at least weaken the Church; and they must transform the school into an accelerator of cultural revolution. This was the natural program of the [Russian] Communists while they performed their Great Experiment.[4]

Just how did the Bolsheviks execute these steps? Answering that will help us understand how to counteract similar patterns today, as part three of this book will explore. So let's journey back in time to read the Bolsheviks' to-do list.

HOW TO BREAK DOWN A SOCIETY

To loosen family ties, here were some boxes the Bolsheviks checked off their agenda:[5]

- ✓ Remove churches' authority to marry couples, erasing reminders of marriage's biblical basis.
- ✓ Alter divorce laws to make marriages quickly dissolvable.
- ✓ Decriminalize incest, adultery, and bigamy (beginning another marriage while already married).
- ✓ Frequently assign husbands and wives to work at separate factories.
- ✓ Enact measures that grant "superiority to the children" over their parents.[6]
- ✓ Legalize abortion.

Meanwhile, the campaign against churches developed like this:[7]

- ✓ Remove private property rights from churches and religious organizations, forcing Christians to use church property as state property, on state terms.
- ✓ Demote ministers to be second-class citizens with restricted rights, higher rent and taxes, and limited access to resources, including ration cards. Additionally, remove the rights of ministers' children to attend a secondary school or university.
- ✓ Forbid "religious instruction" in all public schools, private schools, and any other settings with organized groups of minors.
- ✓ Start to forcibly close churches, desecrate religious items, and imprison, exile, or execute church leaders.

And the schools? The Bolsheviks had apparently beaten Paulo Freire to the idea that schools should be Marxist discipleship centers that shift teachers' authority onto students.[8] As these students grew up and entered the workforce, however, the Bolsheviks started to notice this strategy had backfired. Timasheff explains, "The necessity to stop the school experiment was recognized by the Communist leaders when they saw that the program of industrialization could no longer be pushed forward because of the lack of adequately trained young specialists or even generally educated persons."[9]

The problems didn't end there. The communists' successful attack on the family led to unprecedented surges of broken homes, abortion, and juvenile delinquency in ways that jeopardized the regime.[10] Plunging birth rates threatened Russia's future economic and military strength, while rising hooliganism thrust communities into chaos.[11]

> SUCCESSFUL ATTACK ON THE FAMILY LED TO UNPRECEDENTED SURGES OF BROKEN HOMES, ABORTION, AND JUVENILE DELINQUENCY.

Meanwhile, relentless attacks against the church not only failed to expunge Christianity, but also "bred hostility in large masses of people towards the Soviet regime."[12]

In response, the communists needed to backpedal. They took steps to restore social order, revive academic discipline, and steer family life back in a direction that happened to better align with God's Word.[13] These historical lessons should remind free countries to **hold onto**, **defend**, and (wherever possible) **rebuild** whatever remnant of a biblical foundation they might possess. Meanwhile, learning from past regimes' strategies can help today's

Christians better recognize and respond to social destabilization today.

The Bolsheviks' strategies, for instance, reveal a basic revolutionary goal: break down the beliefs, behavioral patterns, and institutions that stabilized the old society and replace them with new ones. The game plan for this process may feature **blatant attacks** like the Soviets tried or **subtler methods**, which neo-Marxists like Antonio Gramsci preferred. The subtle approach relies less on brute force and more on subversion—infiltrating civil institutions from the inside to convert them into revolutionary agents.

Both the blatant and subtler methods involve harnessing the powers of media, education, and young people to establish a new social order. Meanwhile, Christians may unintentionally further these processes (or make society more vulnerable to them) by passively drifting from commitment to the authority of God's Word. Let's look closer at how all this can happen, starting at a worldview level.

WEAKENED WORLDVIEW FOUNDATIONS

Social change transpires at its most basic level within the worldviews of ordinary people. As chapters 1 and 2 described, totalitarianism represents the zenith of a worldview battle between man's word and God's Word. Humans in totalitarian regimes set themselves in God's position as **the** authority to define reality.

JUST WHAT DOES A "REALITY DEFINER" DO?

Just what does a "reality definer" do? For starters, the job description includes controlling the meaning of language, deciding who deserves human rights, and prescribing moral standards. Lenin's definition of "morality" offers a chilling illustration. In a speech to Russia's communist youth league, Lenin asked, "In what sense do we reject ethics, reject morality? In the sense given to it by the bourgeoisie, who based ethics on God's commandments. . . . Our morality stems from the interests of the class struggle of the proletariat."[14] Redefining morality this way allowed Lenin (and later, Stalin) to execute masses of Christians, all in the name of furthering the interests of oppressed workers.

These active campaigns to control reality aren't the only—or even the most common—ways totalitarian regimes can gain illicit power over truth. Christians themselves may cede their worldview foundations *en masse* during times of freedom. When this happens, free societies that once largely held to a biblical worldview become more vulnerable to totalitarianism.

In part, this vulnerability arises because God's Word provides the foundation for defending the institutions of church and family. Without Scripture as society's authority, totalitarian regimes have an easier task of breaking down these institutions to make way for the new social order. More foundationally, a shift away from biblical authority in times of freedom leaves some version of human reasoning as the authority. But not every human's claim to "truth" can be equally authoritative, or stalemates would arise between conflicting claims.

GOD'S WORD PROVIDES THE FOUNDATION FOR DEFENDING THE INSTITUTIONS OF CHURCH AND FAMILY.

As we saw in chapter 3, Rousseau tried solving this dilemma with his quasi-totalitarian social contract. Rousseau's solution illustrates how abandoning God's Word leaves a vacancy for the role of "truth authority," which totalitarian regimes are only too happy to fill. These regimes cannot tolerate people who stand on God's Word as their highest authority. So nations where most people have already ceded a biblical worldview leave fewer obstacles for totalitarianism to overcome.

COMPROMISED CHURCHES

The kinds of passive concessions and active attacks that weaken society on a worldview level also play out in the church. We've seen examples of **active attacks** against churches in patterns of persecution that unfolded in ancient Rome, the French Revolution, and Russia. One of these patterns was a gradual rise in pressure against Christians to make something besides God's Word their highest authority. Christians may be told they have "religious freedom," **so long** as they compromise on God's Word to accommodate the culture. This pressure usually splinters the local church into two divisions: an official faction that compromises with culture and an underground body that confesses God's Word.

As the Russian communists realized, these frontal attacks don't always work to a regime's advantage. Especially in strongly "Christianized" nations, a subtler strategy comes in handy. At least, that's what Antonio Gramsci decided.

GRAMSCI AND THE SUBTLE METHOD[15]

Gramsci, the Italian communist we met in chapter 5, viewed the Catholicism of Southern Italy's peasants as an obstacle to Marxism. But he knew that coming right out and attacking the clergy would only turn the peasants against communism. What could he do?

In answer, Gramsci noticed that Italian Catholicism consisted of two branches: the "official" religion of Rome and a folksier, grassroots religion that incorporated other beliefs. So Gramsci thought that socialists could create a cultural revolution **within the church** by turning the grassroots church against the dominant church. With institutional religion disempowered, socialism could take the official church's place on the throne of the peasants' affections. Along the way, the socialists could subvert the grassroots church, transforming it into an agent of socialism. The key would be to "rearticulate" ideas and practices already existing within the church by redefining them with Marxist meanings.

Today, we're seeing a similar process where churches allow for redefining biblical terms like **justice** along neo-Marxist lines, as chapter 5 described.[16] Unfortunately, Christians who start compromising on biblical authority only assist the agendas that seek to undermine, subvert, or destabilize the church. This destabilization can happen from the top down as denominations, seminaries, and Christian leaders give in to pressures to compromise. Or it can happen from the bottom up as individual Christians passively drift from God's Word, absorbing unbiblical ideas from culture (including "church culture").

> **AGENDAS WHICH SEEK TO UNDERMINE, SUBVERT, OR DESTABILIZE THE CHURCH**

ABETTING THE AGENDA

These processes accelerate when Christian leaders water down scriptural doctrines, prioritize entertainment over discipleship, and avoid giving biblical answers to controversial topics. Such topics tend to mark the points where

God's Word contradicts our culture's thinking. So these issues are where Christians will face the most pressure to compromise. If churches don't offer Christians biblical answers—and if congregants don't study God's Word themselves to find those answers—what will happen as persecution increases? Compromising Scripture during times of freedom hardly translates to confessing Scripture during times of fire.

Unfortunately, freedom tends to breed passivity. And passivity breeds vulnerability. For just one example of how these trends are playing out, look no further than the worldview that has replaced biblical Christianity's popularity in America.[17] It's a belief system that goes by the name of Moralistic Therapeutic Deism. But let's break down those terms:

PASSIVITY BREEDS VULNERABILITY.

- The **deism** bit refers to the idea that God created the world but doesn't personally relate to humans.
- The term **therapeutic** alludes to the belief that life is all about being happy, comfortable, and carefree.
- The **moralistic** aspect drives at the concept that humans are supposed to "be good."

So moralistic therapeutic deism basically teaches that God just wants us to be happy and do good to each other.[18] This doctrine may sound appealing, but it misses the biblical truth that all humans are sinners who need salvation found only in Jesus Christ. This omission means believers in moralistic therapeutic deism await an eternity without God unless they trust in Jesus rather than their own "good works."

MORALISTIC THERAPEUTIC DEISM = THE BELIEF THAT HUMANS ARE SUPPOSED TO BE GOOD, HAPPY, AND THAT GOD CREATED THE WORLD BUT DOESN'T PERSONALLY RELATE TO HUMANS

Meanwhile, moralistic therapeutic deism can lower society's resistance to neo-Marxist soft totalitarianism for at least two reasons. First, the **therapeutic** aspect conditions people to prioritize comfort over conviction—a danger we'll unpack in chapter 7. Second, wanting to "do good" without having a biblical foundation for defining "goodness" leaves moralistic therapeutic deists vulnerable to messages that redefine **morality as radicalism**.

These are just some of the ways **active attacks** and **passive concessions** can weaken churches—to the advantage of regimes that seek to replace Christianity. But the church isn't the only pillar that advocators for a new social order need to weaken, subvert, and replace. Let's turn to another God-ordained institution: the family.

WHY THE FAMILY MATTERS

From Genesis to Revelation, the big picture of Scripture reveals themes of gender, marriage, and family as fundamental to God's design for humanity. We've seen this design established from the opening chapters of Genesis, which Jesus later quoted when religious rulers questioned him about marriage. He reminded them that "from the beginning of creation, 'God made them male and female.' 'Therefore a man shall leave his father and mother and hold fast to his wife, and the two shall become one flesh'" (Mark 10:6–8).

Here, Jesus reaffirmed the categories **male**, **female**, **father**, **mother**, **husband**, and **wife** as basic to God's intentions for human society from the beginning. Genesis reveals that sin tragically corrupted relationships within families.[19] Even so, the family remained the core social unit through which God would unfold redemptive history from Genesis to Revelation.

EVEN SO, THE FAMILY REMAINED THE CORE SOCIAL UNIT THROUGH WHICH GOD WOULD UNFOLD REDEMPTIVE HISTORY.

God chose Noah's family, for instance, as the unit for preserving humanity during the global flood (Genesis 1:26). Later, God chose Abraham's family—and within it, the family of Israel (Jacob)—as the special people central to God's redemptive plan for creation. To fulfill this plan, God chose the family of Mary and Joseph for raising Jesus, the Creator in human flesh. Finally, at creation's restoration, the institution of earthly marriage will be transcended by the everlasting marriage of Christ and his church.[20]

This centrality of marriage and family within God's purpose, plan, and design for humanity shows why attacks against these institutions oppose Jesus as Creator. Such attacks mark frontline battles in the age-old war of man's word against God's Word. Just like in Eden, Satan continues to leverage this war by tempting God's image bearers to commit self-destructive rebellion, asking, "Did God actually say . . .?" (Genesis 3:1). Only this time, the question arises in reference to family, gender, and marriage.

Today, as in Eden, answering that question in ways that elevate human opinion above God's Word leads to turmoil.[21] Family, therefore, represents a strategic target for **overturning and remaking** society, which is a stated goal of Marxism.[22]

MARXISM VS. THE FAMILY

Practical advantages for destabilizing society aren't the only reason Marxism targets the family. Theoretical reasons also motivate this attack. As earlier chapters revealed, Marxists, neo-Marxists, and utopian socialists have historically viewed the family as the most basic unit, source, and sustainer of social oppression. If any doubts spring up regarding whether Marxism truly opposes the family, the steamroller-like writings of Marxist feminists will quickly flatten them.

Take for instance *The Dialectic of Sex* by radical feminist Shulamith Firestone.[23] In this book, Firestone argued that the patriarchal nuclear family is repressive, oppressive, and the cause of all social ills.[24] She wrote, "Unless revolution disturbs the basic social organization, the biological family . . . the tapeworm of exploitation will never be annihilated. We shall need a sexual revolution much larger than—inclusive of—a socialist one to truly eradicate all class systems."[25]

The reason previous socialist revolutions failed, according to Firestone, is that they **didn't go far enough** in attacking the family.[26] Simply weakening family ties, as the Bolsheviks did, would not do. Firestone advocated for a radical restructuring of society based on the total elimination of family ties, marriage, and the recognition of gender distinctions.[27] She stated:

> And just as the end goal of socialist revolution was not only the elimination of the economic class privilege but of the economic class distinction itself, so the end goal of feminist revolution must be . . . not just the elimination of male privilege but of the sex

> distinction itself: [biological] differences between human beings would no longer matter culturally.[28]

If families no longer existed, then what kind of social system **would**? In a (rather disturbing) reply that would make Freud and Marcuse proud, Shulamith anticipated a "free sexuality" with virtually zero boundaries, taboos, or age restrictions.[29] Not only would children be fully sexualized in Shulamith's future society, but the concept of childhood itself would no longer exist.[30]

Summarizing how Firestone's Marxist ideas fit within the broader scheme of "sexual revolution," Carl Trueman explained:

> [The] sexual revolution ultimately has one great goal, the destruction of the family. It makes sense, of course, for the family is the primary means by which values are transmitted from generation to generation. From a Marxist perspective, that makes the family the means by which false consciousness is passed on and replicated over time. Its demolition is thus essential.[31]

Trueman's comments highlight a final reason why the family matters so much: family is the primary unit God created for intergenerational discipleship. Passages throughout the Bible reflect this reality. For instance, Deuteronomy makes repeated references to older generations teaching God's truths to younger generations.[32] Similar references appear in different Psalms,[33] while multiple Proverbs underscore the indispensable, authoritative mentorship role of parents.[34]

The theme of intergenerational discipleship continues in the New Testament, where Paul exhorted fathers to raise children "in the discipline and instruction of the Lord"

(Ephesians 6:4). This verse emphasizes fathers' responsibility as the primary spiritual leaders. Paul also alluded to mothers' discipleship roles in his second letter to Timothy, who had a believing Jewish mother but a Greek father (Acts 16:1). Having affirmed the faith of Timothy's mother and grandmother, Paul instructed Timothy to continue in the biblical teachings he had learned from childhood (2 Timothy 1:5, 3:14–15).

Ultimately, parents' God-given discipleship roles make the family a high-stakes focal point for both Christians and Marxists. The family represents the central arena in which one generation passes biblical teachings, habits, and lifestyles to the next. This discipleship process isn't just meant to proceed in weekly intervals at churches but on a **continuous**, **daily basis** within families.

DISCIPLESHIP ROLES MAKE THE FAMILY A HIGH-STAKES FOCAL POINT.

Anyone seeking a new social order must replace the family's discipleship role. That's why historically, totalitarian regimes' attacks on the family accompany attacks on students, youth, and children.

CAPTURING THE FUTURE GENERATIONS

In the days of the Cold War with the Soviet Union, America's Central Intelligence Agency (CIA) recognized that communism's success depended on young people. So in the early 1960s, the CIA studied the Freie Deutsche Jugend (Free German Youth League), the official youth organization of East Germany's communist government. This investigation resulted in a secret report, which the CIA produced in 1963 and declassified in 2013. Here's an especially noteworthy statement from the report's introduction:

> All the modern governments which are aiming at the total reorganization of the existing society and at political domination have considered it a matter of very special importance to win a total hold on the youth: in effect, the youth offer this immense advantage over the adults; they have not been familiar with the earlier social structures, and thus cannot generally make unfavorable comparisons; they constitute magnificent virgin soil where one is almost certain that all the seeds which are sown will produce an abundant harvest; and finally they have their intrinsic dynamism.[35]

In other words, the CIA recognized that groups seeking a "new social order" strategically target young people for multiple reasons. Young people are still figuring out what they believe. They have limited life experience. And they haven't lived through much history to be able to evaluate the consequences of different social systems in real time. Compared to older generations who have had more time for gaining life experience, building historical awareness, and establishing their worldviews, **youth** are way easier to influence. They're also more efficient to indoctrinate **en masse**, thanks to education infrastructure. Additionally, young people happen to be the most strategic demographic to target because they're society's future decision-makers. Once a regime has captured the hearts and minds of young people, it can harness their unbounded energy to drive social change in the desired direction.

For all these reasons, regimes that seek a new social order **must** focus on discipling society's youth. These regimes do anything they can to disrupt the God-ordained discipleship process within families. As the CIA observed back in 1963:

> The most important sources of influence on the formation of young people can be considered to be the family, the school, the church and the various youth organizations. The aim of a totalitarian regime—whichever one it may be—will thus be to effect a maximum reduction of the influence of the family and the religious milieu (for want of being able to annihilate them) and to lay hands on the other two sources of influence.[36]

One way the Free German Youth League did this was by organizing "collective vacations" to keep youth away from families during school breaks.[37] Naturally, the vacation itinerary centered around "convincing the children of working people of the truth of socialism."[38] But why wait for school breaks? Today's education systems and mass media platforms together enable the 24/7 mass indoctrination of young people.

STATE SCHOOLS AND MASS MEDIA

With the power to oversee young people's worldview formation for hours every week, schools offer an incredibly effective means to disciple entire generations. Secularists have long recognized this, championing the education system as the key to transforming society. For instance, the prominent humanist Charles Francis Potter wrote back in 1928,

> Education is . . . a most powerful ally of humanism, and every American school is a school of humanism. What can a theistic Sunday school's meeting for an hour once a week and teaching only a fraction of the children do to stem the tide of the five-day program of humanistic teaching?[39]

Schools, Potter realized, have taken the place of families and churches as nations' foremost worldview discipleship centers. Education can direct a new generation to build a new society in line with a new worldview. We saw in chapter 5 how Paulo Freire applied these principles to argue that schools should function as training grounds for revolutionaries.

Because a Marxist worldview sees humans as their own creators,[40] the goal of revolution isn't only to transform **society** but also **humanity**. Education unlocks the way to both these types of transformation. Lev Vygotsky, a Marxist child psychologist in Russia's Soviet Union, understood this. He wrote, "It is education which should play the central role in the transformation of . . . the historical human type. **New generations and new forms of their education represent the main route which history will follow whilst creating the new type of man**"[41] (emphasis in original).

We saw similar themes in writings by occultists, including Robert Owen and Alice Bailey, who championed education for recreating society—and humanity—on a global scale.[42] But education isn't the only channel for shaping future generations along these lines.

EDUCATION ISN'T THE ONLY CHANNEL FOR SHAPING FUTURE GENERATIONS.

Enter mass media.

Antonio Gramsci interpreted media—including cinema, novels, and newspapers—as channels that (like schools) either sustain or revolutionize the old society.[43] Relatedly, Lenin took calculated steps to control the media in Russia.[44] He viewed media as essential to sustaining communism's atheistic foundation, encouraging a Marxist journal to "be a militant atheist organ" that would "propagandise militant materialism" in "an untiring atheist fight."[45]

A century later, we're seeing these same channels of **media** and **education systems** promoting an especially nefarious attack on the family: the sexualization of children.

THE WAR ON INNOCENCE

Dr. Erwin Lutzer wrote, "Perhaps nowhere do we see the work of Satan in America as clearly as we do in the sexualization of children—destroying their identity, confusing their gender, and creating unresolved guilt and self-hatred."[46] Lutzer notes that this attack strikes at the heart of Jesus,[47] who said, "Whoever receives one such child in my name receives me, but whoever causes one of these little ones who believe in me to sin, it would be better for him to have a great millstone fastened around his neck and to be drowned in the depth of the sea" (Matthew 18:5–6).

Encouraging children to practice sexual immorality is a strategic way for Satan to hurt the little ones for whom Jesus so deeply cares. It's also a strategic way for regimes seeking a new social order to destabilize multiple societal pillars at once, using all the most effective tactics. On a worldview level, sexualizing childhood moves society further from a biblical foundation by contradicting God's design for family, marriage, and gender. Meanwhile, Christian leaders, ministries, and institutions face increasing pressure to compromise on God's Word regarding these issues, resulting in weakened churches teaching weakened doctrines.

Lutzer notes that along the way, sexualizing children also destroys the concept of traditional family and leads to broken homes.[48] As this sexualization process escalates, we're seeing society edge closer to something like the no-family, no-childhood, no-taboo scenario Shulamith Firestone envisioned. Meanwhile, policies that deify kids' feelings as the final authority regardless of parental concerns set kids above parents—an experiment that backfired for the Bolsheviks. Related policies that hide children's struggles from parents also help to undercut essential family connections, letting activists disciple children instead.

SEXUALIZING CHILDREN ALSO DESTROYS THE CONCEPT OF TRADITIONAL FAMILY AND LEADS TO BROKEN HOMES.

Education systems and media further disciple kids in the religions of "sexual humanism" and neo-Marxism. Together, these religions promote unbiblical sexuality in the name of equity for oppressed identities. They tell kids who are entering the most vulnerable seasons of their lives that if they identify with such a group, they are stunning, brave, and beautiful. Confuse kids about their God-given purpose and identity, and they'll be that much hungrier to discover a new purpose and identity in activism. While not everyone involved in these processes presumably has **political** revolution in mind (unlike Marcuse and Firestone), neo-Marxists could ask for no greater revolutionary strategy.

SUMMING UP

In the end, we've seen how any attempt to establish a "new social order" must start by firing at the foundations of current society. This process begins on a worldview level, as active attacks against Christianity and passive concessions among Christians condition society to elevate man's word above God's. These attacks and concessions result in weakened churches, which cannot easily resist when totalitarian regimes try usurping God's role as the authority for truth.

To achieve their goals, such regimes must destabilize families, limit kids' connections with parents, and become the next generation's primary source of discipleship. Meanwhile, mainstream media platforms and secular education systems provide an easy, efficient means to capture the hearts and minds of youth. Whoever holds the power to influence these systems holds the power to influence society's future.

When the Bolsheviks wielded these strategies to destabilize society, the results spelled disaster. Such consequences remind us that **there is no right way to build a society on the wrong worldview foundation**. Today, this truth remains more relevant than ever, as neo-Marxist doctrines impact churches, youth, and families—the focal points of past regimes' efforts to destabilize societies.

These efforts mark only the first steps toward neo-Marxism's goals. The next step requires achieving the right kinds of social conditions in which to incubate an army of revolutionaries.

Let's see how this can happen.

ENDNOTES

1. Even in pluralistic societies, the most well-represented beliefs and values among lawmakers, leaders, and citizens shape a society's everyday practices, expectations, and standards of behavior in especially significant ways.

2. E.g., see Matthew 19:4–6; Ephesians 4:11–12; Hebrews 13:7, 17; Romans 13:1–7. While not all institutions of past and present societies were ordained by God, these and other verses suggest that the family, church, and government were, with God remaining the highest authority. (Notably, even before Israel rejected God by choosing a king as 1 Samuel 8 describes, God had established judges as a form of government under his ultimate authority.)

3. More on this in chapter 8.

4. Nicolas Timasheff, "The Family, the School and the Church: The Pillars of Society Shaken and Re-Enforced," in *The Stalinist Dictatorship*, ed. Chris Ward (London: Arnold, and New York: Oxford University Press, 1998), 303.

5. See Timasheff, "The Family, the School and the Church," 303–308.

6. Timasheff, "The Family, the School and the Church," 307.

7. Nicolas Timasheff, *Soviet Religion in Russia* 1917–1942 (New York: Sheed and Ward, 1942), 23–27.

8. Timasheff, "The Family, the School and the Church," 309–312.

9. Timasheff, "The Family, the School and the Church," 309.

10. Timasheff, "The Family, the School and the Church," 304–305.

11. Timasheff, "The Family, the School and the Church," 304–305.

12. Timasheff, "The Family, the School and the Church," 312–313.

13. Timasheff, "The Family, the School and the Church," 305–317. For instance, new laws forbidding "unregistered marriages" made divorce much harder, incentivized childbirth, and prohibited almost all abortions.

14. Vladimir Lenin, "The Task of the Youth Leagues," speech delivered at the Third All-Russia Congress of The Russian Young Communist League, October 1920, English translation accessed July 2024, marxists.org/archive/lenin/works/1920/oct/02.htm#1.

15. This section draws its historical details from Rosario Forlenza, "Antonio Gramsci on Religion," *Journal of Classical Sociology* 21, no. 1 (2021): 38–60, journals.sagepub.com/doi/pdf/10.1177/1468795X19865119.

16. See chapter 5 for more on neo-Marxist redefinitions.

17. See Cultural Research Center, "Counterfeit Christianity: 'Moralistic Therapeutic Deism' Most Popular Worldview in U.S. Culture," Arizona Christian University, April 27, 2021, accessed July 2024, arizonachristian.edu/2021/04/27/counterfeit-christianity-moralistic-therapeutic-deism-most-popular-worldview-in-u-s-culture/.

18. Cultural Research Center, "Counterfeit Christianity."

19. The effects of this corruption are evident right from Genesis 3:16, which indicated how sin's curse would impact Eve in bearing children and in relating to her husband.

20. See Ephesians 5:31–32; c.f. Matthew 22:30; Revelation 19:7–18, 21:9–14.

21. We see this turmoil evidenced in years of research linking the breakdown of the family to heartbreaking social consequences. E.g., Juho Härkönen, Fabrizio Bernardi, and Diederik Boertien, "Family Dynamics and Child Outcomes: An Overview of Research and Open Questions," *European Journal of Population* 33 (2017): 163–184; Ulrike Zartler, "Children and Parents After Separation," in *Research Handbook on the Sociology of the Family*, eds. Norbert Schneider and Michaela Kreyenfeld (Cheltenham, UK, and Northampton, MA: Edward Elgar, 2021): 303–304.

22. E.g., see Karl Marx and Friedrich Engels, *Manifesto of the Communist Party*, trans. Samuel Moore, ed. Fredrich Engels (Chicago: Charles H. Kerr & Company, 1910), 58.

23. Radical feminists including Firestone drew on the thinking of the feminist philosopher Simone de Beauvoir (Elizabeth Fallaize, *Simone de Beauvoir: A Critical Reader* [London: Routledge, 1998], 9). Beauvoir is worth mentioning along with her colleague and long-time lover, the philosopher Jean-Paul Sartre, for their shared cultural impact. Sartre, a vocal neo-Marxist, believed that humans are *not* created beings, meaning there is no divinely designed "human nature" or "essence" that helps define how humans should live. Instead, Sartre essentially believed that humans are characterized by the freedom—and responsibility—to be their own "gods," defining their own existences, meaning, and morality (see R. C. Sproul, *The Consequences of Ideas* [Wheaton, IL: Crossway, 2000], 177–185; see also Gary Gutting, *French Philosophy in the Twentieth Century* [Cambridge, UK: Cambridge University Press, 2001], 121–157). Beauvoir picked up on this belief that there is no created human essence but rather that "the free choices of our consciousness determine what we are" (Gutting, *French Philosophy*, 165). Applying such thinking to the topic of gender, Beauvoir famously stated, "One is not born, but rather becomes, a woman. No biological, psychological, or economic fate determines the figure that the human female presents in society; it is civilization as a whole that produces this creature" (Simone de Beauvoir, *The Second Sex*, trans. ed. H. M. Parshley [New York: Bantam Books, 1952, originally published in French by Librairie Gallimard in 1949], 249). This statement illustrates how the lives and writings of Beauvoir and Sartre offer a glimpse of the worldview foundations of contemporary gender ideology.

24. Shulamith Firestone, *The Dialectic of Sex: The Case for Feminist Revolution* (New York: William Morrow, 1970), 254–255.

25. Firestone, *The Dialectic of Sex*, 12–13.

26. Firestone, *The Dialectic of Sex*, 240.

27. Firestone, *The Dialectic of Sex*, 256–274.

28. Firestone, *The Dialectic of Sex*, 11–12.

29. Firestone, *The Dialectic of Sex*, 236–237, 271–273.

30. Firestone, *The Dialectic of Sex*, 236–237, 271.

31. Carl Trueman, *The Rise and Triumph of the Modern Self: Cultural Amnesia, Expressive Individualism, and the Road to Sexual Revolution* (Wheaton, IL: Crossway, 2020), 262–263.

32. E.g., Deuteronomy 4:9, 6:7, 20–25, 11:19, 32:7.

33. E.g., Psalm 71:18, 78:4, 145:4.

34. E.g., Proverbs 1:8–9, 3:1–2, 4:1–4, 10–11.

35. Central Intelligence Agency (CIA), "Organization, Activities and Aims of the East German Youth Organization, Freie Deutsche Jugend (FDJ)," report (declassified in part—sanitized copy approved for release 2013/02/05), August 1963, General

CIA Records, Digital National Security Archive executive standard document number CIA-RDP80T00246A069500190001-0, accessed July 2024 from cia.gov/readingroom/document/cia-rdp80t00246a069500190001-0 (quote from Introduction, paragraph 2).

36. CIA, "Organization, Activities and Aims of the East German Youth Organization," Introduction, paragraph 3.

37. CIA, "Organization, Activities and Aims of the East German Youth Organization," Section VI, paragraph G.

38. CIA, "Organization, Activities and Aims of the East German Youth Organization," Section VI, paragraph G.

39. Charles Francis Potter, *Humanism: A New Religion* (New York: Simon and Schuster, 1930), 128.

40. More on this in chapter 2.

41. Lev Vygotsky, "The Socialist Alteration of Man," in *Vygotsky Reader*, eds. René van der Veer and Jaan Valsiner (Oxford, UK, and Cambridge, USA: Blackwell, 1994), originally published in 1930 as "Socialisticheskaja Peredelka Cheloveka," *VARNITSO*, the journal of the All-Union Association of Workers in Science and Technics for the Furthering of the Socialist Edification in the USSR; transcribed by Andy Blunden, accessed July 2024, marxists.org/archive/vygotsky/works/1930/socialism.htm.

42. Please see chapter 4 for details.

43. E.g., see Antonio Gramsci, *An Antonio Gramsci Reader: Selected Writings* 1916–1935, ed. Dave Forgacs (New York: Schocken Books, 1988), 370–373, 380–381.

44. Albert Resis, *"Lenin on Freedom of the Press," The Russian Review* 36, no. 3 (1977): 274–296.

45. Vladimir Lenin, "On the Significance of Militant Materialism," in *Lenin's Collected Works*, vol. 33 (Moscow: Progress Publishers, 1972), 227–236, marxists.org/archive/lenin/works/1922/mar/12.htm.

46. Erwin Lutzer, *We Will Not Be Silenced: Responding Courageously to Our Culture's Assault on Christianity* (Eugene, OR: Harvest House Publishers, 2020), 156, ebook version.

47. Lutzer, *We Will Not Be Silenced*, 157, ebook version.

48. Lutzer, *We Will Not Be Silenced*, 159, ebook version.

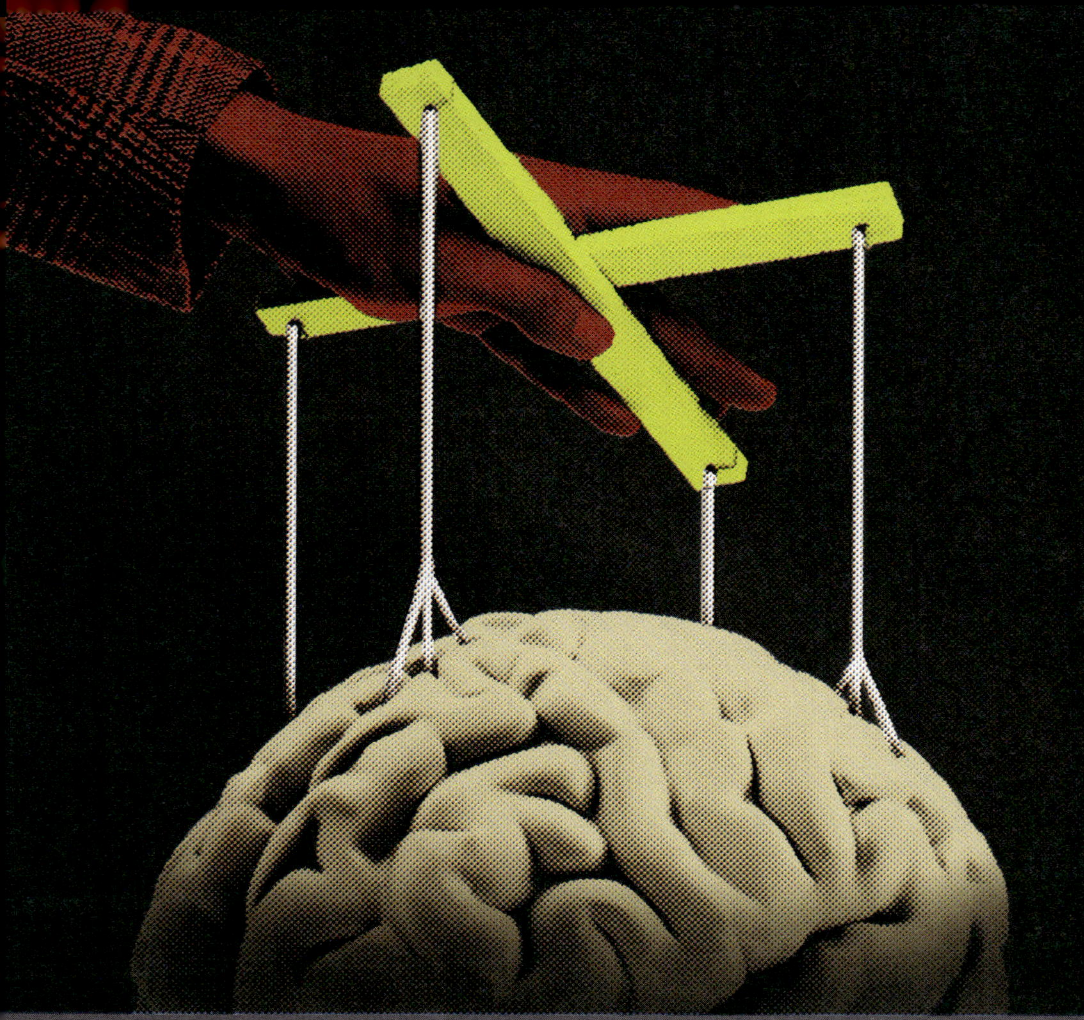

1 THESSALONIANS 5:5-8

FOR YOU ARE ALL CHILDREN OF LIGHT, CHILDREN OF THE DAY. WE ARE NOT OF THE NIGHT OR OF THE DARKNESS. SO THEN LET US NOT SLEEP, AS OTHERS DO, BUT LET US KEEP AWAKE AND BE SOBER. FOR THOSE WHO SLEEP, SLEEP AT NIGHT, AND THOSE WHO GET DRUNK, ARE DRUNK AT NIGHT. BUT SINCE WE BELONG TO THE DAY, LET US BE SOBER, HAVING PUT ON THE BREASTPLATE OF FAITH AND LOVE, AND FOR A HELMET THE HOPE OF SALVATION.

CHAPTER 7

CONDITIONING THE CULTURE

PROCESSES THAT PRIME SOCIETY FOR A SOFT TOTALITARIAN RESET

Never had I seen so many in one place. They filled the windows, lined the walls, and even hung from the ceiling. Everywhere I looked, a wooden face gazed back. I hadn't realized until coming to Prague, the capital of former communist Czechoslovakia, that this city is known for its marionette shops.

In the window of one of these shops, I spotted the most famous marionette of all. With his bright overalls, trademark grin, and (literally) telltale nose, the little guy could only be **Pinocchio**. Originally a nineteenth-century children's novel by Italian author Carlo Collodi, the story of Pinocchio has given generations of youngsters entertainment, instruction, and nightmares about whales.

But there's more to this story than being a whale of a fairy tale. Pinocchio's plight illustrates real-world conditions that make societies vulnerable to hard or soft totalitarianism.[1] Let's look closer at these conditions to better guard against them. As a reminder, the point of this investigation isn't to imply, in the raspy whisper of a conspiracy theorist, that any single organization is orchestrating these conditions. They've been unfolding for too long, on too many levels, to justify that sort of claim. Still, one thing **is** clear. However these conditions arose, their result is a weakened society sleepwalking toward a destiny we must not be lulled into joining.

What **are** the conditions?

Just ask Pinocchio.

FREEDOM WITH STRINGS ATTACHED

The story of Pinocchio as Collodi told it is far longer (and more bizarre) than its most familiar retellings. To recap these retellings' highlights, the story begins with a wood-carver, Geppetto, crafting Pinocchio from an unusually talkative log. A fairy tells Pinocchio he can become a real human **if** he proves himself. With this goal in sight, Pinocchio heads to school.

A series of run-ins with con men, bandits, and assorted talking animals ensues, leading Pinocchio into predicaments from which the fairy helps him escape. Along the way, a cricket (or at least, the ghost of a cricket) offers moral guidance that Pinocchio prefers to ignore. Nowhere does this choice prove costlier than when Pinocchio's classmate convinces him to forsake both school and Geppetto to live in a Land of Pleasure.[2] There the only rule is "Do whatever makes you happy."

THE LAND OF PLEASURE SEEMS LIKE A DREAM COME TRUE.

At first, the Land of Pleasure seems like a dream come true. Kids can run wild, play with anything, and live totally liberated from "repressive" rules. But Pinocchio doesn't realize this kind of freedom comes with strings attached. As he sprouts a pair of furry ears, he realizes too late that the Land of Pleasure eventually turns humans into donkeys. Instead of approaching his goal of becoming **more** human, he's becoming **less**. He leaves the Land of Pleasure and winds up inside a whale (or a dogfish, depending on who you ask), where he conveniently reunites with Geppetto. After they escape, the fairy transforms Pinocchio into a real boy.

Strange, right?

But significant.

LESSONS FROM THE LAND OF PLEASURE

As with many stories, different commentators could interpret this tale to support different conclusions. A Marxist, for instance, might interpret the Land of Pleasure as a capitalistic system that turns humans into beasts of burden for bourgeois coachmen. Along more biblical lines, we could view the Land of Pleasure as partially reflecting the idolatrous, covetous aspects of society that feed humanity's **real** problem. This issue isn't an external **social condition**, as Marx wrongly thought, but an internal **sin condition**.

From this biblical vantage point, we could also see the Land of Pleasure as embracing the "do whatever makes you happy" licentiousness that Marcuse and Firestone championed.[3] These neo-Marxists claimed that freedom from "repressive" sexual morality would make us more human. But like Pinocchio, we'd find the opposite is true.

Looking closer, we might recognize the Land of Pleasure as a breeding ground for soft totalitarianism. It's a place where coachmen are stakeholders who influence the types of social credit systems described in chapter 1. It's a place where people and puppets hear they will own nothing and be happy. It's a place where pleasure, safety, and convenience each cost a degree of freedom.

Pinocchio grew vulnerable to the Land of Pleasure's lies through five conditioning processes, which also make societies susceptible to soft totalitarianism. Let's see how these processes unfolded in Pinocchio's world so we can better recognize them in our own.

1. TRIVIALIZING

According to the Merriam-Webster Dictionary, **trivial** usually means "of little worth or importance" or "relating to . . . the mathematically simplest case."[4] If we ditch the mathematical bit, we can think of trivialization as a process that **simplifies** our God-given rationality and **distracts** us to pursue the insignificant. It's a process that "dumbs society down."

Pinocchio began this process when he ditched school to pursue diversions. This choice not only helped establish a lifestyle of **picking pleasure over purpose** but also left Pinocchio less equipped to resist persuasive lies.

2. ATOMIZING

To atomize something is to break it into smaller pieces—like atoms. Society becomes atomized when people grow isolated from one another. **Isolation**, in turn, makes people vulnerable to **manipulation**.[5] Pinocchio experienced this process by becoming separated from Geppetto, whose influence could have saved Pinocchio endless grief (and a pair of donkey ears).

3. DESENSITIZING

While most people (hopefully) don't take ethical advice from crickets, Romans 2:14–15 affirms that everyone has a conscience for choosing right from wrong. The more we ignore our consciences, like Pinocchio ignored his cricket, the more we grow desensitized to immorality. As a result, soft totalitarian coachmen can more easily leverage our sin nature to their own advantages.

4. THERAPIZING

Although we usually think of "therapies" as medical treatments, American sociologist Philip Rieff talked about "the therapeutic" another way. Rieff argued that Freud had led society to embrace a "therapeutic" mentality, which says inner feelings are the authority, and life's purpose is to be happy.[6]

The Land of Pleasure's "do whatever makes you happy" rule is the creed of therapeutic culture. (Interestingly, given the spiritual connections we saw in chapter 4, this principle is also the central doctrine of Wicca, known as the Wiccan Rede: "An ye harm no one, do what ye will."[7]) As Pinocchio learned the hard way, believing the lie that life's highest priority is **feeling good** means easily falling for certain manipulative messages. These messages promise pleasure, but they don't mention the strings—or chains—attached.

5. SUPERVISING

How did the coachman in Pinocchio's story know what the kids in the Land of Pleasure were up to—and when they became donkeys? He knew because he managed a system of minions who quietly supervised the kids as they pursued their therapeutic lifestyles. Similarly, soft totalitarian systems require surveillance infrastructure, like the data-tracking features of digital technologies.

Let's close Pinocchio's story and look at real-world examples of these five processes. We won't be able to unpack them exhaustively or cover all the other reasons a culture may become vulnerable to soft totalitarianism. Still, these five serve as an important starting point for recognizing and responding to factors that leave our societies open to tyranny.

TRIVIALIZATION: NO THINKING REQUIRED

The first process, trivialization, creates a society of individuals who can't—or worse, don't **want** to—think for themselves. We especially see this happening through two channels the last chapter identified as effective ways to target young people: **education systems** and **mass media**.

THE FIRST PROCESS, TRIVIALIZATION, CREATES A SOCIETY OF INDIVIDUALS WHO CAN'T—OR WORSE, DON'T WANT TO—THINK FOR THEMSELVES.

Regarding education, we saw how Paulo Freire believed schools should exist not to teach academic skills (which Freire thought sustained oppression) but to disciple activists. Students in Freirean classrooms might believe they're learning to "think for themselves" by questioning authority, developing their own curricula, and critiquing every aspect of society. But these activities teach students not to think for **themselves** but to think like neo-Marxists.

Students who **don't** think like neo-Marxists wind up on the wrong side of Marcuse's "repressive tolerance."[8] For instance, a 2023 survey of over 55,000 American college students revealed significantly higher tolerance for liberal speakers on campus than for conservative speakers.[9] The study also found conservative students feel compelled to censor themselves considerably more than do liberal students.[10] Certainly, students are learning to "think critically" in the sense of thinking like critical theorists. But are they learning to think critically in the sense of exercising biblical discernment or logically evaluating arguments?[11]

The answer isn't looking great, given that logic itself—along with math, writing, and grammar—has come under the scrutiny of critical theory-based education. For example, the highly funded curriculum Equitable Math made headlines in 2021 for reportedly saying, "White supremacy culture shows up in math classrooms" that focus "on getting the 'right' answer."[12] Then in 2022, a California teacher went viral for suggesting that schools that teach essay writing, grammar, and syntax contribute to "white supremacy, and misogyny and colonization."[13] As a quick internet search will show, such views are hardly isolated.

WHITE SUPREMACY CULTURE SHOWS UP IN MATH CLASSROOMS.

Active attacks on reading, writing, and arithmetic from critical theory-based educators aren't the only threat to academic skills. Culture has also been passively conceding its intellectual defenses, thanks in part to media consumption patterns. Social commentator Neil Postman sounded alarm bells decades ago in his 1985 book *Amusing Ourselves to Death*.[14] In it, Postman argued that as communication technologies changed in recent centuries, human thinking changed as well—and not generally for the better.

Back when people gained most of their information from books, according to Postman, human thinking reflected the orderly logic of written words. But Postman suggested that as technological changes brought the telegraph, photograph, and television, people started seeing the world differently. They now viewed reality as being less of a coherent whole than a series of disconnected fragments, like images flickering across a screen.[15] Such images can entertain, persuade, and inform us to a degree, but they can't present the level of detailed information, complex arguments, or abstract analyses a book can. Postman thought these changes watered down people's thinking abilities, made everything about entertainment, and softly turned civilization into a puppet show. Whoever controls the television networks holds the marionette strings.

WHOEVER CONTROLS THE TELEVISION NETWORKS HOLDS THE MARIONETTE STRINGS.

If that's what Postman thought about television in 1985, we can only imagine what he'd say about the internet, social media, and generative AI. Internet culture has degenerated the concept of "winning an argument" from "presenting the most logical synthesis of the highest-quality facts" to "posting the most memorable insult." Social media algorithms encourage viewers to spend hours staring at 60-second cat videos. And in theory, generative AI can let humans outsource their writing skills altogether.

Ultimately, a long road of active attacks among educators and passive concessions among consumers has produced a thoroughly trivialized society. The three Rs are no longer **reading**, **writing**, and **'rithmetic** but **radicalism**, **rhetoric**, and **recreation**. (Expand on that last R by legalizing recreational drugs, and the pleasure-seeking, mind-numbing effects of trivialization compound.)

A society that applies the first set of Rs from a biblical foundation can better resist totalitarianism in all its forms. But soft totalitarianism thrives on the second set of Rs. And that's the set which has come to characterize our culture.

ATOMIZATION: DIVIDED AND CONQUERED

Another feature that all too often characterizes society is isolation, with individuals floating like disconnected atoms in a lonely universe. In his 2000 book, *Bowling Alone: The Collapse and Revival of American Community*, political scientist Robert Putnam argued this atomization process began even before the internet.[16] The book's jacket summarizes:

> Putnam shows how we have become increasingly disconnected from family, friends, neighbors, and social structures, whether the PTA, church, recreation clubs, political parties, or bowling leagues. Our shrinking access to the "social capital" that is the reward of communal activity and community sharing is a serious threat to our civic and personal health.[17]

While not all Putnam's suggestions aligned with Scripture,[18] he did bring widespread attention to an important truth from Genesis: "It is not good that the man should be alone" (Genesis 2:18). God designed humans to live in relationship with himself, with the families he gives us, and with the wider body of Christ. Isolation not only thwarts our ability to live out this design but also makes us weaker targets for physical, spiritual, or psychological attacks—aka "brainwashing."

Not many scholars seem to agree on what "brainwashing" means or to what degree it happens.[19] But the term usually refers either to a totalitarian technique of trying to break down and replace people's beliefs or to more subversive indoctrination methods.[20] Whatever its form, "brainwashing" works best when people are separated from family, friends, and access to alternative viewpoints. The more isolated we become, the more alone we feel in our beliefs and the less chance we have of others reminding us what's true.

"BRAINWASHING" WORKS BEST WHEN PEOPLE ARE SEPARATED FROM FAMILY, FRIENDS, AND ACCESS TO ALTERNATIVE VIEWPOINTS.

Unfortunately, it's no secret that many people feel more disconnected than ever—despite our digitally "connected" era. As the world learned in recent years, online connectivity can be a wonderful asset, enabling interactions that couldn't otherwise happen. But communication over screens still isn't a fully satisfying replacement for interacting face-to-face.[21]

Sadly, isolation only worsens with the undermining of the church and family institutions we investigated in chapter 6. The result, as Putnam noted, is a civilization where many people lack a sense of community, belonging, and—thanks in part to a loss of biblical truth—identity. These voids create a vacuum neo-Marxist activism promises to fill.[22]

DESENSITIZATION AND THERAPIZATION: FEEL-GOOD LIES

The next two processes, desensitization and therapization, feed off one another's lies.[23] The more we make our feelings the authority instead of God, the more we give in to temptations our therapeutic culture says will make us happy. Our God-given consciousness numbs, making it easier to pick **pleasure** over **principle** again. When this cycle plays out on a wide scale, we end up with a culture that redefines "good" as "doing whatever makes you feel happy." However, the problem with that is human feelings naturally bend toward sin (Jeremiah 17:9). A society that redefines goodness in terms of feelings will begin to "call evil good and good evil" (Isaiah 5:20).

This consequence reveals a major problem with the ethical decision-making system known as **utilitarianism**. According to utilitarianism, a decision is "moral" if it will bring the greatest happiness to the most people.[24] That idea might sound great at first, especially to our therapeutic culture. But besides raising practical problems of how to define, measure, and triage different people's happiness, utilitarian thinking can rationalize atrocities.

For instance, one bioethicist applied utilitarianism to (seriously) advocate for killing randomly chosen people for their organs.[25] After all, if one such slaughter saved multiple lives, wouldn't that make the most people happy? This example shows how redefining "good" in opposition to God's Word opens the door to justifying limitless evils. This problem remains whether the new definition of **goodness** is "whatever promotes happiness" or something else—like "whatever promotes sustainability benefits the state or empowers the oppressed."

Morality isn't the only value therapeutic culture redefines. Rod Dreher points out that therapization also leads to redefining concepts like **freedom**, **oppression**, and **sin**.[26] "Freedom" comes to mean "liberation from unchosen obligation"—an idea underpinning many pro-abortion arguments.[27] "Oppression" becomes linked with a lack of happiness, such that anything that causes unhappiness counts as "oppressive."[28] As for sin, Dreher observed, "in therapeutic culture, the great sin is to stand in the way of the freedom of others to find happiness as they wish. This goes hand in hand with the sexual revolution."[29]

Therapeutic culture also dovetails with certain watered-down doctrines seeping into churches. One of these doctrines is moralistic therapeutic deism, a worldview we encountered in chapter 6. This worldview dresses Rousseau in a clerical collar to preach that "God just wants you to do good and be happy."[30] Therapeutic messages also surface in "prosperity gospel" teachings, which claim, contrary to Scripture, that faith in Jesus should bring us earthly health, wealth, and luxury.[31]

If churches blend these therapeutic messages with teachings that endorse our culture's moral desensitization, what happens? We wind up with churches saying, "God wants you to embrace whatever sexual lifestyle that makes you happy." Freud has joined Rousseau in the pulpit.

THESE PROCESSES CONDITION SOCIETY FOR SOFT TOTALITARIANISM.

On multiple levels, these processes condition society for soft totalitarianism. Moral desensitization helps break down the family, while therapization helps weaken the church—two foundations totalitarianism must target, as chapter 6 described. Therapeutic culture also trains people to prioritize pleasure, comfort, safety, and convenience over freedom, logic, privacy, and conviction, playing into soft totalitarianism's hand.[32]

SUPERVISION: KEEPING TRACK WITH TECHNOLOGY

One area where we're becoming especially conditioned to choose therapeutic priorities above other concerns—especially privacy—is our use of technology. That's certainly not to imply technology itself is "bad." Various theologians point out that our ability to create and use technology is a **gift** from God.[33] We can apply this gift for endless magnificent purposes such as loving others, stewarding creation, and mitigating the fall's effects. Technological advances have enhanced the length, ease, and quality of life for many people to degrees our recent predecessors could only imagine—and beyond. Today's technologies also unlock opportunities for learning, connecting, and sharing the gospel like never before.

TECHNOLOGY IS A GIFT FROM GOD.

Yes, technology is a gift. In our fallen world, it's also a gift we must use discerningly, responsibly, and with biblical guidelines. After all, not **every** kind of progress necessarily heads in a healthy direction—and not all technologies are created equal. Technologies reflect the values of their users and developers,[34] can be used for **helpful** or **harmful** purposes, and may cause unintended effects—for better or worse. Even positive uses of technologies can affect human thinking, behavior, and relationships in unneutral ways, calling for wisdom.

We especially need wisdom in light of digital technologies' surveillance capacities. From smartphones to search engines to computerized cars, these technologies offer obvious advantages, becoming so ubiquitous that many people (literally) couldn't get by without them.[35] But while these technologies make our lives easier for us, they also make our lives easier for **others** to monitor, track, and manipulate. The result is exactly the surveillance infrastructure soft totalitarianism needs.[36]

Illustrating how complex this infrastructure has become, theologian and software developer Dr. John Dyer has explained:

> For example, if you visit a friend for a few days, you might later see an ad for the same kind of toothpaste they let you borrow at their house. This is not because your phone is recording your conversation about toothpaste; it's because marketers can combine data from your friend's credit card purchases, your GPS movements indicating you were at their house overnight, and the social media connection detailing your relationship.[37]

The more "smart appliances" we buy, apps we download, and time we spend on trackable platforms, the more data we supply for marketing, monitoring, or other objectives. Certainly, legitimate purposes exist for collecting certain data. The questions are whether a specific data collection practice is appropriate and what its consequences might entail.

Take cars, for instance. In 2023, researchers from the Mozilla Foundation (a nonprofit organization promoting internet privacy) reviewed 25 vehicle manufacturers' policies.[38] The team reported, "**Every car brand** we looked at collects more personal data than necessary and uses that information for a reason other than to operate your vehicle and [to] manage their relationship with you." The report continued,

> [Car companies] can collect personal information from how you interact with your car, the connected services you use in your car, the car's app (which provides a gateway to information on your phone), and can gather even more information about you from third party sources like Sirius XM or Google Maps. . . . The gist is: they can collect super intimate information about you—from your medical information, your genetic information . . . to how fast you drive, where you drive, and what songs you play in your car—in huge quantities.[39]

Does all this mean we shouldn't drive cars or use digital devices? No. Many of us can't avoid these technologies without withdrawing from roles to which God called us. But we **can** be aware of embedded surveillance infrastructure. We can recognize that relevant stakeholders are collecting mass data for the purpose of influencing our behavior. And we can exercise wisdom accordingly whenever possible.

DOES ALL THIS MEAN WE SHOULDN'T DRIVE CARS OR USE DIGITAL DEVICES?

We're also wise to hold loosely the technologies we can survive without, knowing they may eventually be integrated into an "access economy" that excludes Christ followers. We glimpsed that possibility in chapter 1, which quoted a World Economic Forum (WEF) publication encouraging organizations to technologically enforce "diversity, equity, and inclusivity" policies.[40] This is soft totalitarianism in motion—and it will foreseeably gain momentum as technology advances.

One near-future stage in technology's advance that some governments have written about is "biodigital convergence."[41] In this convergence, biology and machinery would combine in ways that make human bodies more trackable (or controllable), raising implications for soft totalitarianism. Brain-computer interface (BCI) technologies serve as an especially important example.

BRAIN-COMPUTER INTERFACES: DECODING THE MIND

BCIs are systems where a machine records a brain's activity as input for a computer program—or where a computer inputs signals into a brain.[42] As one research team described, "BCIs can be quickly applied to 'read' the brain to record its activity and decode its meaning and to 'write' to the brain to manipulate activity in specific regions and affect their function." These devices can be **invasive**, requiring surgical implants, or **noninvasive**, touching only the scalp. Both varieties already exist, with multiple noninvasive BCIs available on the market.[43] Meanwhile, breakthroughs continue making interfaces between biology and electronics more efficient than ever.[44]

BCIs = SYSTEMS WHERE A MACHINE RECORDS A BRAIN'S ACTIVITY AS INPUT FOR A COMPUTER PROGRAM—OR WHERE A COMPUTER INPUTS SIGNALS INTO A BRAIN

On the bright side, some BCIs promise astounding medical benefits. BCIs can help restore lost vision, hearing, and communication abilities, and even let paralyzed people mentally control computers, wheelchairs, and prostheses.[45] But other BCIs have nothing to do with therapy, applying instead to militaries, workplaces, and everyday consumers.[46] Still other BCIs go further, enabling **brain-to-brain** interfaces (BTBIs).

Already, BTBI experiments have let humans link brains for wordless communication, collaboration, and problem solving.[47] One early study demonstrated that one person's thinking could jerk another person's hand.[48] But why stop with species boundaries? BTBIs can let researchers mentally move a rodent's tail, guide rats through mazes, and control a cockroach like a robot.[49] Similarly, engineers have applied a technique called optogenetics[50] to transform dragonflies into remote-controlled "living drones" capable of surveillance.[51]

THESE TECHNOLOGIES RAISE NUMEROUS ETHICAL ISSUES.

Clearly, these technologies raise numerous ethical issues. To borrow a phrase from WEF conference speaker Professor Yuval Harari, "Humans are now hackable."[52]

In 2023, another WEF conference speaker, Dr. Nita Farahany, delivered a presentation titled "Ready for Brain Transparency?"[53] Farahany described how BCIs will let workplaces track employees' brain activity, allow hackers to access sensitive mental information, and help corporations gather mountains of neural data. Referring to how companies are releasing devices like earbuds that record brainwaves, Farahany observed, "as healthy people in a widespread way start to have their brainwave data collected, the insights that we can gain through pattern recognition will exponentially increase pretty quickly."[54]

Data collection practices already raise significant concerns **without** major stakeholders accessing consumers' neurological activity, which can reveal sensitive details like banking information.[55] As minds become less viewed as private property, BCIs may additionally raise the stakes for committing "thought crimes." BCIs could also theoretically let law enforcers access mental data about other punishable activities—a concerning prospect in countries that criminalize living out biblical principles.

WILD NEW WORLD: WHEN BCIs MEET OTHER TECH

There's more. Research and resources are pouring into projects that link BCIs with other technologies in ways that relate to global Marxist agendas. Before we survey examples of how researchers are promoting these agendas, below are a few relevant concepts to know.

ARTIFICIAL INTELLIGENCE (AI)

AI is an umbrella term for computer programs that collect, process, and respond to information in ways that mimic the thinking abilities of living creatures.[56] "Narrow AI" programs excel in specific tasks, but a hypothetical technology called "artificial general intelligence" (AGI) would excel in **many** areas.[57]

With capacities to quickly analyze vast amounts of neural data, AI plays an essential role in BCIs.[58] According to one researcher, "the idea of using AI to decode the human brain has been a fast growing commercial venture for many tech giants, who have been investing heavily in . . . neuro-tech related projects."[59]

On another telling note, multiple high-profile individuals have signed a "Social Contract for an AI Age" intended to "provide the foundations for a new society."[60] This contract involves following United Nations and WEF policies, forbidding "online hate," and incentivizing companies to "only do business with" other signatory corporations. Ringing with soft totalitarianism, the contract requests "a system to monitor and evaluate governments, companies, and individuals" based on their upholding the new society's norms.

THE METAVERSE

Still in its early stages, the metaverse is an internet-supported virtual realm where people create digital representations of themselves (avatars) that can interact, shop, game, learn, and more.[61] As one research team observed, "The metaverse is characterized by continuous and pervasive user data acquisition."[62] People can immerse themselves in the metaverse through technologies like virtual reality goggles or haptic gloves (which simulate feelings of touch). But these technologies don't fully replicate real-world sensations and "cannot offer a comprehensive evaluation of user status."[63] In other words, they don't collect enough data.

FUTURISTIC BCI PROJECTS FOR THE METAVERSE TEND TOWARDS INVASIVE SYSTEMS.

Enter BCIs.

The researchers observed, "Futuristic BCI projects for the metaverse tend towards invasive systems."[64] These systems offer a "more immersive experience" while enabling "better study and control" of brains.[65] The researchers noted, "Big technological corporations, such as Meta or Snap, have recently acquired BCI companies" to incorporate BCIs into metaverse-related products.[66]

THE "INTERNET OF THINGS" (IoT)

You know how we can use smartphone apps for controlling anything from appliances to security cameras to light switches? As more everyday objects become digitally connected, the internet of things (IoT) results.[67] This IoT can integrate entire "smart cities," where everything from streetlights to garbage cans contain sensors that monitor, collect, and transmit data.[68]

Add BCIs, and people will be able to control everyday "smart" objects with their minds—even as those objects collect neural data.[69] The resulting network of brains, devices, and sensors would create a prospective "Internet of Everything."[70]

THE GLOBAL BRAIN

If enough BCI users plugged their brains into the Internet of Everything, some researchers believe a "hive mind" would emerge.[71] Every individual brain would function like a single neuron in the larger "global brain," which could also incorporate artificial intelligence.

Hypothetically, people in this global brain could access knowledge from any other connected intelligence, device, or sensor. Philosopher Cadell Last suggests this system "would represent qualities closely associated with the qualities of omniscience, omnipresence, omnipotence, and omnibenevolence."[72] In other words, some people hope the global brain could make people "like God."

Cadell Last noted these aspirations for godlike consciousness reflect the globalist New Age thinking of Peter Teilhard de Chardin (see chapter 4).[73] Last also mentioned the global brain would require a "global system of governance that is inherently more integrated and cooperative," along with a "transition towards a post-capitalist economy."[74]

Last's nod to post-capitalist global governance hints how all these technologies apply to building the kind of globalist socialist society we examined in chapter 4. As one researcher wrote in 2020, "Such a society, which looks like a Marxist utopia, can only occur with both a higher-level of technological development and a universal value system."[75] (Technologies of the world, unite!)

> **A MARXIST UTOPIA CAN ONLY OCCUR WITH A HIGHER-LEVEL OF TECHNOLOGICAL DEVELOPMENT.**

Similar ideas appear in writings by Ben Goertzel, a prominent computer scientist described as "one of the world's foremost experts in Artificial General Intelligence."[76] Cadell Last explained, "Goertzel has developed the idea that the Global Brain will become a medium integrating all socioeconomic and political activities related to the emergence of a sharing economy."[77] An article with Dr. Goertzel as the lead author stated:

> The emergence of artificial general intelligence and the global brain provides new opportunities for realizing humanity's long quest for a more utopian existence. One possibility is a more successful implementation of the state socialist vision of a centrally managed economy, possibly controlled by an AGI "Nanny" instead of a central committee of politicians. An alternative outcome, more in keeping with the original Marxist vision of the withering away of the state, may be the mutualist vision of organizing economic and social life along voluntary lines.[78]

Basically, Dr. Goertzel is outrightly advocating for applying new technologies—which he's leading the charge to develop—for building some version of a Marxist world.

(Notably, some of his other work shows how this agenda ties into the New Age spirituality we examined in chapter 4.[79])

While AGI and Global Brain remain in the future, related technologies like consumer BCIs and the Internet of Things already demand discernment.[80] The more everyday tools become integrated into this internet, the more ordinary necessities can turn into "privileges" that may be canceled, restricted, and subjected to changeable "terms and conditions." This outcome is exactly what totalitarian social credit systems need.

> **EXACTLY WHAT TOTALITARIAN SOCIAL CREDIT SYSTEMS NEED**

Such systems would foreseeably benefit from **(1)** the fact that many people carry (generally) hackable microphones and cameras with them,[81] **(2)** the amount of data our technologies collect, and **(3)** the additional information many of us willingly share online. Previous totalitarian regimes would torture people for information about their contacts, friends, and activities. Now the information is freely available online. As Rod Dreher aptly summarized, "Throughout the past two decades, economic and technological changes—changes that occurred under liberal democratic capitalism—have given both the state and corporations surveillance capabilities of which Lenin and Stalin could have only dreamed."[82]

These realities may seem frightening. But faced with technological powers much stronger than we are, Christians must remember God is infinitely stronger. The tower of Babel reminds us that God can effortlessly overturn humanity's technological ambitions. Even when God allows humans to utilize insidious technologies (like crosses), he orchestrates the outcomes in ways that accomplish his purposes for good (Romans 8:28). Either way, we remain in his loving hands.

CUTTING THE MARIONETTE STRINGS

In the end, we've seen how five processes make people (and puppets) vulnerable to the Land of Pleasure's soft totalitarianism. The first process, trivialization, distracts us with the insignificant, undermines our reasoning abilities, and lowers our intellectual defenses against lies. The second process, atomization, produces a society of isolated individuals more susceptible to manipulation. The next two processes, desensitization and therapization, create a cycle of deception that lures people into prioritizing happiness as the highest "moral" standard.

All these processes converge in the technological arena, where supervision paves the way for soft totalitarianism. If we consume technologies without due biblical wisdom, they can easily distract us with the trivial, desensitize us with the immoral, and atomize us with an isolating "connectivity." All this happens in the therapeutic names of recreation, entertainment, and convenience. Meanwhile, "coachmen" in the real-world Land of Pleasure can leverage the same technologies to monitor, track, and manipulate humanity like never before.

A CYCLE OF DECEPTION THAT LURES PEOPLE INTO PRIORITIZING HAPPINESS AS THE HIGHEST "MORAL" STANDARD

The result is a society where our logical thinking, moral sensitivity, and relational stability are **decreasing**, even as our technological powers are **increasing**. We don't need AI to tell us this equation places society in a precarious position. The situation is especially concerning given all the points where neo-Marxist messages play into the five processes we've examined.

We've seen, for instance, how critical theory-based education contributes to trivialization by producing **activists** instead of **academics**. Activism helps fill the void left by atomization, which arises in part through the breakdowns of families and churches—breakdowns revolutionary agendas need. Moral desensitization and therapization catalyze these breakdowns, spurred by sexual revolutionary messages that neo-Marxists, including Marcuse and Firestone, promoted. As neo-Marxism permeates culture, surveillance infrastructure can favor "good citizens" who conform with this worldview—while **disfavoring** others.

ACTIVISM HELPS FILL THE VOID.

While that's not exactly a happy ending, the good news is the story isn't over. We know from Scripture how history ends. And we know that in the meantime, our lives remain in the hands of a perfect author. Keeping his Word as our authority will protect us from falling, like Pinocchio, for the Land of Pleasure's lies.

Now that we've seen the conditions that make society vulnerable to totalitarianism, let's explore the rise, reign, and resolution of totalitarian regimes. That way we can recognize similar patterns progressing today. To start, we'll need to leave behind the marionette store in Prague and catch a subway to one of the city's coffee shops.

ENDNOTES

1. For more on the differences between hard and soft totalitarianism, see Rod Dreher, *Live Not by Lies: A Manual for Christian Dissidents* (New York: Sentinel, 2020); see also chapter 1.

2. The Land of Pleasure has different names in different retellings but was called the Land of Toys in Collodi's novel.

3. More information on Marcuse, Firestone, and their beliefs is available in chapters 5 and 6.

4. *Merriam-Webster.com Dictionary*, s.v. "trivial," accessed July 2024, merriam-webster.com/dictionary/trivial.

5. See Dreher, *Live Not by Lies*, 31–32, 93 (ebook version).

6. Philip Rieff, *The Triumph of the Therapeutic: Uses of Faith After Freud* (London: Chatto and Windus, 1966). For instance, when explaining the primacy of "inner feelings" (especially happiness) in terms of psychological selfhood, Rieff wrote, "Religious man was born to be saved; psychological man is born to be pleased. The difference was established long ago, when 'I believe,' the cry of the ascetic, lost precedence to 'one feels,' the caveat of the therapeutic" (Rieff, *The Triumph of the Therapeutic*, 24–25). Further discussion on Rieff's concepts of the therapeutic is available in Carl Trueman, *The Rise and Triumph of the Modern Self: Cultural Amnesia, Expressive Individualism, and the Road to Sexual Revolution* (Wheaton, IL: Crossway, 2020).

7. Adler, *Drawing Down the Moon* (New York: Penguin Books, 1979), 97, as cited in Marcia Montenegro, "Wicca and Witchcraft," *World Religions and Cults: Moralistic, Mythical and Mysticism Religions*, vol. 2, edited by Bodie Hodge and Roger Patterson (Green Forest, AR: Master Books, 2016), 191. Notably, attempts to define *liberty* along similar lines failed disastrously in the French Revolution, as chapter 3 described.

8. For a discussion of Marcuse's essay *Repressive Tolerance*, please see chapter 5.

9. Sean T. Stevens, "2024 College Free Speech Rankings: What Is the State of Free Speech on America's College Campuses?" The Foundation for Individual Rights and Expression, accessed July 2024, thefire.org/research-learn/2024-college-free-speech-rankings.

10. Stevens, "2024 College Free Speech Rankings."

11. See "What Is Critical Thinking Anyway—And Why Does It Matter?" Answers in Genesis, July 1, 2020, AnswersInGenesis.org/blogs/patricia-engler/2020/07/01/what-is-critical-thinking-anyway-and-why-does-it-matter/.

12. Paul Bond, "Math Suffers from White Supremacy, According to a Bill Gates-Funded Course," *Newsweek*, February 23, 2021, newsweek.com/math-suffers-white-supremacy-according-bill-gates-funded-course-1571511.

13. Hannah Grossman, "California English Teacher Teaches Kids Grammar Is Part of White Supremacy: 'Undermine that [euphemistic expletive deleted],'" Fox News, December 5, 2022, foxnews.com/media/california-english-teacher-teaches-kids-grammar-is-part-white-supremacy-undermine-bs.

14. Neil Postman, *Amusing Ourselves to Death: Public Discourse in the Age of Show Business* (New York: Penguin, 2006, first published in 1985).

15. The larger worldview issue behind this change is the departure from belief in God as the source of truth toward (eventually) a more postmodern outlook that "everyone has their own truth." Still, if Postman is correct, technological changes contributed to aspects of these that the rejection of God's Word engendered.

16. Robert Putnam, *Bowling Alone: The Collapse and Revival of American Community* (New York: Simon and Schuster, 2000).

17. Putnam, *Bowling Alone*, interior front cover matter.

18. E.g., Putnam apparently advocated for a form of religious pluralism (Putnam, *Bowling Alone*, 409). While treating others as fellow image bearers regardless of their beliefs is one thing, viewing all religions as "the same" is another.

19. Some argue that "brainwashing" doesn't happen at all; generally, these debates hinge on how "brainwashing" is defined.

20. A fuller discussion of brainwashing and its definitions is available in *Prepare to Thrive: A Survival Guide for Christian Students* (Hebron, KY: Answers in Genesis, 2022).

21. E.g., Martha Newson et al., "Digital Contact Does Not Promote Wellbeing, But Face-to-Face Contact Does: A Cross-National Survey During the COVID-19 Pandemic," *New Media & Society* 26, no. 1 (2021): 426–449, journals.sagepub.com/doi/10.1177/14614448211062164 .

22. See Dreher, *Live Not by Lies*, 32 (ebook version).

23. Further discussion of therapeutic culture is available in Rieff, *The Triumph of the Therapeutic*, Trueman, *The Rise and Triumph of the Modern Self*, and Dreher, *Live Not by Lies*.

24. There are different "flavors" of utilitarianism. Some versions prioritize "the most happiness overall," while others prioritize "the most happiness distributed the most fairly among the most people." Some prioritize *rules* that maximize happiness, while others prioritize *actions* that maximize happiness. Still other versions may define the "greatest good" in terms of something other than (or in addition to) happiness. (See "Part VIII, Consequentialism," in *Ethical Theory: An Anthology*, ed. Russ Shafer-Landau, 2nd ed. [Chichester, UK: Wiley-Blackwell, 2013], 411–478.)

25. John Harris, "The Survival Lottery," *Philosophy* 50, no. 191 (1975): 81–87.

26. Dreher, *Live Not by Lies*, 71 (ebook version).

27. Dreher, *Live Not by Lies*, 184 (ebook version).

28. Dreher, *Live Not by Lies*, 33, 184 (ebook version).

29. Dreher, *Live Not by Lies*, 13 (ebook version).

30. See Cultural Research Center, "Counterfeit Christianity: 'Moralistic Therapeutic Deism' Most Popular Worldview in U.S. Culture," April 27, 2021, arizonachristian.edu/2021/04/27/counterfeit-christianity-moralistic-therapeutic-deism-most-popular-worldview-in-u-s-culture/.

31. For more on why prosperity gospel teachings contradict Scripture, see Costi Hinn, "Healthy, Wealthy, and Lies," Answers in Genesis, January 1, 2022, AnswersInGenesis.org/christianity/healthy-wealthy-lies/.

32. See also "Capitalism: Woke and Watchful," in Dreher, *Live Not by Lies*, 71–94 (ebook version).

33. E.g., John Dyer, *From the Garden to the City: The Place of Technology in the Story of God*, rev. ed. (Grand Rapids, MI: Kregel Publications, 2022), ebook version. Key points in the following two paragraphs draw heavily on Dyer's insights. Please note, however, that this book at times gestures toward ideas such as human evolution and systemic oppression so should be read (as any book) with appropriate biblical discernment.

34. For instance, expensive gaming consoles reflect a culture that highly values entertainment, while specific games themselves reflect the themes that our culture tends to value *as* entertainment (e.g., violence).

35. This is why concerns have been raised about the consequences of widescale power grid blackouts in developed nations, where entire systems including healthcare, emergency response, and transportation (and therefore urban food availability) depend on electricity. (E.g., Sukeyuki Ichimasa, "Threat of Cascading 'Permanent Blackout' Effects and High Altitude Electromagnetic Pulse (HEMP)," *NIDS Journal of Defense and Security* 17 [2016]: 3–20.)

36. See "Capitalism: Woke and Watchful," in Dreher, *Live Not by Lies*, 71–94 (ebook version).

37. Dyer, *From the Garden to the City*, ebook version.

38. Jen Caltrider, Misha Rykov, and Zoë MacDonald, "It's Official: Cars Are the Worst Product Category We Have Ever Reviewed for Privacy," Privacy Not Included, Mozilla Foundation, September 6, 2023, foundation.mozilla.org/en/privacynotincluded/articles/its-official-cars-are-the-worst-product-category-we-have-ever-reviewed-for-privacy. See also Matt Burgess, "How Your New Car Tracks You," Wired, June 21, 2023, wired.com/story/car-data-privacy-toyota-honda-ford/.

39. Caltrider, Rykov, and MacDonald, "It's Official."

40. "Diversity, Equity and Inclusion 4.0: A Toolkit for Leaders to Accelerate Social Progress in the Future of Work," June 2020, World Economic Forum (WEF), accessed July 2024, www3.weforum.org/docs/WEF_NES_DEI4.0_Toolkit_2020.pdf. The tool kit contains a disclaimer that the contents are not necessarily official views of the WEF, but the WEF facilitated its development and published it.

41. E.g., Policy Horizons Canada, "Exploring Biodigital Convergence," Government of Canada, February 11, 2020, horizons.gc.ca/en/2020/02/11/exploring-biodigital-convergence/.

42. See also "Questions Christians Need to Ask Before Using Brain-Computer Interfaces," Answers in Genesis, November 25, 2022, AnswersInGenesis.org/human-evolution/questions-brain-computer-interfaces/.

43. Examples of such devices and their applications are listed in Ondrej Kolimár et al., "Current State of Brain-Computer Interface Device Usage in Personal and Professional Applications," Proceedings of ELITECH '23, the 25th Conference of Doctoral Students, May 31, 2023, FEI STU, Bratislava, Slovakia.

44. "Hybrid Transistors Set Stage for Integration of Biology and Microelectronics," ScienceDaily, November 22, 2023, sciencedaily.com/releases/2023/11/231122192301.htm.

45. Andrea Bonci et al., "An Introductory Tutorial on Brain-Computer Interfaces and Their Applications," *Electronics* 10, no. 5 (2021): 560.

46. E.g., Kaido Värbu, Naveed Muhammad, and Yar Muhammad, "Past, Present, and Future of EEG-Based BCI Applications," *Sensors* 22, no. 9 (2022): 3331; Ji-Hoon Jeong et al., "Towards Brain-Computer Interfaces for Drone Swarm Control" (in *2020 8th International Winter Conference on Brain-Computer Interface* [BCI], Gangwon, South Korea, February 2020), 1–4; Christopher Coogan and Bin He, "Brain-Computer Interface Control in a Virtual Reality Environment and Applications for the Internet of Things," *IEEE Access* 6 (2018): 10840–10849; Seonghun Park et al., "Development of an Online Home Appliance Control System Using Augmented Reality and an SSVEP-Based Brain-Computer Interface" (in *2020 8th International Winter Conference on Brain-Computer Interface* [BCI], Gangwon, South Korea, February 2020), 1–2; Gabriel Vasiljevic and Leonardo Cunha De Miranda, "Brain–Computer Interface Games Based on Consumer-Grade EEG Devices: A Systematic Literature Review," *International Journal of Human–Computer Interaction* 36, no. 2 (2020): 105–142.

47. Linxing Jiang et al., "BrainNet: A Multi-Person Brain-to-Brain Interface for Direct Collaboration Between Brains," *Scientific Reports* 9, no. 1 (2019): 1–11.

48. Rajesh Rao et al., "A Direct Brain-to-Brain Interface in Humans," *PLOS ONE* 9, no. 11 (November 2014): e111332.

49. Seung-Schik Yoo et al., "Non-Invasive Brain-to-Brain Interface (BBI): Establishing Functional Links Between Two Brains," *PLOS ONE* 8, no. 4 (April 2013): e60410; Shaomin Zhang et al., "Human Mind Control of Rat Cyborg's Continuous Locomotion with Wireless Brain-to-Brain Interface," *Scientific Reports* 9, no. 1 (2019): 1–12; Guangye Li and Dingguo Zhang, "Brain-Computer Interface Controlled Cyborg: Establishing a Functional Information Transfer Pathway from Human Brain to Cockroach Brain," *PLOS ONE* 11, no. 3 (March 2016): e0150667.

50. Optogenetics involves editing neurons to express a light-sensitive protein so that individual brain cells can be precisely controlled in response to certain wavelengths of light.

51. Emily Matchar, "Turning Dragonflies into Drones: The DragonflEye Project Equips the Insects with Solar-Powered Backpacks that Control Their Flight," *Smithsonian*, February 10, 2017, smithsonianmag.com/innovation/turning-dragonflies-drones-180962097/.

52. In context, Harari stated, "The big story of our era is the ability to hack human beings. And by this, I mean that, if you have enough data and you have enough computing power, you can understand people better than they understand themselves. And then you can manipulate them in ways which were previously impossible. And in such a situation the old democratic system stop[s] functioning. We need to reinvent democracy for this new era in which humans are now hackable animals. You know the whole idea that humans have this soul or spirit, and they have free will . . . that's over." (Statement made by Yuval Harari in "Hebrew University's Prof. Yuval Noah Harari on The Era of the Coronavirus: Living in a New Reality," YouTube video posted by The Hebrew University of Jerusalem Official, October 29, 2020, 24:47–25:49, youtube.com/watch?v=ltJTRnNLYqY&t=1s.)

53. Nita Farahany and Nicholas Thompson, "Ready for Brain Transparency?" session presented at Davos 2023, available at weforum.org/events/world-economic-forum-annual-meeting-2023/sessions/ready-for-brain-transparency.

54. Farahany, "Ready for Brain Transparency?" Notably, Farahany was not necessarily endorsing such data collection. Still, she proceeded to call the prospect of vast neural data collection "frightening but promising," given how the data can help with researching neurological disease.

55. Mario Quiles Pérez et al., "Breaching Subjects' Thoughts Privacy: A Study with Visual Stimuli and Brain-Computer Interfaces," *Journal of Healthcare Engineering* 2021, no. 1 (August 2021), doi.org/10.1155/2021/5517637. See also Ivan Martinovic et al., "On the Feasibility of Side-Channel Attacks with Brain-Computer Interfaces" (in *Proceedings of the 21st USENIX Conference on Security Symposium* [USENIX Security 12], Washington D.C., 2012), 143–158.

56. It's a little more complex than that, as "artificial intelligence" isn't the easiest to define—especially since "intelligence" itself is a debated term. Furthermore, as one team of scholars noted, "The definition of AI and of what should and should not be included has changed over time" (Christoph Bartneck, Christoph Lütge, Alan Wagner, and Sean Welsh, *An Introduction to Ethics in Robotics and AI* [Cham, Switzerland: Springer Nature, 2021], 8). Even so, the *Merriam-Webster* dictionary offers a down-to-earth definition of AI as "(1) the capability of computer systems or algorithms to imitate intelligent human behavior" or "a computer, computer system, or set of algorithms having this capability" and (2) "a branch of computer science dealing with the simulation of intelligent behavior in computers" ("Artificial Intelligence," *Merriam-Webster Online Dictionary*, accessed July 2024, merriam-webster.com/dictionary/artificial%20intelligence).

57. Ben Goertzel, "Artificial General Intelligence: Concept, State of the Art, and Future Prospects," *Journal of Artificial General Intelligence* 5, no. 1 (2014): 1.

58. Janis Peksa and Dmytro Mamchur, "State-of-the-Art on Brain-Computer Interface Technology," *Sensors* 23, no. 13 (2023): 6001; Xiayin Zhang et al., "The Combination of Brain-Computer Interfaces and Artificial Intelligence: Applications and Challenges," *Annals of Translational Medicine* 8, no. 11 (2020); Guillermo Bernal, Sean Montgomery, and Pattie Maes, "Brain-Computer Interfaces, Open-Source, and Democratizing the Future of Augmented Consciousness," *Frontiers in Computer Science* 3 (2021): 661300.

59. Argyro Karanasiou, "On Being Transhuman: Commercial BCIs and the Quest for Autonomy," in *The Cambridge Handbook of the Law of Algorithms* (Cambridge: Cambridge University Press, 2020).

60. AI World Society, "Social Contract for the AI Age," September 9, 2020, ssrc.mit.edu/wp-content/uploads/2020/10/Social-Contract-for-the-AI-Age.pdf. Signatories listed on the document include Google Vice President Vinton Cerf, Zlatko Lagumdzija (former leader of Bosnia and Herzegovina), Vaira Vīķe-Freiberga (former leader of Latvia), Governor Michael Dukakis of the Boston Global Forum, Thomas Patterson and David Silbersweig of Harvard University, Nazli Choucri of the Massachusetts Institute of Technology (MIT) and the Global System for Sustainable Development, Alex Pentland of MIT, and Marc Rotenberg, the executive director and founder of the Center for AI and Digital Policy.

61. Lik-Hang Lee et al., "All One Needs to Know About Metaverse: A Complete Survey on Technological Singularity, Virtual Ecosystem, and Research Agenda," *ArXiv preprint* (2021): doi.org/10.48550/arXiv.2110.05352; Luyi Chang et al., "6G-Enabled Edge AI for Metaverse: Challenges, Methods, and Future Research Directions," *Journal of Communications and Information Networks* 7, no. 2 (2022): 107–121.

62. Sergio Bernal et al., "When Brain-Computer Interfaces Meet the Metaverse: Landscape, Demonstrator, Trends, Challenges, and Concerns," *ArXiv preprint* (2022), doi.org/10.48550/arXiv.2212.03169.

63. Bernal et al., "When Brain-Computer Interfaces Meet," 2.

64. Bernal et al., "When Brain-Computer Interfaces Meet," 19.

65. Bernal et al., "When Brain-Computer Interfaces Meet," 2, 5–6, 19.

66. Bernal et al., "When Brain-Computer Interfaces Meet," 19.

67. Fritz Allhoff and Adam Henschke, "*The Internet of Things: Foundational Ethical Issues*," *Internet of Things* 1 (2018): 55–66; Gianmarco Baldini et al., "Ethical Design in the Internet of Things," *Science and Engineering Ethics* 24 (2018): 905–925; Spyros Tzafestas, "Ethics and Law in the Internet of Things World," *Smart Cities* 1, no. 1 (2018): 98–120.

68. E.g., Mauricio Ramírez-Moreno et al., "Sensors for Sustainable Smart Cities: A Review," *Applied Sciences* 11, no. 17 (2021): 8198; Martin Bauer, Luis Sanchez, and JaeSeung Song, "IoT-Enabled Cities: Evolution and Outlook," *Sensors* 21, no. 13 (2021): 4511; Amir Alavi et al., "Internet of Things-Enabled Smart Cities: State-of-the-Art and Future Trends," *Measurement* 129 (2018): 589–606.

69. The relevant technology for this scenario already exists; e.g., see Faraz Akram et al., "A Symbols-Based BCI Paradigm for Intelligent Home Control Using P300 Event-Related Potentials," *Sensors* 22, no. 24 (2022): 10000.

70. Jordi Vallverdú, Max Talanov, and Airat Khasianov, "Swarm Intelligence Via the Internet of Things and the Phenomenological Turn," *Philosophies* 2, no. 3 (2017): 19; Adelina Kremenska, Anna Lekova, and Georgi Petrov Dimitrov, "EEG Brain-Computer Interfaces for Internet of Everything (IoE)," in *2022 International Conference on Information Technologies* (InfoTech), 1–6, IEEE, 2022.

71. E.g., see Vallverdú, Talanov, and Khasianov, "Swarm Intelligence Via the Internet of Things"; Cadell Last, "Global Brain: Foundations of a Distributed Singularity," in *The*

21st Century Singularity and Global Futures: A Big History Perspective, eds. Andrey Korotayev and David LePoire (Cham, Switzerland: Springer Nature Switzerland AG, 2020), 363–375; Francis Heylighen and Marta Lenartowicz, "The Global Brain as a Model of the Future Information Society: An Introduction to the Special Issue," *Technological Forecasting and Social Change* 114 (2017): 1–6.

72. Last, "Global Brain: Foundations of a Distributed Singularity," 372. Importantly, the scope of these attributes as God possesses them infinitely surpasses whatever range of knowledge, capabilities, or virtual presence humans could glean through their own inventiveness.

73. Last, "Global Brain: Foundations of a Distributed Singularity," 364.

74. Last, "Global Brain: Foundations of a Distributed Singularity," 369.

75. Sergey Dobrolyubov, "The Transition to Global Society as a Singularity of Social Evolution," in *The 21st Century Singularity and Global Futures*, 535–558.

76. Statement from Ben Goertzel's bio for the Ted X video "Decentralized AI," Ben Goertzel, TEDxBerkeley, March 2019, ted.com/talks/ben_goertzel_decentralized_ai?autoplay=true&muted=true.

77. Last, "Global Brain: Foundations of a Distributed Singularity," 365.

78. Ben Goertzel, Ted Goertzel, and Zarathustra Goertzel, "The Global Brain and the Emerging Economy of Abundance: Mutualism, Open Collaboration, Exchange Networks and the Automated Commons," *Technological Forecasting and Social Change* 114 (2017): 65–73.

79. E.g., Dr. Goertzel has written that he hopes technology will "effect a spiritual transformation" in terms of a type of spirituality associated with ideas "from shamanism, from Oriental religion, [and] from gnosticism" (Ben Goertzel, "Science, Wisdom, and the Hierarchy of Being," in *Unification of Science and Spirit*, 1996, accessed July 2024, goertzel.org/books/spirit/uni0.htm.). Dr. Goertzel also spoke for the Davos BlockBase 2019 Planetary SuperNodes Gathering, an event that runs alongside the WEF Annual Meeting and promotes a blend of ideas reminiscent of New Ageism and Transhumanism. See davosblockbase.com/supernode-davos-2019/.

80. See "Questions Christians Need to Ask Before Using Brain-Computer Interfaces," Answers in Genesis, November 25, 2022, AnswersInGenesis.org/human-evolution/questions-brain-computer-interfaces/.

81. For some context of these trends' scale, see Felix Richter, "Charted: There Are More Mobile Phones than People in the World," World Economic Forum, April 11, 2023, weforum.org/agenda/2023/04/charted-there-are-more-phones-than-people-in-the-world/. Not all of these will have cameras or apps, but they certainly have microphones. See also Nancy Luedke, "Research Hack Reveals Call Security Risk in Smartphones," Texas A&M University, August 17, 2023, engineering.tamu.edu/news/2023/08/research-hack-reveals-call-security-risk-in-smartphones.html.

82. Dreher, *Live Not by Lies*, 71 (ebook version).

1 CORINTHIANS 15:58

THEREFORE, MY BELOVED BROTHERS, BE STEADFAST, IMMOVABLE, ALWAYS ABOUNDING IN THE WORK OF THE LORD, KNOWING THAT IN THE LORD YOUR LABOR IS NOT IN VAIN.

CHAPTER 8

STOKING, SUSTAINING & STOPPING A REVOLUTION

PATTERNS IN THE RISE AND FALL OF TOTALITARIAN REGIMES

"There are different types of miracles," said the former journalist across the table from me at the coffee shop in Prague. "There are political miracles. The biggest political miracle I saw in my life was the fall of communism. I could never, ever have believed that in ten days it could be gone."

Those ten days of November 1989 marked the Velvet Revolution, a massive protest movement that helped to topple decades of hard totalitarianism in Czechoslovakia.[1] But this miracle hadn't begun overnight. The spark that lit the Velvet Revolution had ignited more than a year earlier, in the form of five thousand candles.

At the historic Candlelight Demonstration, thousands of people—led by ordinary churchgoers—took a risky stand for "religious freedom and human rights" amidst communism's oppressiveness.[2] Gathering in the city of Bratislava, the demonstrators began to quietly light candles, sing the national anthem, and pray.[3] The communist police answered their peaceful protest with tear gas, water cannons, truncheons, dogs, and arrests.[4] But the spark had caught.

Over the following year, thousands of other demonstrators assembled in Prague on a few other occasions, despite facing communist police violence.[5] When such violence ended a peaceful student march in Prague on November 17, 1989, the public responded with a new wave of mass gatherings. Hundreds of thousands of people participated, catalyzing Czechoslovakian communism's miraculous fall.[6]

Now, more than 30 years later in Prague, I had the chance to talk with a Christian who had witnessed some of these events firsthand.

"Were you there for the Velvet Revolution?" I asked the journalist, who had belonged to an underground Christian student ministry during Czechoslovakia's communist days.

"Yeah," he answered, "I was living in Bratislava." He described how, in response to the November 17 student beatings in Prague, he had joined a small protest in his own city. "There were about 20 of us just standing there for a while and then walking through the streets," he said. "We were followed by guys in long coats—secret police guys. And nothing [else happened]. But

"WERE YOU THERE FOR THE VELVET REVOLUTION?" I ASKED THE JOURNALIST.

then there were more and more people on the streets. And all of the sudden, it became big."

When I asked what role Christians played in the Velvet Revolution, he explained that "many people from the church took part in the protest, and they pleaded for peaceful protests." He added, "It was very spiritual, I would say."

Like the Czechoslovakians who answered the church's plea by lighting candles, Christians today have an opportunity to radiate hope amid the encroaching twilight of totalitarianism. We'll be better able to do so moving forward if we first learn from looking backward. Glancing back in history provides us insights into strategies that stoke revolutions, tactics that sustain totalitarianism, and miraculous ways that God has overturned totalitarian regimes.

RADIATE HOPE AMID THE ENCROACHING TWILIGHT OF TOTALITARIANISM

So let's leave Prague for now, head northeast, and rewind over a century to the origins of the Russian Revolution.

A REVOLUTION BEGINS[7]

The city was St. Petersburg. The year was 1917. The first world war had devastated Russia's economy, disrupted transportation, and dwindled food supplies. But the problems hadn't started with the war. For centuries, Russia's tsars had reigned with absolute power. And the tsars in recent generations hadn't generally exercised that authority well, to say the least.

In response, a revolt arose in 1825 against the tsar's autocracy. But the attempted revolution failed, according to historian Alan Wood, because "there was no revolutionary situation. . . . There was no economic crisis, no external threat, no breakdown in the social order, no mass disturbance—in fact none of the objective circumstances which usually constitute the prerequisite for successful revolution, as was the case in 1917."[8]

All that was about to change. For years, young people in Russia's universities had been proselytizing a religion of socialism.[9] These young socialists included well-to-do students who recognized the suffering in their nation.[10] They experienced "feelings of guilt and shame on account of their unearned privilege."[11] And they rightfully wanted to help the hurting. But in response to the real problems they perceived, these students championed socialist solutions based on a faulty worldview foundation.[12] Historian Yuri Slezkine writes,

THEY RIGHTFULLY WANTED TO HELP THE HURTING.

> As student circles and various "non-party revolutionary organizations" established links with each other and joined formal revolutionary parties, they progressed from just reading to reading and writing essays to reading and writing leaflets . . . to reading and transporting illegal literature, printing proclamations, holding rallies, making bombs, and, in the case of the SR [Socialist Revolutionary] Maximalists, killing state officials. All over the empire, schoolchildren, seminarians, college students, and eternal students were in the grips of a "living, vibrant faith."[13]

One of the main socialist groups attracting young intellectuals was the Bolsheviks, the political faction we met in chapter 6, named for the Russian word for **majority**.[14] The Bolsheviks' dream for the overthrow of Russia's current social system began coming true in February, as violent public protests forced the tsar to abdicate. Historian Ronald Kowalski explained, "A combination of war-weariness, economic hardship, political oppression and numerous other factors precipitated the collapse of the widely hated autocracy."[15]

A (justifiably) unpopular "Provisional Government" stepped in for several months.[16] But the Bolshevik leader Vladimir Lenin was only too happy to call for—and accomplish—its overthrow. The resulting communist dictatorship would spell starvation, imprisonment, and death for millions.[17]

HOW TO START A REVOLUTION

Granted, the Russian Revolution is far more complex than a few paragraphs (or even entire books) can unpack. But the sketch above reveals a few key features of how revolutions begin. Dr. Erwin Lutzer identified three of these features, explaining:

> Revolutions begin with a cultural moment, a pretext that will hide the real agenda to justify the revolution. You need (1) the triumph of an ideology over science, reason, and civil liberties. Then you (2) recruit people who are willing to advance the revolution of anarchy in the name of justice and equality. And finally, (3) you must silence all dissident voices.[18]

For the Bolsheviks, the "cultural moment" arose from the crises that riddled Russia by 1917. Russia's socialist groups could point to these real problems as the supposed justification for a violent revolution.[19] That revolution soon fulfilled Lutzer's first condition, **the triumph of ideology over liberty**.[20] Meanwhile, the Bolsheviks' success at recruiting young people who would champion this revolution out of a thirst for social justice satisfied the second condition. And a widespread purge of "counterrevolutionaries" after October 1917 quickly fulfilled the third.[21]

If that's how revolutions begin, what factors help set these events in motion? When looking at the process of inciting a revolution, we often find several overlapping steps. Specifically, the revolutionaries must **promote division**, **weaponize words**, **leverage crises**, **inflame emotion**, **demand allegiance**, and **erase the past**. Let's see how each of these maneuvers can happen.

PROMOTE DIVISION

As no earthquake can begin without geological fissures, no revolution can arise without sociological divisions. So a vital step to trigger a revolution is to divide society into conflicting factions—or, easier still, exacerbate divisions. An especially effective way to accomplish this step is to partition society into **victims** vs. **villains**. We've seen how different versions of Marxism wield this strategy by automatically labeling people **oppressed** or **oppressor** based on traits like income, gender, and skin tone. Villainizing groups considered oppressors efficiently deepens social schisms, sparks revolutionary outrage, and fuels conflict between factions.

> **PARTITION SOCIETY INTO VICTIMS VS. VILLAINS**

One self-described radical known for promoting this "villainize to polarize" tactic was Saul Alinsky. Although he neither identified as communist nor claimed to support specific ideologies,[22] Alinsky was an all-around activist who wrote a book entitled *Rules for Radicals*. (Strikingly, Alinksy included a statement near his book's table of contents that said, "Lest we forget at least an over-the-shoulder acknowledgment to . . . the first radical known to man who rebelled against the establishment and did it so effectively that he at least won his own kingdom—Lucifer."[23])

The thirteenth rule in Alinsky's book states, "Pick the target, freeze it, personalize it, and polarize it."[24] Alinsky elaborated, "All issues must be polarized if action is to follow. . . . One acts decisively only in the conviction that all the angels are on one side and all the devils on the other."[25] These words sum up the divisiveness of critical theories, which **villainize** and **polarize** with intent to **revolutionize**.

WEAPONIZE WORDS

One way to promote division is by transforming words into weapons for wielding in rhetorical strategies. These strategies rely on different types of fallacies—faulty forms of reasoning—to make arguments sound persuasive without being accurate, true, or logical. Here are five common fallacies that weaponize words.

Bait-and-switch fallacies subtly change a word's definition. This can happen when words like **justice**, **freedom**, and **rights** take on new revolutionary meanings through the process Antonio Gramsci called "rearticulation."[26] Then the word's traditional meaning can bait people into accepting a faulty message without realizing that at some point the word's definition switched.

Take *justice*, for instance. Someone may switch the biblical concept of justice for a neo-Marxist redefinition by arguing something like this: "The Bible tells us to fight injustice. So churches should talk about how unconscious biases contribute to systemic injustices." Chapter 5 mentioned how the biblical concept of **unjust actions** differs from the neo-Marxist concept of systemic, unconscious biases rooted in **unjust identities.**[27] But the argument above talks about both concepts of "injustice" as if they're the same.

To respond to bait-and-switch fallacies, we can ask, "How are the key words in this message defined? Do any meanings change?"

Either/or fallacies present only two possibilities when others also exist. An example we've seen is how neo-Marxism paints people as **either** oppressors **or** oppressed, with "all the angels . . . on one side and all the devils on the other."[28] Other examples include arguments that suggest that **either** you affirm someone's self-identity **or** you must hate or fear them.

Erwin Lutzer identified an even subtler fallacy in arguments that imply that **either** society is perfect **or** society needs to be overthrown: "America is not good unless she is perfect. And because it is clear she is not perfect, her social and legal structures should be destroyed."[29]

In all these cases, we can respond to either/or fallacies by asking, "Is there another possible option?"

Straw man fallacies misrepresent an opposing perspective to make it sound unreasonable—and as easy to knock over as a scarecrow. For instance, say a person shares John 14:6 on social media: "Jesus said to him, 'I am the way, and the truth, and the life. No one comes to the Father except through me.'"

The comments section might begin buzzing with claims that imply, "You obviously hate people from other religions. You can't tolerate cultural diversity. You think we should return to the dark ages!" Do any of these claims accurately reflect what the post said? Nope. They all set up "straw men" in place of the post's real message. The quickest response is to gently bring the conversation back to the actual statement.

Motte-and-bailey fallacies reframe a position that's hard to defend (the "bailey") in terms of one that's easier to defend (the "motte").[30] You've probably seen this in arguments about abortion—a practice the Bolsheviks legalized to help break down family. The observation from biology that preborn individuals are living humans makes abortion a hard-to-defend position for people who accept that killing innocent humans is wrong.[31] So advocates for abortion frequently reframe their arguments in terms of more defensible concepts like **freedom**, **choices**, and **rights**.

Motte-and-baileys often coincide with other fallacies. For instance, arguments that reframe abortion as **women's rights** may contain an either/or fallacy implying that people **either** support abortion **or** oppose women's rights. This implication can then fuel a straw man fallacy, misrepresenting pro-life stances as against women's rights. Meanwhile, a bait-and-switch equates "women's rights" with "the right to have one's child destroyed." Choosing to take an innocent human's life is not normally considered a right. In fact, Genesis 9:6 establishes that God's image bearers have a **prima facie**[32] right **not** to be killed by fellow human beings.[33] By assuming human rights exist, the argument borrows a biblical concept to argue for an unbiblical position. So the argument involves one of the stolen concept fallacies described in chapter 2.

How can we respond to motte-and-baileys? The key is to affirm the importance of the easy-to-defend concept (the motte), but refocus on the hard-to-defend claim (the bailey). Affirming the motte helps establish common ground, fend off straw men, and identify stolen concepts by showing that a biblical worldview underlies the defensible principles. By clarifying those principles' meanings, we can also answer bait-and-switches. For instance, when we hear words like **freedom**, **choice**, and **rights**, we're wise to ask, "The freedom, choice, or rights to do **what**?" Answering this keeps the focus on the bailey.

Fallacies of irrelevant premises try persuading people to accept (or reject) a message based on factors that don't necessarily make the message true (or false). For instance, **appeal to popularity** fallacies claim a message is true just because many people believe it. **Genetic fallacies** incorrectly suggest a message is true or false based only on the kind of people communicating it. ***Tu quoque*** fallacies, for instance, imply a message is false because people who believe it may act hypocritically. Similarly, ***ad hominem*** fallacies attack or ridicule a messenger, even though personal insults don't change a message's truth. Still other fallacies called **appeals to emotion** make messages sound misleadingly true by using emotional language.

The quickest way to answer these (and many other) fallacies of irrelevant premises is to ask, "Is this message true or false **because** . . .?" For instance, "Is a message true because many people believe it?" If the answer is "not necessarily," you've successfully caught a fallacy.

When responding to fallacies, Colossians 4:6 serves as a vital reminder: "Let your speech always be gracious, seasoned with salt, so that you may know how you ought to answer each person." Gracious speech that communicates the truth in love (Ephesians 4:15) will help us turn back weaponized words rather than multiplying them by responding in kind.

LEVERAGE CRISES AND INFLAME EMOTIONS

Along with wielding words as weapons, another strategy for achieving "total social transformation" is to leverage (if not to create or exacerbate) a societal crisis. Famines, wars, recessions, pestilence, political fiascoes, or rising social tensions offer just a few examples. Such crises provide the "revolutionary situation" Wood mentioned regarding the Russian Revolution.

Why are crises so important for revolutions? For starters, crises tend to destabilize societies, accomplishing part of the revolutionaries' work for them. Crises also highlight weak spots in a nation's civil institutions, undermining civilians' trust in them.[34] Even more importantly, crises help ignite anger, fear, and insecurity, which can be transformed into fuel for revolutionary action.

How does this transformation happen? An easy method is to pin the blame for the crisis on "oppressors"—or on any other target sighted for overthrow. This blaming helps to villainize "oppressors," which further exacerbates divisions, stokes revolutionary outrage, and cultivates a sense of guilt among the oppressors. The oppressors then hear they can only cure this guilt by becoming revolutionaries themselves.

Blaming works not only for sparking revolution but also for sustaining the new social order. For instance, Aleksander Solzhenitsyn described how Lenin scapegoated churches in the early 1920s when famine devastated Russia's Volga region.[35] In response to the famine, Lenin's regime arranged for churches to provide disaster relief—through the involuntary "donation" of all church valuables. After some initial protest, the churches eventually gave in. Still, the ordeal not only led to the villainization of pastors in the media but also "provided the legal basis for initiating trials of the clergy."[36]

As handy as crises are for blaming oppressors, inflaming emotions, and destabilizing society, their usefulness doesn't stop there. Crises also offer rationalization for taking undemocratic steps—whether restricting civil freedoms, confiscating property, or illegally arresting dissidents—in the name of public safety. **Evil** becomes way easier to call **good** if it's committed under the auspices of security, freedom, justice, or "rights."

CRISES ALSO OFFER RATIONALIZATION FOR TAKING UNDEMOCRATIC STEPS IN THE NAME OF PUBLIC SAFETY.

The French Revolution offers a chilling example. During the Reign of Terror, the government body responsible for enforcing violent decrees was called "The Committee of Public Safety."[37] As one scholar put it, "Many revolutionaries seemed to be aware that mass killing contradicted the liberties set out in the Declaration of the Rights of Man and the Citizen but they insisted that exceptional measures were legitimate if necessary for the defense of the republic."[38]

We don't need to look far to see parallel—if less gruesome—examples from our own lifetimes. A 2022 survey of nearly 3,000 adults in Spain and Germany found that people expressed higher openness to authoritarian control "in context of the societal crises of COVID-19 and climate change."[39] Relatedly, a 2022 article in *American Political Science Review* argued that "climate change poses an even graver threat to public safety" than COVID-19 and "may require a similarly authoritarian approach."[40] In light of these arguments, we might also remember that neo-Marxist Herbert Marcuse "found the environmental movement to be a particularly promising force for social change."[41] And we might sense how calls for "environmental justice" that go beyond biblical creation stewardship could apply to **initiating** and **sustaining** forms of soft totalitarianism.

IN CONTEXT OF THE SOCIETAL CRISES OF COVID-19

Still another example brings us back to the Diversity, Equity, and Inclusion (DEI) tool kit published by the World Economic Forum.[42] We saw earlier how this document advocates for technologically monitoring adherence to (essentially) neo-Marxist thought patterns. How does the tool kit suggest enacting these soft totalitarian measures? In answer, the document's opening states:

> The start of the decade has seen a convergence of three major trends: the accelerated use of Fourth Industrial Revolution technologies in the midst of the pandemic, job market disruptions to both remote work and work requiring physical presence, and a wide-ranging call for greater inclusivity, equity and social justice. **Now more than ever, in the midst of such sweeping change, organizations have an**

> **opportunity to embed greater diversity, equity and inclusion.**[43] (emphasis added)

In other words, the ideal way to establish soft totalitarian systems that enforce neo-Marxist redefinitions of **equity** is to leverage social crises.

DEMAND ALLEGIANCE

The tool kit's suggestion that organizations ensure **all employees** comply with DEI criteria highlights the next strategy: demanding allegiance. We glimpsed this strategy in chapter 3, examining Christian persecution in ancient Rome and the French Revolution. Both times, Christians were told they had "religious freedom" **so long as** they compromised God's Word to accommodate the culture. Where Scripture contradicts a totalitarian regime's message, the regime requires that Christians side with man's word over God's. But like the apostles concluded, "We must obey God rather than men" (Acts 5:29).

Demands for allegiance also appear in messages suggesting that people who fail to show active support for revolutionary values must be enemies of the state. Such people (the story goes) could only be hateful, violent saboteurs who deserve to be canceled, fired, or worse. This **intolerance of neutrality** regarding the regime's agendas is another hallmark of totalitarianism.

Again, the French Revolution offers telling examples. During the Reign of Terror, people couldn't avoid risk simply by refraining from speaking against the revolution. They had to prove they **supported** it. Historian Timothy Tackett explained:

> By 1793 a whole segment of the most radical militants were attacking not only the counterrevolutionaries, but anyone whose attachment to the Revolution was deemed insufficiently energetic. Moderation and passivity could be treated as crimes. Those who did not support their views in every respect must be against them.[44]

ERASE HISTORY

To achieve their goal of controlling reality, totalitarian regimes must also control people's understanding of history. As Dr. Erwin Lutzer explained:

> Revising history lies at the heart of all social and political revolutions. Perhaps the best example is the bloody cultural revolution in China (1966–1976). Mao Zedong decreed that China was to rid itself of all traces of capitalistic Western influence. The Red Guards took to the streets and monuments were destroyed, Western literature was burned, and buildings renamed along with new designations given for cities and streets to reflect contemporary heroes.[45]

Communist regimes have a history of making history *history*. Lutzer listed examples of similar processes in America, where ideas based in neo-Marxism have motivated everything from destroying statues to altering history textbooks.[46] But it's not just happening in America. Tides of action—like defacing monuments, renaming buildings, and burning books—have swept across the world in the (redefined) names of justice, inclusion, and equity. Headlines from Australia, New Zealand, Africa, Europe, the UK, Latin America, and Canada offer just a few examples.[47] In one striking instance from 2023, libraries in a Canadian school district provoked public outcry by removing—for the purpose of inclusivity—books published before 2008.[48]

Why erase the past?[49] For revolutionaries, selectively censoring history accomplishes at least two purposes. First, our perceptions about the past shape our understandings of how our own lives fit into the broader story of reality. To teach a neo-Marxist rendition of history is to re-story people's identities, setting individuals in a radicalized narrative that demands a revolutionary ending. Erasing the past is a way to **recruit revolutionaries**.

Second, censoring the past keeps people from learning about parts of history that could undermine the revolutionaries' agenda. Today's students might think twice before supporting Marxism if they knew that despairing young people in Czechoslovakia literally lit themselves on fire to protest communism.[50] But a 2020 survey of over 2,000 Americans revealed that 27% of Millennials and 30% of Gen Z expressed a "favorable opinion of the term 'Marxism.'"[51] Furthermore, only 26% of Gen Z (age 16–23 at the time) agreed that "Marxism most looks like a totalitarian state that suppresses the freedom of its citizens," compared to 72% of **respondents age 75 or older**.

History matters—the good, the bad, and the ugly of it. As Lutzer concluded, "This is not a time for us to deny the negative parts of our history and paint a picture that ignores the sins and racism of the past. We can learn from history without needing to destroy it."[52]

SUSTAINING A REVOLUTION

Strategies like erasing the past, demanding total allegiance, and scapegoating "oppressors" help to both **start** and

sustain a revolutionary regime. Once a totalitarian regime is in place, what other factors keep it in power?

To find out, we can backtrack to the early 1950s and journey to Hong Kong. Here we meet a psychiatrist named Robert Lifton heading to his next appointment. But this won't be an ordinary patient-doctor visit. To research "thought reform" ("brainwashing") in totalitarianism environments, Lifton is interviewing people who have either survived communist prison camps or experienced "thought reform" in academia. From these interviews, Lifton will identify eight features of totalitarian environments.[53] Knowing these features can help us recognize similar trends in our own culture.

1. **Milieu control** involves censoring what information people can access, share, and think about. From social media bans to national news biases to school book bans, today's culture comes packed with examples of milieu control.
2. **Mystical manipulation** involves manipulating people's emotions and behaviors, often in the name of some higher purpose. Lifton wrote that during totalitarianism, people aren't allowed to question these manipulations but must accept them "on a basis of ultimate trust (or faith)."[54]
3. **A demand for purity** involves redefining "morality" as "conformity to a certain agenda or ideology." We've seen examples of this in messages that redefine "being good" as "embracing neo-Marxist versions of diversity, equity, and inclusion." Fail to "be good," and you risk the wrath of cancel culture. Lifton wrote that such demands for purity may suggest that "anything done to anyone in the name of this purity is ultimately moral."[55] This idea reflects the Frankfurt School's

view that "truth" (in this case, moral truth) is "whatever promotes radical social change."[56]

4. **A cult of confession** involves creating a culture that's obsessed with confessing breaches of the redefined morality. People may even feel forced to "repent" from crimes they never committed. We might notice this process in today's messages demanding that people **confess** unconscious biases or **repent** from having been born into a group considered "oppressive."
5. **The sacred science** involves presenting human ideas as the unquestionable truth. Lifton elaborated, "The ultimate moral vision becomes an ultimate science; and the man who dares to criticize it, or to harbor even unspoken alternative ideas, becomes not only immoral and irreverent, but also 'unscientific.' . . . The assumption here is not so much that man can be God, but rather that man's ideas can be God."[57]
6. **Loading the language** involves creating clichés that advance the sacred science and silence arguments. Lifton's example of loaded language from communist regimes decades ago was labeling people who accept the sacred science "progressive" while calling those who disagree "oppressive." Again, it's hard to miss the parallels with culture today.
7. **Elevating *doctrine* over *person*** involves dismissing or reinterpreting people's observations or experiences that don't fit the sacred science. The only "facts" allowed are the ones that match the regime's ideology.
8. **The dispensation of existence** begins when regimes set themselves in God's place to the point of deciding which people count as "persons" deserving human rights. Unsurprisingly, qualifying as a "real person"

with full rights tends to require conforming to the regime's agenda.

These eight conditions construct an environment founded on the suppression of truth. But truth cannot remain suppressed forever. Sooner or later, every lie will vanish in the light of the one who is the truth (John 14:6), whom death itself could not suppress. Meanwhile, Jesus' church often plays a vital role in the triumph of truth over totalitarianism. Two encouraging examples come from the fall of Eastern European communism in 1989: the Velvet Revolution and the collapse of the Berlin Wall.

STOPPING A REVOLUTION

As the journalist with whom I spoke in the Prague coffee shop described, many Christians participated in the political miracle that ended communism in Czechoslovakia. An article in the *British Journal of Sociology* details how underground churchgoers helped organize the Candlelight Demonstration, which served as "a precursor to the Velvet Revolution."[58] Calling the demonstration "a world-making event," the article explains that the church had grown into a formidable resistance force, despite persecution:

> Over time this [underground] Church grew in numbers and, in 1987, almost 500,000 people in Czechoslovakia signed a petition demanding the protection of religious rights. This was an unprecedented act of resistance in the country. Out of the success of the petition came the idea to organize the "Candlelight Demonstration"—the first such public demonstration not only in Czechoslovakia but in all of Eastern Europe for over a decade.[59]

The government, hearing of the protest, did everything possible to prevent it.[60] They arranged to broadcast a popular film on TV to keep people home during the demonstration. They altered public transport and blocked roadways to prevent people from easily reaching the protest. They fired water cannons into the crowds and made 138 arrests.[61] Still, thousands came to pray, sing, and light their candles.

As the candles contrasted with the evening's darkness, so the peaceful demonstration contrasted with the communist police violence that answered it. The protest's intentionally peace-focused nature made the demonstration impossible for the police to repress without exposing their regime's inhumanity.[62] Although the communists planted "fake protesters" to try to stir up violence, the real protesters refused to participate in the unrest.[63] They held their peace and prayed.

COMMUNISTS PLANTED "FAKE PROTESTERS" TO TRY TO STIR UP VIOLENCE.

This combination of gentleness and prayer also characterized East German Christians' role in the collapse of the Berlin Wall. An article in *German Politics* by sociology professor Andreas Hadjar explains how movements that resisted East German communism worked closely with the Protestant church.[64] Starting in 1982, **seven years before the wall fell**, Christians prayed for peace every Monday evening at the Nikolai Church in Leipzig. In 1989, weekly peaceful protest marches began to follow these prayer times, with 10,000 people joining the march on October 2. Communist police responded by injuring and arresting some of these protesters, along with demonstrators at subsequent protests that week.

As the weekly prayer and protest scheduled for October 9 drew near, tensions ran high. Hadjar reported,

> But days before it became clear that the GDR state was not ready to tolerate the demonstration. Opposition groups and pastors warned the people against possible police and army operations and demanded strict peacefulness. . . . It was a frightening atmosphere, but nevertheless tens of thousands of people attended the prayer and the demonstration. Many families had decided that only one of the parents should attend this demonstration, so that in the event of any accident there was still one parent left at home to care for the children.[65]

Meanwhile, the church pleaded to keep the protests peaceful. Hadjar quotes several of these pleas from a leaflet that church-based resistance groups distributed before and during the October 9 protest:

> Violence produces violence. Violence cannot solve any problem. Violence is inhuman. Violence cannot be a sign of a new, better society. . . . Abstain from any violence! Do not break any police chains, keep some distance for the cordons! . . . Do not throw any objects and abstain from violent slogans![66]

Although the communist police stood ready to use lethal force, they never received a combat order. A series of political miracles had prevented a massacre![67] Three weeks later, the post-prayer demonstration crowd swelled to 200,000, with a million people joining another protest on November 4. The next Monday's gathering included half a million participants. Hadjar reported, "One day later, the entire [communist] government resigned."[68] On November 9, 1989, the Berlin Wall fell.

SUMMING UP

Whether in Germany, Czechoslovakia, or Russia, historical patterns of how revolutionary regimes rise, remain, and fall offer insights for Christians facing neo-Marxist soft totalitarianism today.

We've seen how regimes **rise** through several overlapping processes. First, the advocates for revolution promote division to polarize society into warring classes. An easy tactic to exacerbate this division is by weaponizing words, especially in ways that vilify "oppressor" classes. Then by leveraging social crises, the revolutionaries can further divide society, scapegoat "oppressors," and transform anger, fear, and anxiety into revolutionary action. Extending zero tolerance for neutrality, the revolutionaries demand total allegiance, labeling individuals who fail to actively support the agenda as "enemies of the state." Meanwhile, erasing history suppresses memories of the old social order and "re-stories" people's identities within the new order.

HISTORICAL PATTERNS OF HOW REVOLUTIONARY REGIMES RISE, REMAIN, AND FALL OFFER INSIGHTS FOR CHRISTIANS.

With the revolution underway, a totalitarian regime sustains its power through the eight methods Robert Lifton identified. Each of these methods represents an attempt to control the truth. But such strategies only work so far as ordinary people let them—and more importantly, so far as God allows it. As the prophet Daniel declared when God provided a humanly impossible way of escape from the wrath of a murderous king:

> Blessed be the name of God forever and ever, to whom belong wisdom and might. **He changes times and seasons; he removes kings and sets up kings**; he gives wisdom to the wise and knowledge to those who have understanding; he reveals deep and hidden things; he knows what is in the darkness, and the light dwells with him. (Daniel 2:20–22, emphasis added)

In the Velvet Revolution and collapse of the Berlin Wall, God changed seasons, times, and kingdoms by working in part through ordinary Christians. Many believers who persevered faithfully under communism did not survive to see the earthly outcome. But others witnessed God perform political miracles as they took a prayerful, peaceful stand. Despite facing brutality for doing so, they resolved not to repay evil for evil but to overcome evil with good (Romans 12:17–21). Against the backdrop of surrounding violence, their Christlike response blazed like candles in the night.

How can we, like these believers, respond to newer types of totalitarianism arising today?

That's what we'll discover in part three.

ENDNOTES

1. Editors of the Encyclopedia Britannica, "Velvet Revolution," *Encyclopedia Britannica*, last updated June 4, 2024, britannica.com/topic/Velvet-Revolution.

2. Editors of the Encyclopedia Britannica, "Velvet Revolution"; see also Klara Jurstakova, Evangelos Ntontis, and Stephen Reicher, "Impresarios of Identity: How the Leaders of Czechoslovakia's 'Candlelight Demonstration' Enabled Effective Collective Action in a Context of Repression," *British Journal of Social Psychology* 63, no. 1 (2023): 153–169, doi.org/10.1111/bjso.12671.

3. Jurstakova, Ntontis, and Reicher, "Impresarios of Identity."

4. Agáta Šústová Drelová, "Trust in the Church Hierarchy Among the Underground Church Community in Post-1968 Slovakia," in *Forum Historiae, Časopis a Aortál Pre Históriu a Príbuzné Spoločenské Vedy*, vol. 15, no. 2 (2021): 104–122, doi.org/10.31577/forhist.2021.15.2.8.

5. E.g., "Police Attack Protesters at Prague Demonstration," *New York Times*, October 29, 1988, nytimes.com/1988/10/29/world/police-attack-protesters-at-prague-demonstration.html; see also Robert Cottrell, *The Czech Republic: The Velvet Revolution* (Philadelphia: Chelsea House, 2005), 111.

6. Cottrell, *The Czech Republic*, 111–117.

7. A fuller but concise synopsis of the following events is available in Alan Wood, *The Origins of the Russian Revolution*, 1861–1917, 2nd ed. (London: Routledge, 1993).

8. Wood, *Origins of the Russian Revolution*, 10.

9. Yuri Slezkine, "The Preachers," in *The House of Government: A Saga of the Russian Revolution* (Princeton, NJ: Princeton University Press, 2017), 21–72.

10. Slezkine, *House of Government*, 26.

11. Slezkine, *House of Government*, 26.

12. Slezkine wrote that while some students tried to blend socialism with Christianity, "Christians tended to think of socialists as atheists or Antichrists, and socialists tended to agree (while considering Christians backward or hypocritical). In standard socialist autobiographies, the loss of 'religious' faith was a prerequisite for spiritual awakening" (Slezkine, *House of Government*, 23). A typical conviction among socialist students was that "to be a true intelligent meant being religious about being secular" (Slezkine, *House of Government*, 24). For a discussion of several core problems with attempts to blend socialism with biblical Christianity, see Erwin Lutzer, *We Will Not Be Silenced: Responding Courageously to Our Culture's Assault on Christianity* (Eugene, OR: Harvest House Publishers, 2020), 171–202, ebook version.

13. Slezkine, *House of Government*, 34.

14. Editors of The Encyclopedia Britannica, "Bolshevik," *Encyclopedia Britannica*, accessed July 2024, britannica.com/topic/Bolshevik.

15. Ronald Kowalski, *The Russian Revolution: 1917–1921* (London: Routledge, 1997), 11. (Notably, however, the revolution was a complex event with multiple layers of possible causes which historians continue to discuss and debate.)

16. Peter Holquist, "Violent Russia, Deadly Marxism? Russia in the Epoch of Violence, 1905–21," *Kritika: Explorations in Russian and Eurasian History* 4, no. 3 (2003): 627–652.

17. See Aleksandr Solzhenitsyn, *The Gulag Archipelago 1918–1956*, trans. Thomas Whitney and Harry Willetts, abridged by Edward Ericson (New York: Perennial Classics, 2002 [originally 1973]).

18. Lutzer, *We Will Not Be Silenced*, 103.

19. Russia's former governments also displayed unjustifiable violence; however, Holquist explains the Soviet violence was "much expanded" and longer-lasting—an intentional tool for revolution and sustained control (Holquist, "Violent Russia, Deadly Marxism?" 646, 651).

20. Illustrating the resulting lack of liberty, Aleksandr Solzhenitsyn documented the sweeping tides of post-revolutionary arrests in his book *The Gulag Archipelago*.

21. Solzhenitsyn, *The Gulag Archipelago*.

22. Saul Alinsky, *Rules for Radicals: A Practical Primer for Realistic Radicals* (New York: Vintage Books, 1972), 4–10.

23. Alinsky, *Rules for Radicals*, front matter.

24. Alinsky, *Rules for Radicals*, 130.

25. Alinsky, *Rules for Radicals*, 133–134.

26. More on this in chapter 6.

27. See Voddie Baucham, *Fault Lines* (Washington, D.C.: Salem Books, 2021), 41–90; Owen Strachan, *Christianity and Wokeness* (Washington, D.C.: Salem, 2021), 4–26, 57–87; Lutzer, *We Will Not Be Silenced*, 78–81.

28. Alinsky, *Rules for Radicals*, 134

29. Lutzer, *We Will Not Be Silenced*, 46.

30. The term *motte and bailey* refers to a style of castle built on a hill called a "motte," which overlooked a courtyard known as the "bailey." The bailey was hard to defend against attacks. So under threat of enemy invasion, the inhabitants of the bailey would retreat to the fortified motte. More information is available in "Logical Fallacies: Motte-and-Bailey Arguments," Answers in Genesis, January 27, 2021, AnswersInGenesis.org/blogs/patricia-engler/2021/01/27/logical-fallacies-motte-bailey-arguments/.

31. More information is available in "The Abortion Controversy: Examining Common Arguments from Opposing Worldviews," Answers in Genesis, January 31, 2023, AnswersInGenesis.org/sanctity-of-life/abortion-controversy-examining-common-arguments-opposing-worldviews/; see also Matt Dawson, "Abortion: A Biblical, Biological, and Philosophical Refutation," *Answers Research Journal* 12 (2019): 13–40, AnswersResearchJournal.org/abortion-refutation/.

32. When used in ethics, *prima facie* (which means "at first appearance") refers to a standard that is always true by default but may not be absolute or binding in every conceivable circumstance. For instance, *prima facie* moral obligations must always be followed unless doing so would irreconcilably conflict with some higher obligation. See Kyle Fedler, *Exploring Christian Ethics: Biblical Foundations for Morality* (Louisville, KY: Westminster John Knox Press), 24–27.

33. For details and nuances, see "God's Image as the Foundation for Human Rights," Answers in Genesis, January 25, 2023, AnswersInGenesis.org/sanctity-of-life/gods-image-as-the-foundation-for-human-rights/.

34. For more on the consequences of this loss of trust, see Rod Dreher, *Live Not by Lies: A Manual for Christian Dissidents* (New York: Sentinel, 2020), 32–34 (ebook version).

35. Aleksander Solzhenitsyn, *The Gulag Archipelago 1918–1956: An Experiment in Literary Investigation*, vols. 1–2, trans. Thomas Whitney (London: Collins & Harvill Press, 1974), 343–346.

36. Solzhenitsyn, *The Gulag Archipelago*, vols. 1–2, 346.

37. Noah Shusterman, *The French Revolution: Faith, Desire, and Politics* (New York: Routledge, 2014), 163, 189. For more on justifying breaches of religious freedom in the name of public security, see Timothy Tackett, *The Coming of Terror in the French Revolution* (London: Belknap Press of Harvard University Press, 2015), 110.

38. Alex Bellamy, *Massacres and Morality: Mass Atrocities in an Age of Civilian Immunity* (Oxford: Oxford University Press, 2012), 48.

39. Magdalena Hirsch, "Becoming Authoritarian for the Greater Good? Authoritarian Attitudes in Context of the Societal Crises of COVID-19 and Climate Change," *Frontiers in Political Science* 4 (2022): 929991.

40. Ross Mittiga, "Political Legitimacy, Authoritarianism, and Climate Change," *American Political Science Review* 116, no. 3 (2022): 998–1011.

41. Charles Reitz, *Ecology and Revolution: Herbert Marcuse and the Challenge of a New World System Today* (New York: Routledge, 2018), ebook version.

42. "Diversity, Equity and Inclusion 4.0: A Toolkit for Leaders to Accelerate Social Progress in the Future of Work," June 2020, World Economic Forum (WEF), 2, accessed July 2024, www3.weforum.org/docs/WEF_NES_DEI4.0_Toolkit_2020.pdf.

43. World Economic Forum, "Diversity, Equity and Inclusion 4.0."

44. Timothy Tackett, *The Coming of Terror in the French Revolution* (London: Belknap Press of Harvard University Press, 2015), 314–315.

45. Lutzer, *We Will Not Be Silenced*, 41–42.

46. Lutzer, *We Will Not Be Silenced*, 42–55.

47. E.g., Samantha Dick, "Police on Watch as Statues of Historical Figures Defaced Around Australia," *The New Daily*, June 15, 2020, thenewdaily.com.au/news/national/2020/06/15/statues-racism-protests/; Nick Perry, "New Zealand City Removes Statue of Its 'Murderous' Namesake," AP News, June 12, 2020, apnews.com/article/dc79b51c4e17317c174fc4863072686f; Jack Guy, "Britain's Imperialist Monuments Face a Bitter Reckoning Amid Black Lives Matter Protests," CNN, June 11, 2020, cnn.com/style/article/uk-statues-protest-movement-scli-intl-gbr/index.html; Debora Patta, "In Africa, Toppling Statues Is a First Step in Addressing Racism, Not the Last," CBS News, June 19, 2020, cbsnews.com/news/in-africa-toppling-statues-is-a-1st-step-in-addressing-racism-not-the-last/; Adam Forrest, "Gandhi Statue Removed from University of Ghana Following Protests Over 'Racist' Indian Leader," *Independent*, December 14, 2018, independent.co.uk/news/world/africa/gandhi-statue-removed-racist-ghana-university-accra-india-africa-a8682901.html; Luke Hurst, "Watch: Statues Under Attack as Europe Confronts Colonial Past" Euronews, June 10, 2020, euronews.com/2020/06/10/watch-statues-under-attack-as-europe-confronts-colonial-past; Augusta Saraiva, "Toppling Statues Isn't Enough in Latin America," *Foreign Policy*, August 10, 2020, foreignpolicy.com/2020/08/10/latin-america-protest-colonial-statues-monuments-indigenous-rights/; Tyler Dawson, "Book Burning at Ontario Francophone Schools as 'Gesture of Reconciliation' Denounced," *The National Post*, September 7, 2021, nationalpost.com/news/canada/book-burning-at-ontario-francophone-schools-as-gesture-of-reconciliation-denounced.

48. Ken Ham, "Canadian School Libraries Remove All Books Published Before 2008," Answers in Genesis, September 28, 2023, AnswersInGenesis.org/culture/canadian-libraries-remove-books-published-2008/.

49. For further discussion on this topic, see also Dreher, *Live Not by Lies*, 116–120 (ebook version).

50. Piotr Żuk and Paweł Żuk, "An 'Ordinary Man's' Protest: Self-Immolation as a Radical Political Message in Eastern Europe Today and in the Past," *Social Movement Studies* 17, no. 5 (2018): 610–617. Importantly, to acknowledge these self-harmful actions happened is not to say they were justifiable. For a biblical discussion of self-harm, see Scott Chadwick, "Suicide and God's Plan for Life," Answers in Genesis, September 14, 2017, AnswersInGenesis.org/sanctity-of-life/suicide-and-gods-plan-for-life/.

51. Victims of Communism Memorial Foundation and YouGov, "U.S. Attitudes Toward Socialism, Communism, and Collectivism," October 2020, accessed July 2024, victimsofcommunism.org/wp-content/uploads/2020/10/10.19.20-VOC-YouGov-Survey-on-U.S.-Attitudes-Toward-Socialism-Communism-and-Collectivism.pdf.

52. Lutzer, *We Will Not Be Silenced*, 60.

53. Robert Lifton, *Thought Reform and the Psychology of Totalism: A Study of 'Brainwashing' in China* (Chapel Hill, NC: UNC Press, 2012, originally published by Norton, 1963), 419–437.

54. Lifton, *Thought Reform and the Psychology of Totalism*, 422.

55. In a tragic twist of irony, such "morality" may include violently exterminating anyone deemed "impure" (Lifton, *Thought Reform and the Psychology of Totalism*, 423).

56. See Martin Jay, *The Dialectical Imagination: A History of the Frankfurt School and the Institute of Social Research 1923–1950* (London: Heinemann, 1973), 63.

57. Jay, *The Dialectical Imagination*, 428.

58. Jurstakova, Ntontis, and Reicher, "Impresarios of Identity."

59. Jurstakova, Ntontis, and Reicher, "Impresarios of Identity."

60. Jurstakova, Ntontis, and Reicher, "Impresarios of Identity."

61. Jurstakova, Ntontis, and Reicher, "Impresarios of Identity."

62. Jurstakova, Ntontis, and Reicher, "Impresarios of Identity."

63. Jurstakova, Ntontis, and Reicher, "Impresarios of Identity."

64. The following historical details are available in Andreas Hadjar, "Non-Violent Political Protest in East Germany in the 1980s: Protestant Church, Opposition Groups and the People," *German Politics* 12, no. 3 (2003): 107–128.

65. Hadjar, "Non-Violent Political Protest in East Germany," 119.

66. Leaflet cited in Hadjar, "Non-Violent Political Protest in East Germany," 121.

67. Details are available in Hadjar, "Non-Violent Political Protest in East Germany," 119.

68. Hadjar, "Non-Violent Political Protest in East Germany," 111.

PRACTICAL TOOLS FOR CHRISTIANS + LIVING OUT AN UNCOMPROMISED BIBLICAL VIEW IN TODAY'S CULTURE

PART THREE

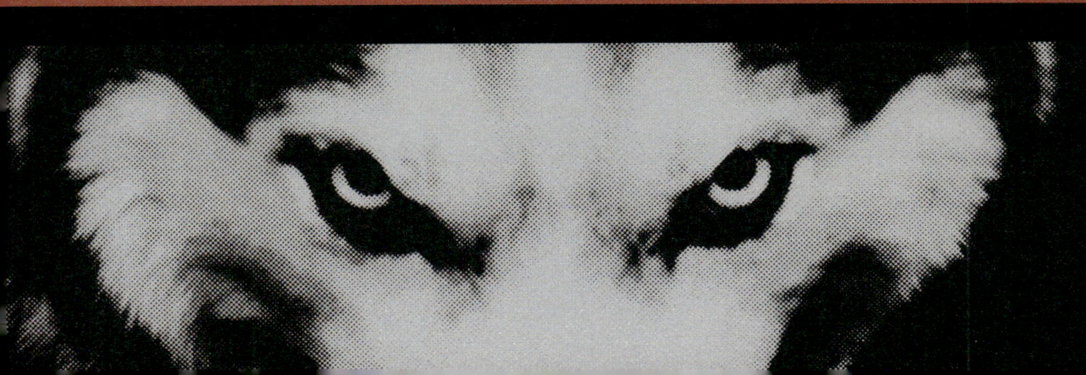

2 PETER 3:17–18

YOU THEREFORE, BELOVED, KNOWING THIS BEFOREHAND, TAKE CARE THAT YOU ARE NOT CARRIED AWAY WITH THE ERROR OF LAWLESS PEOPLE AND LOSE YOUR OWN STABILITY. BUT GROW IN THE GRACE AND KNOWLEDGE OF OUR LORD AND SAVIOR JESUS CHRIST. TO HIM BE THE GLORY BOTH NOW AND TO THE DAY OF ETERNITY. AMEN.

CHAPTER 9

THREE SECRETS TO STANDING STRONG

BUILDING FOUNDATIONS TO WEATHER THE STORM

I wrapped my hands around the metal bars and gave the door a rattle. Beyond the bars, a square patch of concrete floor terminated at a whitewashed wall with a single window. **So this was the solitary confinement cell.**

If I'd run afoul of East Germany's communist government from 1945–1989, I might have lived here—or died here. The notorious Bautzen II prison had been East Germany's primary penitentiary for political prisoners.[1] Now the prison stood open, a silent memorial to its victims. As I walked through its corridors, I could only imagine what being imprisoned for my convictions might be like.

After returning to the US, I had opportunities to meet two Christians who knew firsthand.

Dr. Andrew Brunson knew from spending two years in prison as a missionary in Turkey.[2] And Dr. James Coates, a Canadian pastor, knew from over a month of imprisonment for reopening his church during a wave of lockdowns.[3] These men, together with their wives, graciously shared insights with me and some friends at Answers in Genesis for our podcast, *Zero Compromise*.

As we interviewed these couples, I couldn't help but notice a pattern in their advice for facing persecution. It was the same pattern I'd found a few years earlier while interviewing global Christian students about how they'd kept their faith during secular university. Around the world, students had reported facing diverse challenges that varied by nation, school, and field of study. But strikingly, the strategies that helped them overcome those challenges looked remarkably similar. Everywhere, students pointed to the importance of three personal foundations:[4]

SPIRITUAL FOUNDATIONS:
A CLOSE PERSONAL WALK WITH GOD

INTELLECTUAL FOUNDATIONS:
APOLOGETICS ANSWERS AND BIBLICAL CRITICAL THINKING SKILLS TO DEFEND A BIBLICAL WORLDVIEW

INTERPERSONAL FOUNDATIONS:
A STRONG CHRISTIAN COMMUNITY SUPPORT NETWORK, INCLUDING FAMILY, FRIENDS, A BIBLICAL LOCAL CHURCH, AND GODLY MENTORS

Other studies have uncovered similar themes from surveying church-raised American young adults, finding that individuals with the strongest faith excelled in these foundations.[5] The same foundations also tend to feature in persecuted believers' stories. Check out biographies of Christians whose commitments to biblical authority drove them to impact history, and you'll probably find that these foundations also played significant roles.[6] It's no surprise that Scripture says much about the importance of spiritual, intellectual, and interpersonal foundations.[7]

INSIGHTS FROM PERSECUTED BELIEVERS

These foundations are important for **every believer** to keep a strong biblical worldview in hostile surroundings—and to live out that worldview in ways that impact those surroundings. I unpacked these foundations as they relate to students in the book *Prepare to Thrive*. Now, let's see how the same foundations apply to Christians in soft totalitarian contexts, drawing on insights from persecuted believers.

WHERE FOUNDATION BUILDING STARTS

When builders prepare to lay a foundation, where do they begin? They read their blueprints to mark out where the foundation should go. Similarly, God has given us instructions for where to base our thinking, beliefs, and behaviors—on his Word. The first step to building lasting foundations is committing to stand on biblical authority without compromise.

Dr. Brunson emphasized this step in his video series *Prepare to Stand*, where he shares firsthand insights to help believers weather the persecution he sees coming to Western nations. Echoing New Testament warnings against deception, Dr. Brunson urged Christians to guard the Word of God, because "many people want to dilute it, misuse it, and downgrade its authority."[8] He said, "We must be committed to God's truth as revealed in the Bible. God determines what is true, not man. . . . Here is a principle: say what God says. That is . . . choose to say about everything what God says about it."[9]

Resolving to say what God says shapes how we approach every aspect of life, aligning us to God's unchanging truth. From this basis, we can build and maintain the foundations that will help us live out our commitment to God's Word every day. Let's look at each of these foundations in a persecution context, focusing especially on spiritual foundations. (**More practical ideas for building these foundations are available in this book's appendix.**)

LET'S LOOK AT EACH OF THESE FOUNDATIONS IN A PERSECUTION CONTEXT.

SPIRITUAL FOUNDATIONS

Spiritual foundations refer to a close personal relationship with God. As with any relationship, we cultivate this closeness by **communicating** with God through Scripture, worship, and prayer. The closer we walk with God daily, the more we embrace the life God created us to live.

We're designed for fellowship with God throughout eternity as well as here on earth, whether in seasons of goodness or suffering. Sometimes it's easy to let the blessings in cheery seasons distract us from the giver of these gifts. This temptation permeates our therapeutic culture, which says that life's priority is **feeling good**. But if we remember that life's priority is **knowing God**, we can build the spiritual foundations in sunny seasons that we'll need for stormy seasons. As Rod Dreher notes, "The kind of Christians we will be in the time of testing depends on the kind of Christians we are today."[10]

Nik Ripken, who has interviewed persecuted Christians globally, tells a story that underlines this point. While attending an underground church conference in China, he interviewed two leaders who—to his astonishment—seemed spiritually immature.[11] Later, these believers confessed to the assembly:

> You have honored us and you have made us leaders just because the authorities arrested us and we went to jail for three years. But you never, ever asked us our story. We know that when most of you went to prison, you shared your faith, you preached the word of God, and you brought hundreds if not thousands of people to Jesus. . . . But when we were arrested, we barely knew who Jesus was! We did not know how to pray! We did not know the Bible! We did not know many songs of faith. . . . You can only grow in jail what you take to jail with you. You can only grow in persecution what you take into it.[12]

Like these believers learned, we must intentionally build spiritual foundations beforehand to take into times of testing. Pastor Richard Wurmbrand, who spent 14 years imprisoned for his faith in communist Romania, explained the process this way: "The preparation for underground work is deep spiritualization. As we peel an onion in preparation for its use, so God must "peel" from us what are mere words, sensations of our enjoyments in religion, in order to arrive at the reality of our faith."[13]

Similarly, Dr. Brunson called pursuing God "the most important step we can take to prepare to stand in difficult times."[14] He said, "We have to be very intentional about loving God. It's a lifelong pursuit. Begin building this into your life now and don't wait for hardship to push you to seek God."[15]

How can we follow these believers' advice? Spiritual foundation-building strategies I described in *Prepare to Thrive* include studying and memorizing Scripture, praying, worshipping, grounding our identities in Christ, seeking wisdom, and drawing biblical boundaries. Let's see how these strategies apply to weathering persecution.[16]

STRATEGIES 1 & 2: STUDYING AND MEMORIZING SCRIPTURE

In 2019, the *Christian Post* relayed a report from Christian leaders in China,[17] one of whom described how she'd memorized much Scripture in prison. Even though Bibles weren't allowed in prison, people would smuggle in verses on papers. The prisoners quickly memorized the Scriptures, reasoning, "Even though [the jailers] can take the paper away, they can't take what's hidden in your heart."[18]

Like these prisoners understood, internalizing God's Word is indispensable for faithful living in every season—much less seasons of testing. When Paul wrote about Scripture's significance to Timothy, he himself was a prisoner describing the reality of persecution:

> Indeed, all who desire to live a godly life in Christ Jesus will be persecuted, while evil people and impostors will go on from bad to worse, deceiving and being deceived. But as for you, continue in what you have learned and have firmly believed, knowing from whom you learned it and how from childhood you have been acquainted with the sacred writings, which

> are able to make you wise for salvation through faith in Christ Jesus. All Scripture is breathed out by God and profitable for teaching, for reproof, for correction, and for training in righteousness, that the man of God may be complete, equipped for every good work. (2 Timothy 3:12–17)

Jesus modeled the importance of knowing Scripture during testing. Alone, surrounded by wilderness, and hungry from fasting, Jesus' defenses would have been physically depleted. Satan, never above striking when we're down, didn't miss the opportunity to assail Jesus with temptations (Matthew 4:1–11). But Jesus showed us how to respond by using "the sword of the Spirit, which is the word of God" (Ephesians 6:17).

STRATEGY 3: PRAYING

Peruse the book of Acts, and you'll find a recurring theme of prayer amid persecution. When the apostles first faced opposition from officials, they gathered with friends to pray for boldness (Acts 4:29–30). Then in Acts 7:58–59, Stephen prayed while being stoned. As Peter later lay imprisoned, the church interceded for him (Acts 12:5). Afterward, in Acts 16:25–26, a midnight earthquake rocked another prison where Paul and Silas were "praying and singing hymns to God."

But these early Christians didn't save praying just for emergencies. The book of Acts portrays believers **walking out a lifestyle of prayer**. They prayed as part of their regular fellowship (Acts 2:42), daily worship (Acts 3:1, 10:9, 22:17), and vocational ministries (Acts 6:4). They prayed when making important decisions (Acts 1:24), beginning new assignments (Acts 6:6, 13:3, 14:23), ministering to new believers (Acts 8:14–16), and parting with friends (Acts 20:36, 21:5). Prayer permeated the early church.

Prayer also tends to permeate the lives of persecuted believers. For instance, Pastor Wurmbrand describes fending off the maddening silence of solitary confinement by sleeping during the day and praying through the night.[19] He'd pray for every nation, town, and preacher he could remember, as well as for travelers, prisoners, and families in freedom. He would also review Scripture from memory. "I can tell you from my own experience how I avoided becoming mad," he wrote, "but this again has to be prepared by a life of spiritual exercise beforehand."[20]

I CAN TELL YOU FROM MY OWN EXPERIENCE HOW I AVOIDED BECOMING MAD.

Spiritual exercise not only prepares us for trials but also draws us to God like nothing else can. Another story from China serves as my favorite example, which inspired me to take prayer seriously as a teenager. In a book called *God's Smuggler to China*, I'd read how God worked in incredible ways through a Christian family who experienced severe persecution.[21] When a visitor asked the family how they walked so closely with God, they answered that **any** Christian could experience such a life. However, this life required sacrifice—not of suffering but of prayer.[22]

STRATEGY 4: WORSHIPPING

Leaving China, let's head to a twentieth-century Russian prison to meet another believer, Dmitri. How will we find his prison cell? Easy. As the earliest glimmers of daybreak edge into the sky, we'll just have to follow the sound of someone singing.

For 17 years, this someone—Dmitri—has woken up behind a locked door. And for 17 years, he has begun his days by singing to Jesus. Nik Ripken, who documented Dmitri's story, described how Dmitri and many other persecuted believers have won spiritual battles through worshipful "heart songs."[23]

Worship is always a victory. But it's not always easy. In his videos, Andrew Brunson shared that during his first year of prison, he "had a very difficult time worshiping God. . . . I tried to sing 'Great Is Your Faithfulness,' but I couldn't do it; I would start sobbing."[24] But during his second year of prison, he explained, "I determined to worship, and I sang to Jesus. And this worship was precious to God because it was a declaration of my love for him in very difficult circumstances, in the dark night of my soul."[25]

I WAS SINGING MY GRIEF AND SENSE OF LOSS TO GOD.

At one of the darkest points, Dr. Brunson described, "I was singing my grief and sense of loss to God, and what came out of my mouth is, 'You are Worthy. You are worthy of whatever tears and pain I go through.'"[26] This song represented a turning point. Dr. Brunson chose to continue worshipping every day, even when it hurt. And it transformed him. As he repeated the song, his focus shifted to eternity—to live for standing before Jesus without regrets. The lyrics, said Dr. Brunson, changed from "being a declaration of intent to actually becoming the orientation of my life."[27] He refocused on Jesus as his reward, in line with Hebrews 12:1–3:

> Therefore, since we are surrounded by so great a cloud of witnesses, let us also lay aside every weight, and sin which clings so closely, and let us run with endurance the race that is set before us, looking to

> Jesus, the founder and perfecter of our faith, who for the joy that was set before him endured the cross, despising the shame, and is seated at the right hand of the throne of God. Consider him who endured from sinners such hostility against himself, so that you may not grow weary or fainthearted.

Worship resets our focus, refuels us with truth, and reorients us to live for what (and who) matters. By cultivating a lifestyle of worship, we can prepare to stand faithfully like believers before us, equipped to win battles with praise.

STRATEGY 5: FOCUSING OUR IDENTITY AND PRIORITIES ON JESUS

If you were arrested today for following Jesus, what about your identity would change? Nothing fundamental, if you've grounded your self-understanding on the right foundation.[28] Persecution can take away our careers, degrees, hobbies, friends, families, and the roles that go with them. But as a sermon I once heard emphasized, "Your roles shouldn't inform your identity; your identity should inform your roles." In other words, we can't primarily view ourselves in terms of what we do, who we relate with, where we live, or anything else **on earth**. Instead, God's Word calls us to center our lives on Jesus Christ, who is the same yesterday, today, and forever (Hebrews 13:8).

Basing our identities in Jesus lets us live as "counter-revolutionaries" amid our neo-Marxist culture for three reasons. First, a biblical understanding of identity sets our thinking contrary to neo-Marxism. Neo-Marxism tells us to define ourselves by outward features or inward feelings that supposedly attach us to **oppressed** or **oppressor** identities. But the Bible makes it clear that feelings that contradict God's Word do not define believers (1 Corinthians 6:9–11), who no longer belong to sin but to Jesus (Romans 6:1–23).

As for outward features, Galatians 3:27–28 declares, "For as many of you as were baptized into Christ have put on Christ. There is neither Jew nor Greek, there is neither slave nor free, there is no male and female, for you are all one in Christ Jesus." These words don't imply we lose our ethnicities or genders by following Jesus. Rather, we "put on Christ" like a robe above our other identifiers. Then when we look at others in God's family, we see ourselves not divided by our differences but united in Christ. This oneness makes the divisiveness neo-Marxism requires impossible.

WE SEE OURSELVES NOT DIVIDED BY OUR DIFFERENCES BUT UNITED IN CHRIST.

Second, a biblical view of identity prepares us for "counterrevolutionary" living by building our resistance to soft totalitarian manipulation. Cancel culture threatens to remove the anchors to which many people fasten their identities. But when we anchor our identities in Jesus, cancel culture loses that much more power. We understand that faithfully following Jesus amid cancel culture means that our roles, status, wealth, careers, reputations, and relationships could quickly change. Yet these factors do not ultimately define us. And besides, they could change anyway, even in the best societies. We must ground our identities in what—and who—doesn't change. No matter what happens, Christians can rest assured that God knows us, loves us, saved us, is with us, and that we belong to him.

Third, grounding our identities in Jesus gives us an eternal perspective. Dr. Brunson called this perspective one of two keys (along with developing a fear of God above man) to having courage amid persecution.[29] Dr. Coates and his wife, Erin, also emphasized the importance of an eternal perspective during their interview with *Zero Compromise*.[30] Their statements demonstrated how when Jesus is the defining center of our lives, our priorities realign to "seek first the kingdom of God" (Matthew 6:33). This mindset helps to disarm fear, which **often involves the fear of losing something**, whether comfort, freedom, people, possessions, or more time on earth.

Truthfully, these earthly goods are not our lives, first love, or reward. Jesus is. Colossians 3:1–4 describes this mindset perfectly:

> If then you have been raised with Christ, seek the things that are above, where Christ is, seated at the right hand of God. Set your minds on things that are above, not on things that are on earth. For you have died, and your life is hidden with Christ in God. When Christ who is your life appears, then you also will appear with him in glory.

With our identities, priorities, and focus calibrated to Jesus, we're better prepared to lower our expectations regarding the things of earth.[31] Along these lines, Pastor Richard Wurmbrand suggested "counting the cost" of following Jesus ahead of time, saying,

> We have to make the preparation now before we are imprisoned. In prison you lose everything. You are undressed and given a prisoner's suit. No more nice furniture, nice carpets or nice curtains. You do not have a wife anymore and you do not have your children. You do not have your library and you never

> see a flower. Nothing of what makes life pleasant remains. Nobody resists who has not renounced the pleasures of life beforehand. . . . The Christian who prepares himself for this now will not suffer the loss of them when he is in prison.[32]

We, like Pastor Wurmbrand, must resolve to follow Jesus regardless of the cost. As missionary martyr Jim Elliot famously said, "He is no fool who gives what he cannot keep to gain what he cannot lose."[33]

STRATEGIES 6 & 7: SEEKING WISDOM, SETTING BOUNDARIES

"You cannot separate religion and culture here," a Christian woman once told me in a restricted access nation I visited while interviewing students. "If you don't make your stand clear and say that as a Christian, you choose not to do this or that, you are lost."

As this believer urged, Christians need clear biblical boundaries for interacting with their societies. I've written before about the importance of Christian students drawing such boundaries ahead of time regarding pressures and temptations they'll face at a university.[34] That way when the moment of pressure arrives, students will already have decided how to respond. The same strategy applies for Christians in other hostile contexts, including today's soft totalitarianism.

Determining these boundaries isn't always easy. Sometimes Scripture doesn't clearly address an issue, making biblical boundaries trickier to draw. Broader biblical principles—like the importance of truth or the value of human life—help us think through such cases. Depending on **which** biblical principles believers prioritize, different

Christians may reach different conclusions about certain boundaries, despite sharing the same commitment to God's Word. (A classic example surrounds the question "Is it right to prioritize **life** over **truth** by lying, if necessary, to save innocent lives?")

Even in the early church, Christians drew varied boundaries regarding practices like eating meat sacrificed to idols (1 Corinthians 8:1–13). Romans 14 offers vital advice for these cases. Verses 3, 5, and 13 summarize,

> Let not the one who eats despise the one who abstains, and let not the one who abstains pass judgment on the one who eats, for God has welcomed him. . . . One person esteems one day as better than another, while another esteems all days alike. Each one should be fully convinced in his own mind. . . . Therefore let us not pass judgment on one another any longer, but rather decide never to put a stumbling block or hindrance in the way of a brother.

The importance of these verses surfaced when I asked the journalist in Prague about underground church strategies. He responded, "You had to be strategic to survive. We were constantly facing the question 'How far should we go?' . . . Some parents would join communist organizations, some even the communist party, so that their children could study. There were difficult decisions." In many situations, he explained, Christians faced decisions between **no** ideal alternatives—like the choice between lying or risking someone's life. When I asked what helps with such decisions, he responded,

> There is nothing to recommend. Every situation is so specific that you have to follow your faith, and that's

> it. Some people would be much more radical than I was; some people would be much more compromised than I was. The only thing you have to keep in mind is that you have to tolerate others in their situations, and trust them, and support each other. That's all you can do.

As we seek to follow God when confronting such decisions, he may reveal paths with minimal compromise. For instance, Pastor Wurmbrand described the following story from Russia:

> A brother had been taken to the police and was asked, "Do you still gather at meetings?" He answered, "Comrade captain, prayer meetings are forbidden now." To this the captain replied, "Well, it is good that you conform with this. Just go." The brother had not said that he conformed; he had not said that he did not go to meetings.[35]

This episode illustrates how for **drawing** and **abiding** by boundaries, we must seek wisdom from God. Jesus spoke in the context of persecution when he told his disciples, "Behold, I am sending you out as sheep in the midst of wolves, so be wise as serpents and innocent as doves" (Matthew 10:16). By praying for wisdom (James 1:5), familiarizing ourselves with Scripture, and drawing boundaries where possible now, we can prepare to live as doves and serpents in a wolfish world.

INTELLECTUAL FOUNDATIONS

Strong spiritual foundations help us **grow** in and **live out** a biblical worldview. But how do we defend the truth of this worldview? That's where intellectual foundations come in, which involve two aspects: apologetics answers and critical thinking skills.

Apologetics is the field of study and practice focused on giving logical answers for our biblical beliefs. Apologetics knowledge helps us respond to questions like "How do we know the Bible is true? Doesn't science contradict the Bible? And how does Christianity compare to other belief systems?" The concept of apologetics comes straight from Scripture, based on the Greek word for **defense** (*apologia*) in 1 Peter 3:15. But when Christians (including me) cite this verse to define apologetics, we don't often mention the context is about persecution. Here's the wider passage including verses 13–17:

> Now who is there to harm you if you are zealous for what is good? But even if you should suffer for righteousness' sake, you will be blessed. Have no fear of them, nor be troubled, but in your hearts honor Christ the Lord as holy, always being prepared to make a defense [*apologia*] to anyone who asks you for a reason for the hope that is in you; yet do it with gentleness and respect, having a good conscience, so that, when you are slandered, those who revile your good behavior in Christ may be put to shame. For it is better to suffer for doing good, if that should be God's will, than for doing evil.

These verses show that apologetics' original purpose was to answer for our hope in Christ **amid persecution**. As our culture grows increasingly hostile toward Christianity, apologetics becomes more relevant than ever. The reason we need solid answers for our faith isn't just to defend against opposing worldviews, equip the church, and share the gospel. It's also to encourage ourselves that God's Word is **certain**, **true**, and **worth clinging to despite the cost of suffering**.

Illustrating these realities, Pastor Wurmbrand relayed how, when the communists began applying pressure to Christians, liberal theologians caved in first. He described their thinking this way:

> Why should I die for a dead God and a problematic Bible?—If the stories of Adam and Eve are not true, if Joshua did not stop the sun, if the prophecies were written many years after they were fulfilled, if Jesus was not born of a Virgin and He did not rise bodily from the dead—then there are more lies in the Bible than in "Pravda."[36] Why should I go to death for what is not true or at least remains problematic?[37]

For foundations that weather storms, we need not only apologetics answers for **known** questions but also biblical critical thinking skills for **novel** questions. These skills help us think like apologists ourselves to process any new faith-challenging message we encounter. The framework I often share for arming Christian students with these skills revolves around "Three Rules and Seven Checks of Critical Thinking."[38] But this critical thinking framework doesn't just apply to students. **Any** Christian can use this system to break down unbiblical messages in today's neo-Marxist culture. Here's a quick rundown.

RULE 1: DON'T PANIC

When you hear a persuasive message that contradicts Scripture, take a breath and remember what you know: God's Word is true. And as my favorite anonymous quote says, "Truth fears no questions." The Bible always stands up to scrutiny. Meanwhile, I encourage you to jot down any questions about the message right away. Having this record of your questions lets you seek answers when you have a chance. Writing the message in quotation marks will also remind you it's just a human idea—not necessarily a fact.

RULE 2: BREAK IT DOWN

The next step is to "break the message down" by separating everything that's fact and logic from everything that isn't. Here are **Seven Checks of Critical Thinking** to help:

1. **Check Scripture.** What does God's Word say about this topic? What biblical truths or principles are relevant for thinking through this issue?
2. **Check the challenge.** Does this message genuinely contradict God's Word, as opposed to challenging a human-made idea from outside the Bible?
3. **Check the source.** Who's communicating this message? How was the information collected? (Remember that while the most credible human sources are relevant experts, even experts can make mistakes, believe wrong ideas, and are biased by their worldviews.)
4. **Check the definitions.** Do any words' meanings need clarification? Have the meanings changed? (This helps with catching bait-and-switch fallacies.)
5. **Check for propaganda.** Propaganda is communication that persuades by appealing to something other than logic (or by misusing facts). Why does the message sound persuasive? Is that reason relevant to whether the message is true?
6. **Check the interpretations.** Which parts of this message are facts we can observe in the present?

Which parts are interpretations about the past (or something else we can't directly observe)? What's an alternative, biblical explanation for the facts?

7. **Check the logic.** Does the message contain any other faulty reasoning?[39]

RULE 3: FOLLOW UP

While these seven checks will help you filter tons of persuasive untruths from the information you encounter, you might still have some unresolved questions. But—rule #1—don't panic. As humans, we won't understand everything. We can know that God understands the answer; we can ask him for it, but we can also trust him even if he never reveals it. Like Peter, we can ask, "Lord, to whom shall we go? You have the words of eternal life, and we have believed, and have come to know, that you are the Holy One of God" (John 6:68–69).

By practicing these biblical critical thinking skills and teaching them to others, we can stay grounded in the truth while combating popular lies.

INTERPERSONAL FOUNDATIONS

The final secret to standing strong is to stand with other strong believers. The importance of interpersonal foundations—a community network including godly family, friends, church, and mentors—emerged as one of the most significant themes from my student interviews. It's also a key theme you'll find in stories of persecuted Christians. Here are just three reasons why networking with other believers committed to God's Word will only grow more essential.

1. RESISTING ATOMIZATION

Spending time with fellow Christians helps us combat isolation, reminding us that we're not alone in standing on God's Word. Andrew Brunson describes this reality well:

> Over the years, I had taught about the importance of strengthening relationships in the church and building community. But I came to really believe it in prison. I felt very isolated in prison. . . . I had no fellow believer to encourage me, no one to pray with me. And when I was overwhelmed with doubt and became confused, I had no one to challenge my wrong thoughts and correct me.[40]

Explaining from 1 Peter 4:8–9 how building community is a biblical strategy, Dr. Brunson added,

> I think it's especially important now to build relationships that will strengthen us in times of pressure. . . . I'm talking about intentionally growing love, prayer, faithfulness, and trust with a smaller circle of friends. In our individualistic society, it takes more effort to get close to people and to let them get close to us. But it is worth it.[41]

2. BUILDING LIKE-MINDED CHRISTIAN COMMUNITY NETWORKS

At the end of his book *Live Not by Lies*, written for Christians facing soft totalitarianism, Rod Dreher stated:

> My greatest hope is that readers who finish this book convinced of its warnings will come together with like-minded others and start building resistance cells and networks like [a faith-based group in communist

> Czechoslovakia]. The key method of [their] resistance was gathering small groups together to discuss current events in light of the teachings of their faith, determine what to do about it, and then do it.[42]

Among the greatest forms of resistance cells, says Dreher, is the Christian family. One family who famously modeled Christian resistance during a totalitarian regime was that of Corrie ten Boom. Driven by a strong biblical worldview, the ten Booms offered their home to shelter Jewish people in Nazi-occupied Holland.[43] The family also worked alongside other ordinary people—including an "army of teenagers"—to overcome evil with good at every opportunity.[44]

3. REFUELING WITH FREEDOM

When I asked the journalist in Prague about positive experiences during communism, he responded,

> One of the positive things about communism was that for Christian communities, they became islands of freedom. So, for example, we could meet with [the student ministry group] somewhere in Slovakia for a week, and it was like experiencing absolute freedom—unbelievable freedom.

He described how just like eating feels like a miracle after going without food, being around other Christians felt like a miracle during communism. Food refreshes, restores, and sustains us. By God's design, so does Christian fellowship.

As essential as community is, Dr. Brunson warns that not just any fellowship will do.[45] The kind of believers we must network with are those who share an uncompromising commitment to the authority of God's Word.

SUMMING UP

Whether they are Christian students facing university, Christian leaders facing imprisonment, or Christian citizens facing hostile cultures, three biblical foundations help believers stand strong amid hardships. Spiritual foundations fueled through Scripture, prayer, and worship keep us close to God. This closeness lets us navigate culture wisely, set biblical boundaries, and align our identities and priorities rightly in Christ. Meanwhile, intellectual foundations, including apologetics answers and critical thinking skills, help us defend our biblical worldview in an oppositional culture. And interpersonal foundations help us strengthen, maintain, and live out this worldview in community with other believers.

These foundations will become increasingly essential for every Christian, regardless of what lies ahead. God may never call us to a solitary confinement cell like the one I saw at the Bautzen II prison. But in whatever trials we **do** encounter, we will be far better prepared for them if we build strong spiritual, intellectual, and interpersonal foundations now.

With these foundations in place, how can we live as Christian "counterrevolutionaries"? How do we resist the unbiblical aspects of neo-Marxism and counter its revolutionary strategies?

That's what we'll examine next.

ENDNOTES

1. See "Bautzen II, the 'Stasi Prison,'" Gedenkstätte Bautzen, Stiftung Sächsische Gedenkstätten (Bautzen Prison, Saxon Memorials Foundation), accessed July 2024, en.stsg.de/cms/node/987.

2. See Andrew Brunson and Craig Borlase, *God's Hostage: A True Story of Persecution, Imprisonment, and Perseverance* (Grand Rapids, MI: Baker Books, 2019).

3. See Nathan Busenitz and James Coates, *God vs. Government: Taking a Biblical Stand When Christ and Compliance Collide* (Eugene, OR: Harvest House Publishers, 2022).

4. While not every student in every country pointed to every foundation, these three foundations were the general trends that emerged. I found that students tended to emphasize spiritual and interpersonal foundations almost invariably, with references to intellectual foundations varying more but still appearing across diverse cultural contexts. Details from these interviews are available in a 30-part blog series at AnswersInGenesis.org, starting at "360° in 180—The Adventure Begins! (Part 1)," Answers in Genesis, November 6, 2019, AnswersInGenesis.org/blogs/patricia-engler/2019/11/06/360-in-180-the-adventure-begins-part-1/. A summary of interview themes and practical foundation-building advice for students is also available in *Prepare to Thrive: A Survival Guide for Christian Students* (Hebron, KY: Answers in Genesis, 2022).

5. E.g., see David Kinnaman and Mark Matlock with Aly Hawkins, *Faith for Exiles: 5 Ways for a New Generation to Follow Jesus in Digital Babylon* (Grand Rapids, MI: Baker Books, 2019). Although Kinnaman et al. categorized their findings using different groupings than I did for my student interviews, the five themes these researchers identified overlapped significantly with the three foundations described above (see *Prepare to Thrive*, 103).

6. A few examples are available in chapter 14 of *Prepare to Thrive*, but I encourage you to keep an eye out for these themes in other stories you encounter of faithful believers.

7. We'll see some examples as we go, with further examples available in part two of *Prepare to Thrive*.

8. Andrew Brunson, "Prepare to Stand Session 6," Family Research Council, YouTube, June 7, 2022, 12:23–12:30, youtube.com/watch?v=Xfdx5Lv-H2U&list=PLmNx2j3x-22Q-I3HDk3hLaMg6X8-h7RoD&index=7.

9. See Brunson, "Prepare to Stand Session 6," 12:30–12:53.

10. See Brunson, "Prepare to Stand Session 6," 12:30–12:53.

11. Nik Ripken, *Insanity of God: A True Story of Faith Resurrected* (Nashville: B&H Publishing Group, 2013), 249. (Although I'm not a fan of the title personally, I did appreciate the book's powerful testimonies of persecuted believers.)

12. Ripken, *Insanity*, 252.

13. Richard Wurmbrand, *Preparing for the Underground Church* (Christian Mission to the Communist World, 1982), 11. (Please note that while this is an insightful resource, it must be read, as always, with biblical discernment.)

14. Andrew Brunson, "Prepare to Stand Session 4—Pursuing God's Heart," Family Research Council, YouTube, June 7, 2022, 0:38–0:54, youtube.com/watch?v=usXbBT-kGIE&list=PLmNx2j3x-22Q-I3HDk3hLaMg6X8-h7RoD&index=5.

15. Brunson, "Prepare to Stand Session 4," 14:16–14:32.

16. All these strategies are important, so their numbered order isn't necessarily to suggest hierarchical significance.

17. Leah MarieAnn Klett, "Chinese Christians Memorize Bible in Prison: Gov't 'Can't Take What's Hidden in Your Heart,'" *The Christian Post*, June 11, 2019, christianpost.com/news/chinese-christians-memorize-bible-prison-cant-take-whats-hidden-in-your-heart.html.

18. See Klett, "Chinese Christians Memorize Bible."

19. Wurmbrand, *Preparing for the Underground Church*, 30–31.

20. Wurmbrand, *Preparing for the Underground Church*, 30.

21. Brother David, Dan Wooding, and Sarah Bruce, *God's Smuggler to China* (Wheaton, IL: Tyndale House Publishers, 1981).

22. See David, Wooding, and Bruce, *God's Smuggler to China*, 218.

23. Ripken, *Insanity*, 155–160.

24. Andrew Brunson, "Prepare to Stand Session 4," 5:16–5:35. See also Brunson and Borlase, *God's Hostage*.

25. Brunson, "Prepare to Stand Session 4," 5:35–5:53.

26. Andrew Brunson, "Prepare to Stand Session 2—Overcoming Fear," Family Research Council, YouTube, June 7, 2022, 6:40–7:00, youtube.com/watch?v=TJsn75mJ-3Q&list=PLmNx2j3x-22Q-I3HDk3hLaMg6X8-h7RoD&index=8.

27. Brunson, "Prepare to Stand Session 2," 8:14–8:41.

28. For more on developing a biblical understanding of identity, see Martyn Iles, *Who Am I? Solving the Identity Puzzle* (Green Forest, AR: Master Books, 2024).

29. See Brunson, "Prepare to Stand Session 2."

30. See episode 41 of the *Zero Compromise* podcast (aired November 21, 2023), available on YouTube, Spotify, and Apple Podcasts.

31. See also Dreher, *Live Not by Lies*, 103 (ebook version).

32. Wurmbrand, *Preparing for the Underground Church*, 12–13.

33. See Elisabeth Elliot, *Shadow of the Almighty: The Life and Testament of Jim Elliot* (New York: Harper & Brothers, 1958), 15.

34. See *Prepare to Thrive*, 112–113; see also Daniel 1:8.

35. Wurmbrand, *Preparing for the Underground Church*, 23.

36. The official newspaper of the Soviet Union.

37. Wurmbrand, *Preparing for the Underground Church*, 13.

38. An in-depth look at how to use this framework is available in *Prepare to Thrive* chapters 9–12; see also *Critical Thinking Scan* on Answers TV.

39. You can learn more about how to identify different types of logical fallacies through resources including AnswersInGenesis.org, the *Critical Thinking Scan* video series on Answers TV, or Appendix B of *Prepare to Thrive*.

40. See Brunson, "Prepare to Stand Session 6," 8:26–19:16.

41. See Brunson, "Prepare to Stand Session 6," 10:44–11:37.

42. Dreher, *Live Not by Lies*, 241 (ebook version).

43. See Corrie ten Boom, John Sherrill, and Elizabeth Sherrill, *The Hiding Place* (Old Tappan, NJ: Spire Books, 1971).

44. For an autobiography of one of those teenagers, see Hans Poley, *Return to the Hiding Place* (Elgin, IL: LifeJourney Books, 1993), 25.

45. See Brunson, "Prepare to Stand Session 6," 11:53–12:23.

PHILIPPIANS 1:27-29

ONLY LET YOUR MANNER OF LIFE BE WORTHY OF THE GOSPEL OF CHRIST, SO THAT WHETHER I COME AND SEE YOU OR AM ABSENT, I MAY HEAR OF YOU THAT YOU ARE STANDING FIRM IN ONE SPIRIT, WITH ONE MIND STRIVING SIDE BY SIDE FOR THE FAITH OF THE GOSPEL, AND NOT FRIGHTENED IN ANYTHING BY YOUR OPPONENTS. . . . FOR IT HAS BEEN GRANTED TO YOU THAT FOR THE SAKE OF CHRIST YOU SHOULD NOT ONLY BELIEVE IN HIM BUT ALSO SUFFER FOR HIS SAKE.

CHAPTER 10

COUNTER-REVOLUTIONARY STRATEGIES

PRACTICAL TACTICS FOR CHRISTIAN RESISTANCE

"For every action, there is an equal and opposite reaction."

So goes Sir Isaac Newton's Third Law of Motion, beloved and feared in physics classrooms everywhere. Basically, Newton meant that whenever something moves or pushes in one direction, something else moves or pushes back. Push an oar against a lake while you're canoeing, and the lake pushes back, propelling you forward. But what if this principle applies not just in classrooms and canoes but—in a sense—also in culture?

Clearly, not every revolutionary strategy (say, storming castles with pitchforks) should engender an equivalent response from Christians—quite the contrary. Romans 12:17 commands, "Repay no one evil for evil, but give thought to do what is honorable in the sight of all," while verse 14 urges, "Bless those who persecute you; bless and do not curse them." Still, many revolutionary strategies we've looked at suggest biblically "counterrevolutionary" responses. For instance, where neo-Marxism tears families down, Christians can build families up.

Let's look at 12 broad categories of ways to be biblically counterrevolutionary Christians who overcome evil with good (Romans 12:21). This list isn't exhaustive, and countless creative avenues exist to apply each strategy in specific contexts, inviting further prayerful brainstorming among Christian individuals, families, and churches. Still, identifying these general countermoves will launch us off to a solid start.

1. DEFEND CHURCHES AND FAMILIES

Throughout this book, we've seen how revolutionary regimes seek to weaken churches and undermine families, making way for a new social order. For instance, chapter 6 described how Lenin targeted families by attacking marriage, inhibiting family togetherness, and disrupting parents' roles as loving authority figures above their kids. Another revolutionary strategy involved sexualizing children.

A counterrevolutionary response is to defend the God-given institution of family wherever it's attacked. This begins with defending God's Word from Genesis as the basis for family life as God designed. Here are several other broad ways to counter anti-family strategies:

- Standing for the biblical institutions of marriage and parenthood.
- Supporting initiatives to strengthen individual families and marriages.

- Seeking to develop, strengthen, and model godly family lives ourselves. (For many Christians—and **all** Christians during certain seasons—this includes modeling godly singleness.[1])
- Discipling others (especially young people) to become all that God intends for them within their current or future families.
- Watching for opportunities to protect and strengthen families as parents, community participants, and voters.

Families aren't the only pillar under attack—churches are too. One response is taking opportunities to protect religious freedom. Even more fundamentally, we can defend biblical doctrine, following Dr. Brunson's advice to "guard the Word" against dilution, misuse, and assimilation with our therapeutic culture's lies.[2] Meanwhile, it's vital not to underestimate the power of keeping individual churches, families, and the wider institutions they represent in our prayers.

2. DISCIPLE YOUTH

As the CIA report in chapter 6 highlighted, any movement that wants to capture a culture needs to capture society's youth. In response, Christians must be at least as intentional about discipling young people as secularists are.

Unfortunately, I find that well-meaning churches too often give young people the opposite of what they need in terms of spiritual, intellectual, and interpersonal foundations. This consequence can flow from factors like emphasizing entertainment **over** discipleship, not equipping youth to think biblically about tough questions, or invariably segregating age groups. (While age-appropriate teaching serves an important function, **always** keeping age groups separated cuts off essential mentorship opportunities.) Imagine what could happen if churches focused strategically on equipping youth with the personal foundations every Christian needs?

Importantly though, the responsibility for discipling the next generation doesn't rest primarily on the church. Discipleship begins at home, with parents intentionally investing in children's spiritual formation, teaching them God's Word, and modeling biblical living throughout the week. And outside the home, we can all seek opportunities to mentor, serve, and pour into younger people—many of whom absorb much of their thinking from secular culture.

> **WE CAN ALL SEEK OPPORTUNITIES TO MENTOR, SERVE, AND POUR INTO YOUNGER PEOPLE.**

Whether in churches, households, or communities, a practical game plan is to help young people implement the foundation-building strategies chapter 9 unpacked. Starting with spiritual foundations, how can we spark young people's excitement about walking closer with God? While no magic formulas exist, I remember several things that helped stoke this excitement in me as a teenager.

1. My parents modeled enthusiasm about the Bible, prayer, and their own walks with God.
2. My family introduced me to stories of missionaries, martyrs, and other ordinary Christians who saw God work in extraordinary ways. These accounts made me want to know God more myself.
3. Getting involved in outreaches, interacting with Christians in ministry, and becoming more intentional about prayer gave me opportunities to see God work firsthand.

4. Plugging into apologetics resources fortified my convictions that God's Word is true, essential, and trustworthy.
5. Participation in Bible memorization programs armed me with scriptures God would remind me of when I needed them in the future.

Again, these aren't magic formulas. We never know how God might draw a young person to himself. We can only do **our** best to be faithful in intentionally, prayerfully discipling the next generation with spiritual foundations, entrusting the results to God.

What about intellectual foundations? Ministries like Answers in Genesis offer tons of resources for equipping the next generation with apologetics answers and biblical critical thinking skills.[3] Armed with these tools, young people can better resist the onslaught of persuasive—but unbiblical—messages bombarding them from secular culture, classrooms, and mass media. We can also find opportunities to help youth develop solid reasoning, communication, and literacy skills to combat the trivialization processes chapter 7 described.

As for interpersonal foundations, a vital strategy is to encourage intergenerational connections within the body of Christ. Major studies affirm meaningful relationships with older Christian adults to be a common denominator among youth who keep a thriving faith.[4] But these older Christians must be committed to biblical authority. The more churches and families bolster intergenerational connections grounded in this commitment, the stronger

ENCOURAGE INTERGENERATIONAL CONNECTIONS WITHIN THE BODY OF CHRIST.

the foundations Christians can foster for resisting the neo-Marxist tide.

3. HARNESS THE POWER OF MEDIA, ART, TECHNOLOGY, AND EDUCATION

We've seen that one way revolutionaries capture young people (and their wider society) is by leveraging media, art, technology, and education to promote faulty worldviews. While education systems especially shape the worldviews of young people, what tools exist for influencing adults' more solidified beliefs? Long-established thinking patterns often stand like fortresses against mere **arguments**. But **stories** can bypass our defenses in ways arguments can't, inviting us to new places where we'll encounter truths (or lies) from a novel perspective.[5]

That's where art and media come in, telling stories in formats ranging from video to music to live drama. Neo-Marxists like Marcuse reflected long and hard about the revolutionary potential of visual arts.[6] For decades, the secular world has poured untold billions of dollars into telling stories in ways that promote a secular worldview. Christians don't always have access to the same financial or technical resources, but we do have access to God. Leaning on **God's** resources, believers have increasingly found ways to produce high-quality cultural products, utilizing the technologies, formats, and platforms that best reach today's audiences.

> THE SECULAR WORLD HAS POURED UNTOLD BILLIONS OF DOLLARS INTO TELLING STORIES.

4. COUNTER FALSE NARRATIVES

Along with creating cultural products that promote **true** narratives, we must intentionally resist **false** narratives. One of these narratives is the story therapeutic culture tells: "Once upon a time, there was you. Your feelings determine what's true for you. So be true to yourself by following your heart, putting yourself first, and doing whatever makes you happy. Because that's what life is all about."

A second false narrative is the "gospel according to Marx." We've seen how this narrative divides humanity into **oppressed** or **oppressor** identity groups, insisting that "all the angels are on one side and all the devils on the other."[7] According to this story, the oppressed can do no wrong and are justified in inflicting any violence necessary to disempower their oppressors. Only revolution, the story goes, can redeem humanity from its grievances.

ACCORDING TO THIS STORY, THE OPPRESSED CAN DO NO WRONG.

Combine this revolutionary story with a Freudian version of the therapeutic story above, and you wind up with the Frankfurt School's narrative: "The feelings of oppressed identity groups determine truth. Only when these groups help overthrow society's oppressive structures represented by the family unit can we all be free to do whatever makes us happy."

As Christians, we must reject all three of these narratives for the Bible's true account of history starting in Genesis. Aligned with the truth of God's Word, we have everything we need for resisting the influence of false narratives in our own lives.

How does this resistance look in practice? For starters, we can resist allowing unbiblical "woke" ideologies into our own thinking and churches.[8] We can also reject the therapeutic messages we encounter in everyday life rather than letting them influence our mentalities. For instance, when advertisements assure me that I "deserve" to buy a certain product, I try remembering that biblically, even the fact that I'm alive is undeserved grace.

We can build further resistance to therapeutic culture by trying biblical disciplines like fasting. People practice different forms of fasting, but these practices all share one important commonality. They all train us for saying "no" to comforts, conveniences, and pleasures that beg for priority over biblical convictions. A related practice Pastor Wurmbrand suggested is to walk through a supermarket, look at the delicious fares on offer, and say of each item, "That looks very nice, but I can go without it."[9] All of this certainly isn't to say we shouldn't enjoy the gifts God makes available (Ecclesiastes 9:7–10; 1 Timothy 6:17–19). But by training ourselves not to unduly **prioritize** or **depend** on earthly comforts, we become more resistant to manipulation by soft totalitarian threats to cancel these comforts.

THAT LOOKS VERY NICE, BUT I CAN GO WITHOUT IT.

5. USE TECHNOLOGY WISELY

One way we've seen how people can become vulnerable to soft totalitarianism is through certain uses of technology. Under the auspices of capitalism, various corporations have taught us to prioritize technological comfort, pleasure, and convenience over privacy, freedom, and conviction.[10] We saw in chapter 7 how today's technologies give totalitarian regimes unprecedented surveillance capacities, providing new ways to incentivize conformity, identify dissenters, and censor information.

Recognizing these realities doesn't entail rejecting technology. A biblical view enables us to appreciate technology as a gift. This gift reflects our God-given creativity, helps us mitigate the fall's effects, and lets us share God's truth. We must, however, use this gift wisely. And that begins with embracing a biblical worldview founded in Genesis. From this foundation, we can understand human purpose, flourishing, and morality in ways that inform our values, principles, and guidelines for engaging with technology.[11] We can also understand that our world is fallen. Technology places power tools in the hands of sinful humans, demanding the types of ethical boundaries that a biblical worldview enables.

THIS AWARENESS MOTIVATES US TO SEEK EXTRA WISDOM.

As opposition to this worldview increases, we're wise to beware of how our technological usages contribute to the surveillance system soft totalitarianism needs. This awareness motivates us to seek extra wisdom for engaging in online activities, making consumer decisions, and interacting with devices. Meanwhile, we can notice ways to practice simply "being human" in a digital age—for instance, by interacting in person, spending time in God's creation, or enjoying other "real-world" activities. The less we're **dependent** on certain technologies, the more we can resist soft totalitarian threats to cancel our access to them.

Again, none of this suggests we should all smash our phones, retreat to the desert, and eat lizards for the rest of our lives. For many of us, fulfilling our God-given assignments means engaging in a digitally driven society. We just need to do so with wisdom. We need to draw biblical boundaries, beware of certain technologies' usefulness to totalitarianism, and consider possible positive and negative effects from specific applications of technologies. That way we can be wise as serpents and gentle as doves in a digital world (Matthew 10:16)—no lizards required.

6. SPEAK THE TRUTH IN LOVE

Naturally, living as serpents and doves doesn't just apply to using technology but also to every other aspect of navigating culture. The apostle Paul, in Colossians 4:5–6, urges believers to "walk in wisdom toward outsiders, making the best use of the time. Let your speech always be gracious, seasoned with salt, so that you may know how you ought to answer each person." We also see this theme of wisdom and gentleness in Ephesians 4:15, with Paul's famous phrase about "speaking the truth in love." The same theme reappears in 2 Timothy 2:24–26, where Paul says,

> And the Lord's servant must not be quarrelsome but kind to everyone, able to teach, patiently enduring evil, correcting his opponents with gentleness. God may perhaps grant them repentance leading to a knowledge of the truth, and they may come to their senses and escape from the snare of the devil, after being captured by him to do his will.

What are some practical ways to live out the Bible's call for wisdom and gentleness in today's culture? Here are three, for starters.

PICK YOUR BATTLES

Ecclesiastes 3:7 observes that there is "a time to keep silence, and a time to speak." Mordecai commanded Esther to speak in response to one threat (Esther 4:14); Hezekiah commanded his people to keep silent in response to another (2 Kings 18:36). Knowing the difference requires biblical wisdom.

In this regard, Rod Dreher advised, “cherish truth-telling, but be prudent.”[12] He aptly elaborated, “Ordinary life, in every society, requires assessing which fights are worth having in a given context. Though one must guard against rationalization, prudence is not the same thing as cowardice.” Prayer, godly counsel, familiarity with Scripture, and sensitivity to convictions from God will be vital as we seek wisdom to pick our battles well.

ORDINARY LIFE, IN EVERY SOCIETY, REQUIRES ASSESSING WHICH FIGHTS ARE WORTH HAVING.

HONE THOUGHTFUL CONVERSATION SKILLS

While interviewing Christians at secular universities, I heard several believers mention the importance of knowing discussion skills for conversing with people from other worldviews. One method that students (including me) have found useful is **asking questions** that get people thinking about the problems with their worldviews. Jesus himself often answered questions with questions, especially when he knew that people were trying to trap him in his words.[13]

Other helpful conversation skills include remembering to clarify key word definitions, responding to fallacies graciously, and pointing out how our differences come down to worldviews. That is, the reason we think differently from the other person isn't because we have different personal preferences but a different foundation for truth. God determines truth; his Word is our authority, and we can do nothing but obey him. Along the way, we can also demonstrate that Christians are kind, normal individuals who genuinely care about others. And we can pray for God's Holy Spirit to give us the right words for every situation (Matthew 10:20).

FIGHT LIKE A CHRISTIAN

In a conference presentation titled "How to Fight Like a Christian," Bible-believing attorney Michael Farris called for Christians to "sing sweetly, boldly, and faithfully."[14] By **singing sweetly**, he meant that our job isn't just to speak the truth, analogous to singing the correct lyrics for a song. We also need to do so in gentleness, grace, and love—analogous to singing a sweet melody **along with** the right words. Our mission, he explained, is to represent Christ well by standing for truth graciously, courageously, and persistently, relying on God to accomplish the results.

7. DEFEND HUMAN LIFE

One cultural arena that especially calls for "fighting like a Christian" surrounds the defense of human life. Chapter 8 described how psychiatrist Robert Lifton identified several hallmarks of totalitarianism, the last of which most blatantly attacks human life.[15] In "the dispensation of existence," a person or organization[16] presumes to redefine the truth about who qualifies for human rights—and for life itself.

This outcome can develop subtly as totalitarian regimes start prioritizing **ideologies** over **individuals**. For instance, Nazism prioritized the concept of "attaining a perfect human race" over the value of human life, leading to horrific genocides. Similarly, communist regimes throughout the twentieth century prioritized versions of Marxism above human life in ways that spelled death for millions. And, although not always enforced by totalitarianism, pro-abortion laws in many places prioritize still other cultural concepts over the value of preborn human life.

Abortion offers just one example of lethal dehumanization occurring **en masse** in our own societies.[17] In rejecting God's Word, our societies forfeited a consistent, stable basis for understanding the value of human life. Now the door to endless forms of dehumanization stands wide open. As history's darkest episodes remind us, such dehumanization can happen easier than we think. Dehumanization also follows readily from the **villainization** strategies we saw associated with revolutions in chapter 8.

ADAMANTLY OPPOSE THE DEVALUATION OF IMAGE BEARERS.

What's a counterrevolutionary response? Simply put, Christians need to take an uncompromised biblical stance for the value of human life. If we don't speak up for the voiceless during freedom, who will speak during persecution? Now is the time to resist narratives implying that human meaning, worth, or rights are based in group identity, state decrees, social contribution, or **anything else** besides bearing God's image. Now is the time to adamantly oppose the devaluation of image bearers. And now is the time to stand **for** the value of human life.

Countless ways exist to stand for life, from supporting pro-life ministries to voting for life-protecting laws to sharing life-affirming resources from ministries like Answers in Genesis. As always, we can also defend and proclaim the truth of God's Word beginning in Genesis, which shows why every human life is priceless.

8. LIVE NOT BY LIES

When totalitarianism tries to hijack truth, the result is a world where people live by lies. In his 1974 essay "Live Not by Lies" (which inspired the title of Rod Dreher's 2020 book), Aleksander Solzhenitsyn called citizens to a different standard. Writing to other people under Soviet communism, Solzhenitsyn declared:

> The simplest and most accessible key to our self-neglected liberation is this: personal non-participation in lies. . . . Let us admit it: we have not matured enough to march into the squares and shout the truth out loud or to express aloud what we think. It is not necessary. It's dangerous. But let us refuse to say what we do not think.

As Christians, we can practice taking this advice by refusing to promote ideas that go against God's Word. We should never be forced to say anything we know is untrue. Let's pray for grace to stand like Shadrach, Meshach, and Abednego, who refused to bow before a god they knew was false (Daniel 3:1–30). Following their example in **living not by lies** means **living by God's Word** as the standard for truth. A helpful litmus test to identify whether we're being told to compromise on this standard is to ask, "Is someone forbidding what God has commanded or commanding what God has forbidden?"[18]

Another way to live not by lies is to resist neo-Marxist redefinitions of language. In past chapters, we've seen how redefinitions of concepts including **justice**, **equity**, **freedom**, **rights**, **oppression**, and **morality** play a central role in revolutionary strategies. The redefinition of language also ties into the totalitarian quest to control truth.[19] But we can spot manipulated language by defining terms, asking how words' meanings have changed, and questioning whether current definitions match a biblical view. Affirming unbiblical redefinitions means living by lies.

9. RESIST "BRAINWASHING"

One way to live not by lies is to resist the other "thought reform" processes Robert Lifton identified.[20] Many of these processes boil down to **being told what to think** by an illegitimate authority for truth.

- The "sacred science" tells us what to think.
- "Loaded language" encourages us to keep thinking it.
- The "demand for purity" tells us we're immoral if we think otherwise.
- The "cult of confession" tells us to repent if we ever thought differently.
- "Milieu control" ensures that we can't access information that supports other thinking.
- "Doctrine over person" dismisses people whose perceptions might encourage different thinking.

One of the most counterrevolutionary actions we could dare to perform is to think. But we'll only have a true foundation for thinking if we begin from the Word of our all-knowing God. Biblical critical thinking is indispensable for resisting totalitarianism in all its forms.

Unfortunately, totalitarian "thought reform" environments can make critical thinking extra difficult. Under classical "brainwashing" conditions at communist prison camps, people contend with malnourishment, sleep deprivation, and other factors that can weaken mental defenses. People in such environments may also experience isolation, which prevents them from interacting with others who could offer a "reality check."

Noting that university students can face similar challenges—albeit to lesser degrees—I suggested strategies in *Prepare to Thrive* for resisting "brainwashing" conditions on campuses.[21] The same strategies also apply to helping other Christians maintain their biblical critical thinking defenses for withstanding "thought reform" in wider culture. Here's a quick summary.

- **Take care of yourself spiritually** by building and maintaining the strong spiritual, intellectual, and interpersonal foundations we saw in the last chapter and by staying in God's Word.
- **Take care of yourself physically** by aiming for the sleep, nutrition, and exercise your brain needs to function at its finest.
- **Take care of yourself mentally** by maintaining your spiritual and physical health and by taking breaks for simple, spirit-lifting activities. Just a few ideas include spending time with people, getting outside, tackling creative projects, or playing music—especially worship songs.

Silvester Krčméry, a doctor imprisoned in communist Czechoslovakia, offered similar advice. In his book *This Saved Us: How to Survive Brainwashing*, Krčméry emphasized the role of spiritual foundations in preparing to withstand "brainwashing."[22] He urged Christians to minimize isolation, fear, and depression during persecution by "engaging in an intensive spiritual life" including prayer, Scripture study, and Bible memorization. Krčméry also highlighted interpersonal foundations for combating isolation, saying, "When there is danger of a nervous breakdown, it is imperative to do everything to break the isolation and feeling of despair, even at the cost of personal risk, that is arrest of oneself or with other friends."[23]

By staying connected with fellow believers and by taking steps to keep our minds alert, applied, and awash with **Scripture**, we'll be best positioned to live out Romans 12:2: "Do not be conformed to this world, but be transformed by the renewal of your mind, that by testing you may discern what is the will of God, what is good and acceptable and perfect."

10. KNOW YOUR LEGAL RIGHTS

In his Nobel Prize-winning book *Gulag Archipelago*, which documented the oppressiveness of Soviet communism, Aleksandr Solzhenitsyn asked this question: "Should we not say . . . that if people had been heroic in exercising their civic responsibilities, there would never have been any reason to write either this chapter or this whole book?"[24]

Solzhenitsyn described how, as people toiled in labor camps after arbitrary arrests, all these prisoners could do was wonder what might have happened differently. What turmoil could they have prevented if they had taken a stronger stand for freedom when they'd had the chance? Solzhenitsyn concluded, "We didn't love freedom enough. And even more—we had no awareness of the real situation."[25]

WHAT TURMOIL COULD THEY HAVE PREVENTED?

It was too late for them. But it's not too late for us. There's still a window of opportunity to learn, use, and defend our legal rights as Christians, parents, students, and citizens. Along the way, we'll need to "sing sweetly," remember our citizenship is in heaven, and pick our battles in ways that prioritize God's kingdom.[26] For Jesus, prioritizing God's kingdom meant not standing up for his own rights during his trial—in obedience to his Father's will. For Paul, prioritizing God's kingdom meant **standing up** for his own rights when doing so aligned with his God-given mission to further the gospel.

I still remember one of the best (and only) sermons I ever heard about this topic. Drawing on examples from Acts, the pastor examined how Paul made use of his legal rights as a Roman citizen. Take, for instance, the dramatic accounts of Acts 22:22–29. When a series of adrenaline-pumping events landed Paul in front of a mob demanding his blood, the Roman commander whisked Paul away for interrogation under flogging. Verse 25 recounts, "But when they had stretched him out for the whips, Paul said to the centurion who was standing by, 'Is it lawful for you to flog a man who is a Roman citizen and uncondemned?'" When the plot twist of Paul's citizenship sank in, "those who were about to examine him withdrew from him immediately, and the [commander] also was afraid, for he realized that Paul was a Roman citizen and that he had bound him" (Acts 22:29; see also Acts 16:37).

THE PLOT TWIST OF PAUL'S CITIZENSHIP SANK IN.

Like Paul, we can only keep relevant officials accountable to uphold citizens' rights if we know what those rights are. Silvester Krčméry, the dissident doctor, urged free citizens to "read the Penal Order and Criminal law codes, especially the sections dealing with the police and human rights, even if it is only to acquire information."[27] Relatedly, Aleksandr Solzhenitsyn illustrated the importance of watching for, identifying, and calling out ill-defined sections of criminal codes.[28] These are the sections that could most easily be interpreted in ways that undermine basic freedoms (especially for Christians).

Keeping silent may be easier than speaking up. But not even silence offers safety when totalitarianism's demands for total allegiance arise. Writing about the evils of totalitarian repression, Solzhenitsyn warns, "In keeping silent about evil . . . we are **implanting** it, it will rise up a thousandfold in the future."[29]

11. LIVE ABOVE REPROACH

Ask for advice about living in hostile contexts from Christians who have "been there," and you'll find they often emphasize **living as a good witness**.[30] From how we treat others to how we present ourselves to how we make daily decisions, we represent Christ to the world by how we live.

The ultimate way to represent Christ is to obey his commands, as Jesus indicated in John 13:34–35: "A new commandment I give to you, that you love one another: just as I have loved you, you also are to love one another. By this all people will know that you are my disciples, if you have love for one another."

WE REPRESENT CHRIST TO THE WORLD BY HOW WE LIVE.

Following Jesus' commands entails honoring Christ as Lord, as 1 Peter 3:16 says: "Having a good conscience, so that, when you are slandered, those who revile your good behavior in Christ may be put to shame." Relatedly, Titus 2:7–8 urges, "Show yourself in all respects to be a model of good works, and in your teaching show integrity, dignity, and sound speech that cannot be condemned, so that an opponent may be put to shame, having nothing evil to say about us." Reiterating the importance of not giving opponents anything evil to say, 1 Peter 4:15–16 states,

"But let none of you suffer as a murderer or a thief or an evildoer or as a meddler. Yet if anyone suffers as a Christian, let him not be ashamed, but let him glorify God in that name."

Along with keeping a clean conscience, we can live as good witnesses simply by being normal, kind, caring, gracious, respectable participants in society. When visiting Slovakia on my backpacking journey to research Marxism, I had the chance to interview a Christian who had modeled this lifestyle during communism. He told me the communist regime not only treated Christians as "second-class citizens" but also tried to paint believers as "backwards thinking." But many Christians—including him—gained social relevance by becoming credentialed experts in their fields. As an engineer who had won a national award for his scientific contributions, he stood as living disproof of the communists' anti-Christian propaganda.

HE STOOD AS LIVING DISPROOF OF THE COMMUNISTS' ANTI-CHRISTIAN PROPAGANDA.

Two or three times a year, the KGB (secret police) would question this engineer about his church-related activities. The interrogator respected him for winning the award and asked why, as an engineer, he felt the need to be so involved with the church. This question gave the engineer an opportunity to tell his interrogator how he had seen Jesus restore broken lives. "And from that moment," said the engineer, "I haven't really had a fear to go into that kind of meeting with [the interrogator]." We never know how God might use our stories to impact others as we seek to follow him faithfully.

12. OVERCOME EVIL WITH GOOD

Living above reproach keeps us from contributing to evil. But combating evil doesn't end there. Romans 12 offers multiple practical mandates to help believers shine the light of Christ in a sin-filled world, concluding with verse 21: "Do not be overcome by evil, but overcome evil with good."

One of the ways Romans 12 shows us how to overcome evil is by loving our enemies. We demonstrate God's reality to the world in a profound way when we display a love that we could never summon ourselves. Just ask Corrie ten Boom. After the Nazis arrested the ten Booms for protecting God's people, Corrie spent years in dehumanizing concentration camps. There, her beloved father and sister paid the price of their lives. But Corrie survived. After experiencing a miraculous release from imprisonment, she began traveling to tell others that "there is no pit so deep that [Jesus] is not deeper still."[31]

After speaking one day, Corrie stopped short at the sight of one of her former Nazi jailers approaching her. As he told her that Jesus had forgiven his sins, this former Nazi extended his hand to Corrie. She recounted in her book, *The Hiding Place*:

> I tried to smile, I struggled to raise my hand. I could not. . . . And so again I breathed a silent prayer. **Jesus, I cannot forgive him. Give me Your forgiveness.** As I took his hand the most incredible thing happened . . . into my heart sprang a love for this stranger that almost overwhelmed me. And so I discovered that it is not on our forgiveness any more than on our goodness that the world's healing hinges, but on His. When He tells us to love our enemies, He gives, along with the command, the love itself.[32]

Every act of love matters. And Jesus, not the world, defines what love is. He modeled love himself by showing compassion to crowds, washing his disciples' feet, and proving by his substitutionary death that "greater love has no one than this, that someone lay down his life for his friends" (John 15:13).

Serving others like Jesus modeled offers countless little ways to overcome evil with good. And the most profound way to serve and love others is by sharing the message of Christ. The gospel alone offers the hope that revolutionary activists are seeking. When we defend, proclaim, and advance the gospel, we hold up the one true solution for humanity's problems.[33] Only in Jesus can humans find the freedom, redemption, and restoration that no version of Marxism will ever deliver.

ONLY IN JESUS CAN HUMANS FIND FREEDOM, REDEMPTION, AND RESTORATION.

SUMMING UP

Ultimately, these "counterrevolutionary" categories suggest ways we can resist soft totalitarian neo-Marxist agendas demanding a new social order. Many of these categories represent an "equal and opposite" approach to revolutionaries' own strategies. Where revolutionary agendas disrupt families, we can defend families. Where revolutionary agendas target youth with a false worldview, we can disciple youth to live out a biblical worldview. Where revolutionary agendas leverage media, art, technology, and education to promote false gospels, we can harness the same powers to advance the gospel of Jesus Christ.

Other counterrevolutionary strategies represent further forms of "resistance." We can resist totalitarianism's digital powers of manipulation by using technology wisely. We can resist totalitarianism's inherent dehumanization by defending the value of human life. And we can resist totalitarianism's truth-twisting oppressiveness by striving to live not by lies, guarding against brainwashing, and understanding our legal rights. Along the way, we'll shine as lights against a shadowy world by speaking the truth in love, living above reproach, and overcoming evil with good.

These biblical counterrevolutionary strategies, tested and tried by Christians before us, remind us that we are not helpless to respond to the gathering storm. Not by might, nor by power, but by God's Spirit (Zechariah 4:6) we have much to do. But first, a few final words of encouragement.

ENDNOTES

1. For biblical perspectives on modeling godly singleness, see "Encouragement for Single Christians—Episode 36," *Zero Compromise* podcast, October 10, 2023.

2. Andrew Brunson, "Prepare to Stand Session 6—Avoiding Deception," Family Research Council, YouTube, June 7, 2022, 11:56–14:23, youtube.com/watch?v=Xfdx5Lv-H2U&list=PLmNx2j3x-22Q-I3HDk3hLaMg6X8-h7RoD&index=7

3. AnswersInGenesis.org and Answers TV are great places to start checking out these resources. If possible, I'd also encourage you to bring young people to visit the Ark Encounter or Creation Museum.

4. E.g., David Kinnaman and Mark Matlock with Aly Hawkins, *Faith for Exiles: 5 Ways for a New Generation to Follow Jesus in Digital Babylon* (Grand Rapids, MI: Baker Books, 2019); Rick Hiemstra, Lorianne Dueck, and Matthew Blackaby, "Renegotiating Faith: The Delay in Young Adult Identity Formation and What It Means for the Church in Canada," Faith Today Publications, 2018, p2c.com/renegotiating-faith/; see also Christian Smith and Patricia Snell, *Souls in Transition: The Religious and Spiritual Lives of Emerging Adults* (New York: Oxford University Press, 2009).

5. I'm grateful to Dr. Christina Bieberlake for highlighting this point in her presentation at the Center for Bioethics and Human Dignity's 2023 Annual Conference, The Christian Stake in Bioethics Revisited, June 23, 2023.

6. A summary of Marcuse's reflections on art is available in Arnold Farr, "Herbert Marcuse," *The Stanford Encyclopedia of Philosophy* (Summer 2021 Edition), ed. Edward Zalta, plato.stanford.edu/entries/marcuse/.

7. See Saul Alinsky, *Rules for Radicals: A Practical Primer for Realistic Radicals* (New York: Vintage Books, 1972), 133–134. While Alinsky himself did not profess allegiance to communism, his statement nicely captures the binary worldview of Marxist conflict theories.

8. See Owen Strachan, *Christianity and Wokeness: How the Social Justice Movement Is Hijacking the Gospel—and the Way to Stop It* (Washington, D.C.: Salem Books, 2021).

9. See Richard Wurmbrand, *Preparing for the Underground Church* (Christian Mission to the Communist World, 1982), 13.

10. See also Rod Dreher, "Capitalism: Woke and Watchful," in *Live Not by Lies: A Manual for Christian Dissidents* (New York: Sentinel, 2020), 71–94 (ebook version).

11. Examples of how a Genesis-based view can inform our technological usage are available in "7 Genesis Truths for Thinking About Any New Technology," Answers in Genesis, September 20, 2024, AnswersInGenesis.org/technology/genesis-truths-for-new-technology/.

12. Dreher, *Live Not by Lies*, 105 (ebook version).

13. E.g., Matthew 21:23–27, 22:15–22. See also Matthew 22:41–46.

14. Michael Farris, "How to Fight Like a Christian" (presentation, 2023 Answers for Pastors Conference, Contending for a Biblical Worldview, Ark Encounter in Williamstown, KY, October 5, 2023).

15. Robert Lifton, *Thought Reform and the Psychology of Totalism: A Study of "Brainwashing" in China* (Chapel Hill, NC: UNC Press, 2012, originally published by Norton, 1963), 419–437.

16. Or in today's context, an artificially intelligent entity or a combination of human and artificial intelligence.

17. For some further examples, see Dr. Georgia Purdom, "Eugenics, Abortion, and Our Future: The Quest for Perfection," a presentation available on Answers TV.

18. See John Lillie, *Lectures on the First and Second Epistles of Peter* (New York: Charles Scribner & Co., 1869), 142.

19. See Dreher, *Live Not by Lies*, 14–15 (ebook version).

20. See Lifton, *Thought Reform and the Psychology of Totalism*, 419–437. See also chapter 8 of the present book.

21. See *Prepare to Thrive* (Hebron, KY: Answers in Genesis, 2022), 245–250.

22. Silvester Krčméry Sr. M.D., *This Saved Us: How to Survive Brainwashing*, ed. trans. Madeleine Rivest and Benedict Hayas (Bratislava, Slovakia: Silvester Krčméry, 1996, originally published in Slovak by Slovak Publishing Houses, 1995), 219.

23. Krčméry, *This Saved Us*, 219.

24. Aleksander Solzhenitsyn, *The Gulag Archipelago: An Experiment in Literary Investigation*, vol. 1, trans. Thomas Whitney (New York: Harper Perennial Modern Classics, 2007, originally published in 1973), 49.

25. Solzhenitsyn, *The Gulag Archipelago*, 13.

26. See point 6 above; see also Philippians 3:20 and Farris, "How to Fight Like a Christian," available on Answers TV.

27. Krčméry, *This Saved Us*, 219–220.

28. See Solzhenitsyn, *The Gulag Archipelago*, 60–67.

29. Solzhenitsyn, *The Gulag Archipelago*, 178.

30. For examples from Christians in Western academic and cultural contexts, see Karina Altman's story on Episode 23 of the *Zero Compromise* podcast (aired July 10, 2023) and Martyn Iles, "Living in Babylon" (presentation, 2023 Answers Homeschool Experience: Equipping Generations for the King, Ark Encounter in Williamstown, KY, August 15, 2023), available on Answers TV.

31. Betsie ten Boom, quoted in Corrie ten Boom with John and Elizabeth Sherrill, *The Hiding Place* (Minneapolis: World Wide Publications, 1971), 215.

32. Corrie ten Boom, *The Hiding Place*, 233 (emphasis added).

33. Practical tools for evangelism are available at AnswersInGenesis.org; see also Ken Ham, *Gospel Reset* (Green Forest, AR: Master Books, 2018).

ROMANS 8:35-39

WHO SHALL SEPARATE US FROM THE LOVE OF CHRIST? SHALL TRIBULATION, OR DISTRESS, OR PERSECUTION, OR FAMINE, OR NAKEDNESS, OR DANGER, OR SWORD? . . . NO, IN ALL THESE THINGS WE ARE MORE THAN CONQUERORS THROUGH HIM WHO LOVED US. FOR I AM SURE THAT NEITHER DEATH NOR LIFE, NOR ANGELS NOR RULERS, NOR THINGS PRESENT NOR THINGS TO COME, NOR POWERS, NOR HEIGHT NOR DEPTH, NOR ANYTHING ELSE IN ALL CREATION, WILL BE ABLE TO SEPARATE US FROM THE LOVE OF GOD IN CHRIST JESUS OUR LORD.

CHAPTER 11

MORE THAN CONQUERORS

FINAL ENCOURAGEMENT

"JESUS IS VICTOR."

Those words, etched in stone, lay thousands of miles from the university where I stood reading posters, signs, and banners at the pro-communist protest in Berlin. At the time, I could only hear the protesters applauding. The crowds cheering. The German speeches echoing from the megaphone.

But meanwhile, across the ocean, a stone was crying out a louder message. When the protesters packed up their signs and left, the stone and its message remained. And its message will still be resounding after every voice extolling "man's word" as the authority has fallen silent.

You can read the stone's message yourself if you visit Santa Ana, California, enter Fairhaven Memorial Park, and find the grave of Corrie ten Boom. Alternatively, you can read the truth that **Jesus is victor** in its original source, God's Word—which, unlike the gravestone, will last **forever** (Isaiah 40:8). In John 16:33, Jesus assured his disciples, "I have said these things to you, that in me you may have peace. In the world you will have tribulation. But take heart; I have overcome the world."

Accounts of Christians like Corrie ten Boom, Richard Wurmbrand, Andrew Brunson, and other Christ-followers who have faced tribulation before us harbor goldmines of practical encouragement. These Christians' testimonies also offer three reminders for going forward faithfully as we follow Jesus wherever he calls us.

1. RESOLVE TO FOLLOW JESUS UNCONDITIONALLY

If Jesus is truly our Lord, then we're committed to following him under all circumstances, at all costs, regardless of whether he does what we'd like. This sort of surrender may be scary, but it's also liberating. We release our claim to a control we never had, and we find that "the eternal God is [our] dwelling place, and underneath are the everlasting arms" (Deuteronomy 33:27).

> **THIS SORT OF SURRENDER MAY BE SCARY, BUT IT'S ALSO LIBERATING.**

This liberation comes in part because when we belong to God, the worries we encounter are no longer primarily our job to handle. Our job is simply to commend our lives to God, trust him, and faithfully complete whatever current task he has set before us. As 1 Peter 4:19 says, "Therefore let those who suffer according to God's will entrust their souls to a faithful Creator while doing good."

What does it entail to unconditionally resolve to follow Jesus this way? Here are three aspects.

1. Committing to stand on the authority of God's Word without compromise.

2. Pursuing a life of faithful obedience to Jesus, including by seeking to maintain integrity in the "little things." (This is part of "living above reproach," as chapter 10 described.)
3. Making Jesus our life focus—the center of our priorities, identities, and pursuits—as "living sacrifices" to him (Romans 12:1).

Dr. James Coates, who was imprisoned in Canada for church-related activities, has shared compelling insights regarding this third aspect. When we interviewed Dr. and Mrs. Coates for our *Zero Compromise* podcast, one of my cohosts asked what helps Christians walk through persecution. How can believers stay committed to the authority of God's Word, love their enemies, and persevere amid hardships?

The Coates replied that the key is to live "a gospel-centered life" in all respects, fueled by a three-fold focus. First, we recognize that Jesus forgave the infinite debt we could never pay. Second, we remember that all humans await eternity **somewhere**—a reality that kindles in us both heavenly hope and earthly love for those without Christ. And third, we realize that through hardships, God grants us opportunities to share the gospel.

> **HOW CAN BELIEVERS STAY COMMITTED TO THE AUTHORITY OF GOD'S WORD, LOVE THEIR ENEMIES, AND PERSEVERE AMID HARDSHIPS?**

Dr. Coates added, "I think it's important to highlight that with the gospel, you give up your life." Through the gospel of Jesus, he said, we don't only gain eternity. We also lose our earthly lives. We lay them down to walk in obedience to Jesus through the power of God's Spirit, becoming increasingly like Jesus as we follow him. "The goal of it all," concluded Dr. Coates, is to be "perfectly conformed into his image, to be with him, and to behold his glory for all eternity."

An eternal focus reminds us that life on earth is just a short-term mission trip. The purpose of our time here isn't to be comfortable, pain free, wealthy, successful, or well received. Instead, God's Word reveals that love for God and for others—the kind of love defined by God himself—is what ultimately matters.[1] Love lasts forever,[2] human souls last forever, and eternity lasts forever. And matters of **eternal permanence** call for **earthly perseverance**, as Hebrews 10:32–36 exhorts:

> But recall the former days when, after you were enlightened, you endured a hard struggle with sufferings, sometimes being publicly exposed to reproach and affliction, and sometimes being partners with those so treated. For you had compassion on those in prison, and you joyfully accepted the plundering of your property, since you knew that you yourselves had a better possession and an abiding one. Therefore do not throw away your confidence, which has a great reward. For you have need of endurance, so that when you have done the will of God you may receive what is promised.

These concepts reflect the eternal perspective that Andrew Brunson pinpointed as essential for overcoming fear.[3] As breathing sacrifices who no longer live for ourselves,[4] we've already forfeited our claims to the earthly things we might fear losing. We can't keep them forever anyway, and anything we do give up for following God's will counts as a valuable love offering to him. Jesus said it best:

> Whoever loves father or mother more than me is not worthy of me, and whoever loves son or daughter more than me is not worthy of me. And whoever does not take his cross and follow me is not worthy of me. Whoever finds his life will lose it, and whoever loses his life for my sake will find it. (Matthew 10:37–39)

Granted, this message of denying ourselves, taking up our crosses, and following Jesus runs contrary to the most cherished values of our therapeutic culture. So does the reality that God's Word guarantees we'll experience trouble (John 16:33), persecution (2 Timothy 3:12), and hatred (John 15:18–19; 1 John 3:13). But what if letting go of our therapeutic culture's priorities freed us to live for a higher purpose—one we were **created** to pursue? We might come to fully glimpse how our culture's ambitions, like those of Paul's pharisaical culture, count as **less than worthless** compared to gaining Christ. In Paul's words,

> Indeed, I count everything as loss because of the surpassing worth of knowing Christ Jesus my Lord. For his sake I have suffered the loss of all things and count them as rubbish, in order that I may gain Christ and be found in him, not having a righteousness of my own that comes from the law, but that which comes through faith in Christ, the righteousness from God that depends on faith—that I may know him and the power of his resurrection, and may share his sufferings, becoming like him in his death, that by any means possible I may attain the resurrection from the dead. (Philippians 3:8–11)

With these declarations, Paul exemplified the gospel-centered life the Coates and Brunsons talked about. How does this kind of living look in practice? In answer,

Nik Ripkin offers a remarkable example from Christians in China, demonstrating why a fully surrendered, gospel-centered, eternity-focused life helps with overcoming fear.[5]

Ripkin had asked these believers to explain why Christianity threatens totalitarianism. The Christians replied by describing the kind of scenario that might unfold when a communist police officer confronts a house-church property owner. Every time the police threatened to take something away, the Christians reframed that threat in terms of their freedom in Christ. If their homes were taken, the Christians would be "free to trust God for shelter" and for sustenance. If the Christians were beaten, they would "be free to trust Jesus for healing." If they were imprisoned, they'd be free to share their hope in Christ with other prisoners. And if they were killed, they'd be free to live forever with Jesus.

> **EVERY TIME THE POLICE THREATENED TO TAKE SOMETHING AWAY, THE CHRISTIANS REFRAMED THAT THREAT.**

This example illustrates how when Christians resolve to follow Jesus unconditionally as Lord, remembering their lives belong completely to **him**, totalitarianism loses its absolute power. In response, the regime may kill believers' bodies for honoring Jesus as the highest authority. But when this happens, the believers have won. From an earthly perspective, they seem to have lost. Yet they've triumphed in the battle that matters most. As a result, they stand forever as overcomers, like the saints described in Revelation 12:11: "And they have conquered him by the blood of the Lamb and by the word of their testimony, for they loved not their lives even unto death."

The victorious part of that passage sounds great to me. The "self-denial to the point of death" part . . . not so much.

But as the verse suggests, victory and suffering often go together. This point brings us to the next lesson from persecuted Christians.

2. IT WILL BE HARD

When we interviewed the Brunsons on *Zero Compromise*, this comment from Dr. Brunson stood out to me: "Grace is not an anesthetic."[6] We can expect that persecution will be more difficult than we imagine. God does not promise that we will never face more hardships than we can handle.[7] Paul wrote in 2 Corinthians 1:8–9 during one set of troubles, "We were so utterly burdened beyond our strength that we despaired of life itself. Indeed, we felt that we had received the sentence of death. But that was to make us rely not on ourselves but on God who raises the dead."

On the plus side, Paul also wrote that **because** we humans are weak, we demonstrate God's power in a unique way. In 2 Corinthians 12:9–10, for instance, Paul famously relayed a time when God didn't answer a prayer in the way that Paul had hoped:

> But [God] said to me, "My grace is sufficient for you, for my power is made perfect in weakness." Therefore I will boast all the more gladly of my weaknesses, so that the power of Christ may rest upon me. For the sake of Christ, then, I am content with weaknesses, insults, hardships, persecutions, and calamities. For when I am weak, then I am strong.

Similarly, Paul was talking about contentment in all circumstances—even hardships—when he wrote, "I can do all things through him who strengthens me" (Philippians 4:13). Paul didn't sugarcoat the need for endurance in this process. Neither did Dr. Brunson, who advised Christians in *Prepare to Stand*:

> Pray for the grace of endurance. The truth is that underlying all our efforts is God's faithfulness. We could not endure on our own, and he doesn't ask us to. Ultimately, he carries us through. And we should rest in this. But let's not minimize that he expects us to exert ourselves to persevere—and that this can be very difficult and [push us] to our limits and even beyond. We must commit ourselves to persevere.[8]

Building that perseverance, observed Dr. Brunson, starts with "being faithful in the small things now."[9] Choosing faithfulness in everyday decisions that require a little self-denial **now** equips us to choose faithfulness in decisions demanding greater sacrifice **later**.

No sacrifice is especially pleasant. But the need to persevere through the difficulty doesn't suggest we just have to "buck up," "grin and bear it," or otherwise try squelching valid grief. In God's Word, an entire category of Psalms exists for lament. Lament is a legitimate response to a fallen world wracked with evil, suffering, and genuine injustices that God himself hates.[10] We rightfully long for the day when "he will wipe away every tear from their eyes, and death shall be no more, neither shall there be mourning, nor crying, nor pain anymore, for the former things have passed away" (Revelation 21:4). Meanwhile, torn by the shards of our sin-broken world, we join the psalmists and the martyrs of Revelation 6:10 in asking, "O Sovereign Lord . . . how long?"

LAMENT IS A LEGITIMATE RESPONSE TO A FALLEN WORLD.

God completely understands our pain. Jesus was "despised and rejected by men, a man of sorrows and acquainted with grief" (Isaiah 53:3). He experienced the anguish of Gethsemane. Fully God and fully man, Jesus fully felt an appropriate human response to the horrors he was about to endure. With drops of sweat like blood, he prayed, "Father, if you are willing, remove this cup from me. Nevertheless, not my will, but yours, be done" (Luke 22:42). As Hebrews 12:2 says, Jesus "who for the joy that was set before him endured the cross, despising the shame, and is seated at the right hand of the throne of God."

Part of Jesus' suffering required bearing the alienation of our sin, crying, "My God, my God, why have you forsaken me?" (Matthew 27:46). But because Jesus was forsaken, we who belong to him are not. Psalm 34:18 promises, "The LORD is near to the brokenhearted and saves the crushed in spirit." Amid the hurt, Psalm 62:8 assures us, "Trust in him at all times, O people; pour out your heart before him; God is a refuge for us."

BECAUSE JESUS WAS FORSAKEN, WE WHO BELONG TO HIM ARE NOT.

Personally, I still don't for a minute like the thought of walking through suffering, even for amazing payoffs. But when faced with the biblical truth that **following Jesus will be difficult**, I find encouragement from John 6. These verses quote Peter's words when Jesus' teachings became so challenging that many disciples started walking away. When Jesus asked his 12 followers if they wanted to leave as well, John recounts, "Simon Peter answered him, 'Lord, to whom shall we go? You have the words of eternal life, and we have believed, and have come to know, that you are the Holy One of God'" (John 6:68–69).

These verses helped me at university by reminding me that the certainty of my faith far outweighed the uncertainty of any questions my studies raised. The same verses also helped the Brunsons resolve to follow Jesus despite the costs, disappointments, and unanswered questions of persecution.[11]

The way home won't be easy. But as these verses remind us, there is no other way. Jesus assured his disciples in John 14:6, "I am the way, and the truth, and the life. No one comes to the Father except through me." He also guarantees his presence for every step (Matthew 28:20; Hebrews 13:5). Regardless of whether we always "feel him" with us, we know that we are never alone. We know that God has given us his Holy Spirit as our Helper.[12] And we know that God remains in sovereign control, working all things together for the good of those who love him (Romans 8:28).

We also know something else, which brings us to the third lesson from persecuted believers.

3. IT WILL BE WORTH IT

The truth is, no earthly price we could be called to pay comes anywhere close to the worth of the goal we're pursuing. Just ask the Apostle Paul. As we've seen, he was no stranger to suffering. Stoning, flogging, imprisonment, shipwreck, and other dramatic escapes for his life were only some of the highlights on his résumé.[13] Yet he declared with total confidence,

> So we do not lose heart. Though our outer self is wasting away, our inner self is being renewed day by day. For this light momentary affliction is preparing for us an eternal weight of glory beyond all comparison, as we look not to the things that are seen but to the things that are unseen. For the things that are seen are transient, but the things that are unseen are eternal. (2 Corinthians 4:16–18)

These verses encourage us to persevere in following Jesus, no matter the cost, because eternity is worth it. And most importantly, Jesus himself is worth it. Paul realized this truth when he spoke of counting everything else as loss to gain Christ (Philippians 3:8–11). Dr. Brunson realized this when he wrote the worship song described in chapter 9. And one of the persecuted believers Nik Ripkin spoke with realized this when admitting his greatest fear.[14]

This Christian confided that his worst nightmare was the prospect of his family being called to suffer the type of persecution he'd endured. But Nik Ripkin challenged him with the question "Is Jesus worth it?" Through his tears, the man soon concluded, "Jesus is worth it. He is worth my life, my wife's life, and He is worth the lives of my children!"[15]

SUMMING UP

Ultimately, Jesus is the rock to whom we must anchor our lives in preparation for the gathering storm. Preparation matters because, like the signs I saw in Berlin forewarned, tides of opposition to Christianity have risen under the banner of a false gospel. We've uncovered how this gospel draws from neo-Marxist messages, which rend society into villains and victims, coronating the latter's feelings as the authority for truth. These messages rest on a faulty worldview foundation that neglects God as our **Creator**, sin as our **problem**, and Jesus as our **Savior**. As a result, when the neo-Marxist "gospel" identifies (or exacerbates) real problems, it tends to propose destructive solutions.

While classical Marxism yielded systems of hard totalitarianism, neo-Marxism invites a softer tyranny. This soft totalitarianism features modified forms of societal control including cancel culture, social credit systems like ESG scores, and technological surveillance for "equity" training purposes.[16] Historical patterns of persecution, revolution, and church compromise offer today's Christians vital insights into the ways hostility under soft totalitarianism appears to be escalating.

Given the unsavory spiritual roots we unearthed beneath certain agendas relevant to these trends, we can expect the battle around us will only intensify. As Ephesians 6:12 reveals, "We do not wrestle against flesh and blood, but . . . against the spiritual forces of evil in the heavenly places." The destabilization of society's pillars, the rise of conditions leaving culture vulnerable to totalitarianism, and the reappearance of revolutionary strategies highlight earthly aspects of this battle. Christians will likely not **win** the battle in the sense of reclaiming a church-friendly society. But by God's grace, we can still **overcome** in ways that truly matter.

BY GOD'S GRACE, WE CAN STILL OVERCOME IN WAYS THAT TRULY MATTER.

Overcoming begins with committing to God's Word as our highest authority, which means choosing to side with Scripture wherever God's Word disagrees with our culture. From this biblical starting point, we can build strong spiritual, intellectual, and interpersonal foundations essential for weathering—and positively impacting—our hostile environments. These foundations will position us to walk as counterrevolutionary Christians who love our enemies, live above reproach, and overcome evil with good.

This kind of faithful living amid opposition will require embracing an eternal perspective grounded in an unconditional resolve to follow Jesus.

We can expect it will be hard.

But we know it will be worth it.

Jesus is worth it, eternity is worth it, and human souls are worth it. So persevering through persecution is worth it. Standing for truth is worth it. Walking in consistent integrity is worth it. Faithfulness is worth it, even if we never see the results.

Despite temporary appearances—and whether or not we live to see the outcome—we know day overcomes night, good overcomes evil, and truth overcomes lies. To stand with the overcomers, we need to stand with Jesus.

Jesus is victor.

ENDNOTES

1. See 1 Corinthians 13.

2. See 1 Corinthians 13:8–13.

3. See Andrew Brunson, "Prepare to Stand Session 2 – Overcoming Fear," Family Research Council, YouTube, June 7, 2022, youtube.com/watch?v=TJsn75mJ-3Q&list=PLmNx2j3x-22Q-I3HDk3hLaMg6X8-h7RoD&index=8.

4. See Romans 12:1 and 2 Corinthians 5:15.

5. Nik Ripken, *Insanity of God: A True Story of Faith Resurrected* (Nashville: B&H Publishing Group, 2013), 262–263.

6. Statement by Andrew Brunson, "He Was Sentenced to Prison for Life for Sharing the Gospel: Episode 013—Zero Compromise," *Zero Compromise*, YouTube, May 2, 2023, 7:55–8:00, youtube.com/watch?v=RZLKMA3E1_w&t=734s.

7. The closest God's Word comes to promise is in 1 Corinthians 10:13 that God "will not let you be tempted beyond your ability."

8. Andrew Brunson, "Prepare to Stand Session 5 – Building Perseverance," Family Research Council, YouTube, June 7, 2022, 16:00–16:34, youtube.com/watch?v=8u4vDBlC6C4&list=PLX54JHEGsMzPdjjzod_OmhlJTkL5T108R&index=9.

9. Andrew Brunson, "Prepare to Stand Session 5 – Building Perseverance," 15:28–16:00.

10. E.g., see Psalm 11:5; Proverbs 6:16–19, 11:2, 20:23.

11. See Andrew and Norine Brunson, "Prepare to Stand Session 8 – A Conversation Between Andrew and Norine," Family Research Council, YouTube, June 7, 2022, 23:05–24:20, youtube.com/watch?v=BET_nr3isHg&list=PLX54JHEGsMzPdjjzod_OmhlJTkL5T108R&index=8.

12. E.g., see John 14:16–26, 16:7–14; Luke 12:11–12.

13. See 2 Corinthians 11:23–28.

14. Ripkin, *Insanity of God*, 286–287.

15. Ripkin, *Insanity of God*, 286–287.

16. See chapter 1 for details.

ADDITIONAL PRACTICAL FOUNDATION-BUILDING TIPS + ANSWERING COMMON OBJECTIONS + KEY HISTORICAL FIGURES & EVENTS + GLOSSARY

APPENDICES: SUPPLEMENTARY TOOLS

APPENDIX A

PRACTICAL FOUNDATION-BUILDING TIPS

These ideas are based on tips originally presented in *Prepare to Thrive: A Survival Guide for Christian Students*. Here they have been adjusted from the context of student life to citizenship.

SPIRITUAL FOUNDATIONS

PRACTICAL TIPS FOR DIGGING DEEPER INTO SCRIPTURE

- Find a Bible reading plan that works for you—and stick with it.
- Try listening to an audio Bible or Scripture songs while going about other tasks.
- Make sure you're not missing out on reading the Old Testament (including parts that Sunday schools rarely cover).
- Set a goal to read the whole Bible if you haven't already.
- Join (or start) a solid Bible study group.

- Post Bible verses where you'll see them in your home, car, or office as daily reminders of truth.
- Tap into free Bible study tools, including online commentaries (just remember they're not themselves the inspired words of God).

PRACTICAL TIPS FOR MEMORIZING MORE SCRIPTURE

- Read it! In a Bible memorization program which I participated in as a teenager, a friend of mine developed a helpful chapter memorization tool she called the Five-Verse Method. She would read each verse five times, each paragraph five times, and the chapter five times until she'd learned the whole thing.
- Listen to it! As a Bible quizzer, I enjoyed listening to New Testament audio dramatizations to memorize passages. Sometimes I'd edit the audio files to repeat each verse several times. Then I'd go for a walk and listen to them.
- Say it! One tactic I've found especially useful is to combine the powers of repeated reading, listening, **and** speaking by recording myself saying each verse several times.
- Sing it! Setting verses to music, whether a song you like or a tune you invent yourself, helps you remember them long term.

PRACTICAL IDEAS FOR PEPPING UP YOUR PRAYER LIFE

- To help structure your designated prayer times, try posting prayers or prayer points near a specific place you like to pray or listing them in a notebook you can take with you anywhere.

- Try prayer journaling, where you tell God about your day and write him your thoughts.
- Start or join a prayer group. Praying with others can't replace your personal prayer times, but it **can** supply encouragement, support, and accountability.
- Post verses and quotes about the importance (and rewards) of prayer where you'll see them.
- Try turning thoughts, feelings, disappointments, joys, mental conversations, worries, or anything else you find on your mind into prayers. (This is also part of "taking every thought captive," as 2 Corinthians 10:5 mandates.)

PRACTICAL IDEAS TO "AMP UP" YOUR WORSHIP LIFE

- Tune into worship music throughout the day. Even playing instrumental background music while focused on other tasks lets your mind keep working while your spirit sings along.
- Try kicking off your daily prayer time with worship.
- Check yourself throughout the day: what song is in your head?
- Write out your favorite worship lyrics (Psalms count too) to post where you'll see them. Or if you're the creative type, try incorporating them into artwork.
- Take breaks from other tasks to sing or play an instrument.

PRACTICAL TIPS FOR IDENTITY AND PRIORITY CALIBRATION

- Pray for a Christ-centered focus in everyday life.

- Worship with lyrics which, like those in Dr. Brunson's song (see chapter 9), realign your focus to Jesus as your priority, identity, and reward.
- When studying Scripture, highlight or write down passages that reveal who you are in Christ.
- How do you think about who you are? Are you basing your identity in fading landmarks or in who Christ is, what he's done, and who he's created and called you to be?
- Watch the messages your mind plays about yourself, recalibrating them to Scripture as necessary.

PRACTICAL IDEAS FOR SETTING BOUNDARIES AND SEEKING WISDOM

- Think about various pressures or temptations today's culture presents. Study what Scripture says about each and consider a biblical response.
- Study how the Bible speaks to different controversial topics so you can graciously respond from **Scripture** rather than from secondhand convictions.
- Consider the nonnegotiables of your biblical worldview, ask someone to respond if they notice you compromising on those beliefs, and formulate a plan for handling questions and doubts.
- Bring godly family, friends, or mentors into your boundary setting and accountability plan so you know you're not standing alone.
- Read Proverbs to grow in wisdom. Conveniently, this Bible book includes 31 chapters—one for each day of the month.
- Learn from godly mentors. Anyone who's known God for years has likely stockpiled gems of wisdom to share.

- Read books by wise Christians who share what they've learned from years of life with Christ.
- Ask God for wisdom, read his Word expecting to find it, and write down what happens.

INTELLECTUAL FOUNDATIONS

PRACTICAL TIPS FOR LEARNING TO DEFEND A BIBLICAL WORLDVIEW

- Take advantage of apologetics resources from solid, biblical platforms like AnswersInGenesis.org and Answers TV.
- Try incorporating intellectual foundation-building into everyday life—for instance, by taking a few minutes a day to read about an apologetics topic or by listening to apologetics podcasts, videos, and audiobooks while performing routine tasks.
- Take time to learn basic answers to common apologetics questions, like "Did Jesus really claim to be God? Does evolution disprove the Bible? And if God exists, why is there death and suffering?" (AnswersInGenesis.org and *The New Answers Book* series are great places to start.)
- Remember not to hinge your faith on any one argument or apologist but in God and his Word.
- Learn how to sharpen your biblical critical thinking skills for responding to new information.[1]
- Beware that not all pro-Bible arguments may be logically sound (or even biblical). Apply biblical critical thinking even to faith-based sources, avoiding

weak apologetics arguments to present a thoroughly credible case.[2]

- Learn about unbiblical worldviews—while being wise. Accurately understanding non-Christian perspectives keeps us from being blindsided when we encounter other viewpoints and can help us share the gospel with others. However, if we expose ourselves continuously to the false messages of other worldviews, their lies may start to sound persuasive (even when we know they can't be true). That's why, when I studied science at a secular university to better understand evolution, I made sure to first have (and then continuously maintain) strong spiritual, intellectual, and interpersonal foundations—including a mentor. Earlier, when I was still just starting to build these foundations, I would learn about evolutionary arguments from godly sources by researching biblical **responses** to evolutionists.
- Find a biblically grounded mentor who can talk through apologetics topics with you, point you to solid resources, and follow up on remaining questions.

INTERPERSONAL FOUNDATIONS

PRACTICAL TIPS FOR BUILDING CHRISTIAN COMMUNITY NETWORKS

- Make sure you're plugged into a biblical local church committed to **believing**, **teaching**, and **living out** God's Word.[3]
- Consistently take (or make) opportunities to forge and strengthen friendships with godly believers.

- Use your God-given gifts to serve other Christians (or serve **alongside** other Christians) where you can, whether by joining an established ministry or by offering your strengths in a new way.
- Be wise who you spend time with (see Dr. Brunson's advice on that regard in chapter 9). Godly churches, friends, and small groups can be hard to find. There may always be aspects of a church or Christian group which aren't fully your style, but that doesn't necessarily mean the assembly is biblically compromised. Three questions can help you make a discerning decision: (1) Are there doctrinal issues within the leadership? (2) How is spending time here likely to impact my spiritual health? (3) Will my involvement with this group likely lead me to compromise?
- Pray that God would help you connect (or reconnect) with the right people, that he would guide your interactions, and that his will would be done in and through these relationships.
- Intentionally build intergenerational mentorship connections. A mentor is anyone willing to personally share valuable experience, knowledge, and insights that can benefit someone else—especially someone younger. To **be mentored**, you can seek opportunities to interact with and learn from older godly Christians who you'd like to emulate. To **be a mentor**, you can look for ways to encourage, support, and disciple younger people.[4]

PRACTICAL IDEAS FOR CHURCHES AND MINISTRY GROUPS TO PROMOTE INTERGENERATIONAL MENTORSHIP CONNECTIONS

- Provide service and leadership opportunities for young people to use their God-given gifts, passions, and ideas. Have older Christians available to support the youths' efforts.
- Approach trusted older adults about getting involved with youth or student ministries. For instance, older Christians could host Bible studies, become mentors, participate in a Q&A night, join students for outreach and prayer initiatives, or help with special events.
- Create opportunities for believers to share their testimonies with others. As a Christian student ministry leader in Holland described, a mentor can be anyone with a story of God's faithfulness to share.[5]
- Host monthly men's or women's events specifically designed to foster intergenerational relationships.
- Bring people from different age groups together for a series of sessions designed to encourage intergenerational connections and discipleship. These sessions might include time for Scripture study, discussion, intellectual foundation-building, application activities, and service projects.[6]
- Run mentorship initiatives to connect church members with students in their occupational or academic fields. For instance, a pastor in Dubai explained how a church he attended ran a program where business leaders from the congregation met weekly with senior-year students to equip them in matters of career and faith.
- Encourage the development of intergenerational small groups whenever possible.

ENDNOTES

1. Resources for doing this include Answers in Genesis' online *Critical Thinking Scan* course, the *Critical Thinking Scan* video series available on Answers TV, multiple articles related to logic and critical thinking at AnswersInGenesis.org, and part three of the book *Prepare to Thrive* (Hebron, KY: Answers in Genesis, 2022).

2. For examples of arguments to avoid, see AnswersInGenesis.org/creationism/arguments-to-avoid/.

3. While no church is *perfect*, you can find practical advice for what to look for in a good church in Scot Chadwick, "How to Find a Good Church," Answers in Genesis, April 30, 2018, AnswersInGenesis.org/church/how-to-find-good-church/.

4. For more information and ideas on becoming or finding a mentor, see "Why Mentorship Matters," Answers in Genesis, July 1, 2021, AnswersInGenesis.org/christianity/christian-life/why-mentorship-matters, and chapter 8 of *Prepare to Thrive* (Hebron, KY: Answers in Genesis, 2022).

5. See "360° in 180—What It Takes to Be a Mentor: A Conversation in Holland (Part 24)," Answers in Genesis, May 6, 2020, AnswersInGenesis.org/blogs/patricia-engler/2020/05/06/360-in-180-mentor-conversation-holland-part24/.

6. For a 15-week series of sessions geared toward intergenerational groups that include teens and young adults who might be considering secular college, see the *Prepare to Thrive Leader Guide* and *Prepare to Thrive Study Guide* available at AnswersInGenesis.org.

APPENDIX B

ANSWERING COMMON OBJECTIONS

This appendix provides responses to a few common objections Christians may face when discussing neo-Marxism, though it does not offer detailed rebuttals to every possible objection. The goal is to portray each objection briefly but accurately, sketching a reasoned response in biblical gentleness.

OBJECTION 1

"SOCIAL MARXISM IS A CONSPIRACY THEORY."

CLAIM

The idea that neo-Marxist movements and thinkers infiltrated Western social institutions to promote a "cultural revolution" is a conspiracy theory. Sure, institutions like the Frankfurt School may have drawn from some aspects of Marx's thinking, but reports of neo-Marxism's contemporary influence have been greatly exaggerated.

QUICK ANSWER

In order to say whether neo-Marxism's influence is a conspiracy theory, we first need to ask, "What **is** a conspiracy theory?" The *Merriam-Webster Dictionary* defines **conspiracy theory** as "a theory that explains an event or set of circumstances as the result of a secret plot by usually powerful conspirators."[1] This definition raises the question "What does 'theory' mean?"

In science, a theory is a broad explanation shown to be consistent with vast quantities of experimental data.[2] But when it comes to conspiracy theories, we usually mean **theory** in the sense of what the *Merriam-Webster Dictionary* calls "an unproved assumption" or "conjecture."[3] So a key step in identifying, evaluating, and responding to potential conspiracy theories is separating fact from conjecture.[4]

In this case, is the influence of neo-Marxism in Western societies an unproven assumption or conjecture? People do at times make unproven or exaggerated conjectures about topics related to neo-Marxism. For communication purposes, such speculation tends to be unhelpful and unnecessary. This book steers clear of unproven conjectures by striving to provide careful documentation wherever applicable, emphasizing a reliance on primary sources, and avoiding unsubstantiated sweeping speculations. The details presented here about the rise and reign of neo-Marxism in today's culture are not speculative theory but readily verifiable data.

OBJECTION 2

"NEO-MARXISM ISN'T REALLY MARXISM."

CLAIM

This book isn't really about Marxism. Neo-Marxists like the Frankfurt School thinkers not only critiqued Karl Marx but also held fundamentally different views from "classical" Marxism. For instance, Marx primarily focused on economics, emphasized material conditions over ideas as the forces that drive history, and believed in economic determinism. He thought socioeconomic conditions set a predetermined course for history, which **must** result in workers' revolutions that create communist societies. To abandon these concepts is to abandon Marxism. The neo-Marxists shared none of these core beliefs and even criticized communist societies that tried to implement classical Marxism.

QUICK ANSWER

As chapters 2 and 5 unpack, it's true that twentieth-century neo-Marxists generally rejected Marx's economic determinism. They returned to emphasizing the importance of not just outward material conditions but also inward ideas, emotions, and mental processes. And they often (though not always[5]) critiqued hard totalitarian communism. Neo-Marxists also tended to blend Marx's ideas with those of other thinkers, such as Sigmund Freud.

Although the neo-Marxists recognized the problems with some of Marx's core economic assumptions, **they kept many of his faulty worldview beliefs**.[6] For instance, the neo-Marxists reapplied Marx's basic ideas.

- History is the story of class conflict between oppressors vs. the oppressed.
- The present form of society is inherently oppressive.
- Humanity's hope lies in some form of reorganized society.
- The oppressed must actively work to bring about this new social order.

You might say that Marxists and neo-Marxists ultimately view society through the same "conflict-tinted" binoculars. These binoculars color **everyone** as either a powerful oppressor or a disempowered victim and **everything** as either sustaining or reversing this power imbalance. Marx had "zoomed in" his binoculars to focus on conflict between economic classes—specifically oppressive business owners vs. oppressed workers. Neo-Marxists picked up the **same binoculars** and widened the field of focus to encompass conflict between additional groups, such as men vs. women, "white" vs. "colored," and colonialist vs. indigenous.

This zoomed-out focus helps explain the main differences between Marx and neo-Marxists. Namely, the neo-Marxists no longer needed to describe history solely in Marx's narrow terms of materialistic economic determinism. But the neo-Marxists still used Marx's binoculars. Despite their differences with Marx, neo-Marxists, including Antonio Gramsci and the Frankfurt School founders, expressly based their beliefs on reformulations of Marx's thinking.[7] While it's important to recognize that neo-Marxism isn't identical to classical Marxism, it's also important to recognize the ways neo-Marxism shares basic tenets with—and historically stems from—Marx's worldview.

OBJECTION 3

"CRITICS OF MARXIST AND NEO-MARXIST WRITINGS JUST MISUNDERSTAND THESE WRITINGS."

CLAIM

People who critically cite Marxists or neo-Marxists tend to take quotes out of context, misunderstand the sources, or simply can't understand. This inability to understand may result from having "false consciousness" (thinking society is fine as it is) or from being an oppressor who cannot know the lived experience of the oppressed. For such reasons, critics of Marxism and neo-Marxism are generally wrong, despite their efforts to provide primary source documentation.

QUICK ANSWER

As ambassadors for Jesus, who **is** the truth (John 14:6), Christians are called to love the truth, to represent Christ well, and to practice "sound speech that cannot be condemned" (Titus 2:8). While unfortunately not everyone **applies** these standards consistently, Christian commentators on Marxism must strive to explain Marxist and neo-Marxist writings as accurately as possible.[8] This is not always easy, as these writings can be ambiguous, opaque, and tricky to pin down. Nearly two centuries after Marx lived, scholars of Marxism continue debating the details of what Marx himself believed—let alone different neo-Marxists. Despite these difficulties, maximum accuracy remains the goal.

Striving for accuracy requires taking time to seek sufficient familiarity with the other person's views. Doing so involves both examining the original sources' writings and, as necessary, reading other scholars' interpretations of these writings. Mistakes are always still possible, but that's where careful footnotes provide accountability. Quotations of longer works can only include so much of the original text in a limited space, but footnotes enable readers to verify the full quotes in their original contexts. If the quotes can be validly interpreted in multiple ways, or if other writings shed important light on the quotes, then thorough footnotes will include this information if it's available. Critiques that demonstrate a rigorous pursuit of accuracy, transparency, and verifiability by applying such standards are more difficult to summarily dismiss.

What about the claims that people who disagree with Marxist writings (despite careful reading) still inevitably (1) misinterpret them, (2) have "false consciousness," or (3) simply cannot understand? The first claim implies the Marxist writers **really** mean something different from what they **seem** to mean, and only their followers can understand. The second and third claims likewise suggest that only people who already wear Marxist worldview "glasses" are enlightened enough not to critique Marxist perspectives. Instead of functioning as persuasive arguments, each of these claims (and the glasses required to agree with them) must simply be accepted as a matter of faith.[9]

OBJECTION 4

"MARX WAS RIGHT IN MANY WAYS, BUT HIS IDEAS HAVE JUST BEEN MISAPPLIED."

Marx's core ideas were correct. The problem is that nobody has managed to implement these ideas in the right way to fully liberate society. For instance, nations that attempted communist revolutions in the past were not mature capitalistic societies ready for the kind of revolution Marx envisioned. Many other factors can help explain the problems of historical attempts at communism: the leaders too flawed, the regime's power too concentrated, the people too undermotivated, or the technology too undeveloped. With a few tweaks, and given today's technological powers, we could make a communist utopia work.

QUICK ANSWER

It's true that Marx made some perceptive observations. For instance, he drew attention to the destructiveness of greed, the significance of material realities, and the problems of exploitative working conditions during the Industrial Revolution.[10] It's also true that communist revolutions never played out the way Marx predicted. These revolutions didn't happen in developed capitalist societies; they didn't move beyond dictatorships, and they didn't liberate humanity—in fact, they precipitated the deaths of untold millions.[11]

Does all this mean Marx's ideas were simply misapplied? Or are these ideas—and their spinoffs—inherently flawed? In answer, Marx's beliefs contained deep internal flaws on two levels: faulty economic assumptions and faulty worldview beliefs. As chapter 2 noted:

> Regarding the first set of mistakes, Marx seemed to incorrectly assume history must progress along a certain path set by socioeconomic conditions. He ignored that many problems with Industrial Revolution capitalism are not necessarily built into all free market systems. And he overestimated how motivated real people would be to contribute to a

> collectivist society without directly getting much back for themselves in return.[12]

Law professor Ilya Somin has outlined a number of further problems with communist systems.[13] For instance, a lack of free markets leaves workers with "little incentive" to diligently produce goods suited to consumer needs, which market prices normally help producers to determine.[14] Somin also argued that even communist states that try to be democratic don't sustain democracy for long due to the inevitable suppression of other political parties. Worse, as chapter 2 of this book explained:

> But even more significant was Marx's shaky worldview foundation. Rejecting God's Word left Marx with a wrong view of humanity's nature, core problem, and redemptive hope. He mistakenly looked at real Industrial Revolution-era problems through the lens of this faulty worldview and proposed the wrong solutions.

There is no right way to build a society on a flawed foundation. A repeatedly attempted construction project that always starts with a faulty foundation will fail every time—easily harming people in the process. We must learn from history and build on a foundation of truth, the authority for which is our Creator's Word.[15]

OBJECTION 5

"CAPITALISM AND RELIGION HAVE DONE, AND CONTINUE TO DO, MORE DAMAGE THAN SOCIALISM EVER COULD."

CLAIM

Capitalism and religion (especially Judeo-Christianity) motivate immense evil—from historical examples of war, slavery, and violent colonization practices to current systems of discrimination, environmental destruction, and exploitative labor conditions. Capitalism also creates artificial "needs" that distract people from pursuing liberation from these harms. Although evils have also been committed in the name of Marxism, Judeo-Christianity and capitalism are the **real** enemies to defeat for humanity to make progress.

QUICK ANSWER

First, we can agree that evil is a problem. From a biblical worldview, Christians recognize wrongdoings, exploitation, and hypocrisy as grievous. It's grievous when people who identify as Christians commit great wrongs. It's grievous when people try citing Scripture—however incorrectly—to rationalize those wrongs. And it's grievous when people abuse capitalism by idolizing money, by entangling themselves and others in the "deceitfulness of riches" (Mark 4:19), or by prioritizing profits over God's image bearers.

With that common ground established, let's back up and think about worldview starting points. When we're evaluating a worldview based on its consequences, we need to look at the results of applying that worldview **consistently**—not inconsistently. Doing so requires examining what the worldview teaches holistically and considering what happens when people consistently live out those teachings. So let's think about the consistent application of a biblical worldview in contrast to Marxism-based worldviews.

As chapter 2 explains, a biblical worldview provides the foundation for truth, morality, human value, justice, and rights in the first place. God's Word lets us recognize that the issue behind problematic practices in capitalist societies is **sin**. Scripture also establishes mandates, principles, and paradigms that best enable human flourishing while adding "guardrails" to prevent abuses of these practices.

For example, passages throughout Scripture **support** the idea of people privately owning the resources they've worked for, inherited, or received as a gift, recognizing that God is the ultimate owner.[16] Scripture teaches how to use these resources for **good**—for instance, by practicing generosity and hospitality—while also forbidding sinful misuses of them, such as greed, covetousness, discontentment, bribery, usury, extortion, exploitation, oppression, and idolatry. Professing Christians who acted hypocritically in these regards were being **inconsistent** with a biblical worldview. Similarly, people who have killed or abused others in the name of Christianity were acting **contrary** to Jesus' teachings. But Christians who have sought to uphold the value of life, reform exploitative economic practices, and "love their neighbors as themselves" acted consistently with their worldview.[17]

In contrast, chapter 2 examined how the secular worldview behind Karl Marx's thinking lacked a solid foundation for truth, meaning, morality, justice, and human value. Secular worldviews allow for redefining morality in ways that permit abuses against innocent[18] human lives—while being consistent with secularism. For example, neo-Marxism allows for redefining truth and morality so that any violence that changes society's power balance in favor of oppressed groups can be considered "good." A similar redefinition of morality enabled the French revolutionaries to slay thousands of people in the name of "the greater good," as chapter 3 recounts. Atheistic communist regimes throughout the twentieth century likewise committed atrocities in line with their beliefs.

While these historical revolutionaries were not always acting consistently with some of the **ideals** they espoused, they nonetheless acted consistently with their secular **worldviews**, which did not provide a stable foundation for those ideals. A biblical worldview, by supplying that foundation along with "guardrails" against abuses, remains society's hope. God's Word offers the basis for achieving earthly progress. And most importantly, Scripture reveals the way to eternal redemption through Jesus.

OBJECTION 6
"SOCIALISM IS JUST ABOUT HELPING PEOPLE."

CLAIM

Socialism's primary goal is to help impoverished, exploited, and marginalized populations. Economic inequality has led to an unjustifiable gap between the extremely wealthy and the majority of the world's population. Socialism is the answer to an inherently unfair society.[19]

QUICK ANSWER

Helping the poor is an essential goal, as God's Word mandates loving others, bearing one another's burdens, and meeting earthly (as well as spiritual) needs.[20] But is that the real gist of socialism?[21] The *Merriam-Webster Dictionary*'s definitions of **socialism** focus on these elements:[22]

1. The "collective or governmental ownership and administration of the means of production and distribution of goods"
2. A "system of society or group living in which there is no private property" and in which "the means of production are owned and controlled by the state"
3. A transitional stage between capitalism and communism

The first two definitions overlap significantly with the dictionary's definition of communism—which, again, focuses on a system where people own goods in common, the state controls the means of producing goods, and private property may be eliminated.[23] If dictionary definitions are any indication, the real gist of socialism is **communism**. The question now becomes is communism the best or most effective way to help the poor?

The events of the twentieth century suggest otherwise. Marxism (and neo-Marxism) overwhelmingly tend to worsen the problems they're implemented to solve.[24] Again, there's no effective, lasting way to build a flourishing society on a faulty foundation.

If Marxism-based "solutions" are **not** the best (much less the only) way to help the poor, what **can** mitigate poverty? While analyzing the complex factors behind poverty—and cycles of poverty—goes beyond the scope of this discussion, one point is clear. To respond effectively to real problems, we need to begin from a true foundation: God's Word. The consistent application of a biblical worldview—which provides a foundation for combating poverty to begin with—is the starting point for genuine social progress.

OBJECTION 7

"MARXISM AND THE BIBLE ARE COMPATIBLE, IF NOT COMPLEMENTARY. THE BIBLE EVEN TEACHES A FORM OF SOCIALISM."

CLAIM

There is no need to choose between a Marxist worldview and a biblical worldview. Marxism (or neo-Marxism) and Christianity share many important overlaps. For instance, Old Testament gleaning laws required landowners to leave part of their crop to the poor. In the New Testament, the early church practiced a form of socialism, sharing their goods in common. Furthermore, social justice is a gospel issue. Marxism or neo-Marxism can be appropriate expressions of Christian concern for the oppressed.

QUICK ANSWER

On the surface, certain biblical and Marxist or neo-Marxist concepts might seem to overlap. Both worldviews affirm that exploitation, injustice, and poverty are problems and that combating these issues is morally right. One key issue is that although Marxism and Christianity use some similar **terms, the definitions or underlying meanings** of key words can often look very different.[25]

Even more foundationally, neo-Marxism and Christianity contradict at a worldview level. Chapter 2 summarizes just a few of these differences. For instance, God's Word reveals that humanity's core **problem** is sin. Scripture does call believers to alleviate sin's effects in the world by loving others, defending the vulnerable, and meeting earthly needs. But humanity's ultimate hope lies not in human effort but in redemption, reconciliation, and restoration through Jesus Christ.

Marxism, in contrast, teaches that social or economic conditions are humanity's core problem, with the solution being revolution—which may involve groups considered oppressed obtaining power at any cost. Chapter 5 also illustrated how, classically, neo-Marxism endorses an anti-biblical view of marriage, gender, and family.

The reality that Christianity and Marxism are very different worldviews helps explain why they define important concepts in vastly discordant ways. As chapter 5 unpacked, God's Word and Marxism teach different understandings not only of **justice** but also of **truth**, **morality**, **oppression**, and **guilt**. For example, neo-Marxism defines people as "bad" or "good"—guilty or innocent, oppressor or oppressed, sinner or saint—based on traits such as gender and skin tone. This redefinition of **guilt** helps explain why neo-Marxists interpret society's "sin condition" as a disbalance of power between oppressed and oppressor groups.

Neo-Marxism believes humanity's salvation from this "sin condition" demands breaking down the current society and rebuilding a new social order. The resulting transfer of power from oppressor to oppressed groups is considered "social justice." To support this version of justice, neo-Marxism redefines morality in terms of "whatever takes power away from 'oppressors.'" Along the way, neo-Marxism considers the authority for truth not to be God's Word but the inner feelings of the oppressed. These unbiblical redefinitions of guilt, sin, salvation, justice, morality, and truth illustrate how neo-Marxism teaches a different gospel from God's Word.[26] Social justice is not a **gospel** issue but a **false gospel** issue.

These differences in biblical and neo-Marxist **concepts** lead to further differences in **practice**. For instance, the Bible teaches people to practice generosity by voluntarily giving of their own wealth (which ultimately belongs to God).[27] This is what Zacchaeus, the formerly exploitative tax collector, did after he encountered Jesus (Luke 19:1–10). In drastic contrast, Marxism teaches people to practice "generosity" by confiscating **other** people's wealth.[28]

What about Old Testament harvest laws? These laws allowed landowners to gather in most of their harvests while tithing a portion and leaving a remnant available for the poor to diligently glean. This system assumed private control over the **means of** and **profits from** production and did not entail equal outcomes for everyone, regardless of personal diligence, motivation, or responsibility.[29] Clearly, such a society looks quite different from the dictionary definition of socialism described.

Not even the early church that "shared everything in common" biblically validates socialism. These early Christians shared their goods through voluntary generosity in a way that didn't involve state control. So the early church's practices are also not comparable with a contemporary understanding of socialism.

To recap, Marxism (including neo-Marxism) and Christianity significantly differ on three levels: **worldview, definitions**, and **practice**. Despite some overlapping terms, these two worldviews rest on incompatible foundations. As chapter 2 explains, today's form of Marxism represents one more battlefront in the ancient war of man's word vs. God's Word.

OBJECTION 8

"WHILE ON EARTH, JESUS PROMOTED AND PRACTICED EARLY FORMS OF SOCIALISM OR NEO-MARXISM. SO CHRISTIANS SHOULD TOO."

CLAIM

Jesus clearly stood on the side of the marginalized, exploited, and oppressed. He associated with sinners, Samaritans, and tax collectors. He affirmed the value of women. He told a rich man to sell everything and give to the poor. He opposed privileged religious rulers who were abusing their social power. He identified with the needy and imprisoned, saying that what we do for the least of these, we do for him. Jesus also quoted Isaiah 61 to reveal himself as the Messiah whom God anointed "to proclaim good news to the poor . . . liberty to the captives and recovering of sight to the blind, to set at liberty those who are oppressed" (Luke 4:18). In all these ways, Jesus advanced aspects of an early form of socialism or neo-Marxism—and so should his followers.

QUICK ANSWER

Most of this claim—at least until the last sentence—is completely biblical.[30] Jesus did associate with the marginalized, validate women's dignity,[31] and minister to **earthly** needs as part of his wider purpose to meet **spiritual** needs. He did oppose religious rulers who hypocritically prioritized human ideas above God's Word at the expense of God's image bearers. Jesus did counsel the rich young ruler to sell everything and give to the poor.[32] He does command us to serve "the least of these" in his name. And (praise

God) Jesus did identify himself as the anointed one—the Messiah—of Isaiah 61.

But does all this mean our Savior endorsed an early form of socialism or neo-Marxism?[33]

Jesus, the living Word of God, would not promote anything that contradicts the written Word of God. As we saw earlier, neo-Marxism revolves around worldview assumptions, definitions, and practices that **do** contradict God's Word. By fundamentally contradicting Scripture, neo-Marxism fundamentally opposes Jesus.

This opposition remains even though aspects of neo-Marxism may seem to align with Christ by expressing concern for liberating the oppressed—the language of Isaiah 61. The key issue, as we saw earlier, is that neo-Marxism uses words like **liberation**, **justice**, **oppression**, and **guilt** so differently from Scripture. Take liberation, for instance. Given the big picture of Jesus' mission revealed throughout Scripture, it's reasonable to think Jesus was primarily concerned with liberating people from **sin**.[34] Part of Jesus' ministry—healing diseases, raising the dead, driving out demons—did involve freeing people from instances of sin's oppressive hold on creation.[35] However, these miracles' ultimate purpose was to validate Jesus' power to liberate humanity—and ultimately creation—from **sin and its effects**.[36]

We see this ultimate purpose revealed from Genesis 3:15 to Revelation 21:14. The goal of liberating creation from sin provides the wider context for Jesus' earthly actions—including every example given to argue that Jesus endorsed socialism. We see his ultimate mission reflected in Jesus' words to Pilate: "My kingdom is not of this world. If my kingdom were of this world, my servants would have been fighting, that I might not be delivered over to the Jews. But my kingdom is not from the world" (John 18:36). Contrary to popular expectations among first-century Jews, Jesus had **not** come to lead a revolution against the truly oppressive power of Rome. He came—ultimately—to liberate his image bearers from the oppression of sin.

At a practical level, Jesus' actions affirm his primary concern was not about earthly socioeconomic conditions, power dynamics, or coercive wealth redistribution.[37] For example, Luke's Gospel records that a man once asked Jesus, "Teacher, tell my brother to divide the inheritance with me." Although this man was presumably entitled to economic equality with his brother, Luke records that Jesus answered, "Man, who made me a judge or arbitrator over you?" Jesus then declared, "Take care, and be on your guard against all covetousness, for one's life does not consist in the abundance of his possessions" (Luke 12:13–15). Jesus clearly cares about people's earthly needs but did not suggest—or enforce—the idea of necessarily equal economic outcomes.

Jesus' practices differ from socialism and neo-Marxism in other respects as well. For instance, while neo-Marxism demands partiality toward groups considered oppressed, Jesus, being God, shows no partiality.[38] Jesus did not solely befriend, benefit, or minister to the poor. He also ministered to noblemen, rulers, and a centurion—who, despite showing love to the Jews, was a powerful, privileged representative of the oppressive Romans.[39] Jesus additionally befriended tax collectors like Zacchaeus, who were marginalized **because** other Jews (often with good reason) considered them to be traitorous, wealthy oppressors.[40]

Zacchaeus' response to meeting Jesus illustrates how the gospel is the solution to genuine oppression. Jesus, who was not himself a revolutionary, offers the real liberation that earthly revolutions consistently fail to deliver. One day, Jesus will return as the triumphant warrior king and reign in genuine justice. He will create a new heaven and earth, where the oppressive effects of sin will be no more. Meanwhile, Jesus commands us to live out our faith by being like him and loving others—including by defending the vulnerable, speaking for the voiceless, and meeting earthly needs (Matthew 25:31–46).[41] All these practices help mitigate the effects of our fallen world and point toward Jesus' reign in the restored creation.

Christians **rightfully emphasize** these practices, which neo-Marxism has hijacked for its own agenda by using the similar-sounding—but differently defined—language of "justice" and "liberation." As we practice biblical justice, we must be careful not to fall for this hijacking. Following Jesus will never mean endorsing a worldview that opposes him.

OBJECTION 9
"THIS BOOK IS OPPRESSIVE."

CLAIM

By defending authority structures like the church, the family, and marriage, this book contributes to sustaining an inherently unjust status quo and is therefore oppressive.

QUICK ANSWER

Whether we see institutions like the family as oppressive social constructs or as God-given paradigms for human flourishing comes down to our worldview "glasses." A person wearing Marxist glasses will see everything as either sustaining oppression or working toward liberation (revolution). Meanwhile, someone with biblical glasses will interpret reality through the lens of God's Word. The question is which glasses are best?

In answer, we can evaluate a worldview based on three factors.[42]

1. INTERNAL CONSISTENCY

How well does the worldview support **itself**? For instance, does the worldview contradict itself by relying on concepts it can't self-consistently explain? Does embracing the worldview require people to accept—or **act** as though they accept—conflicting ideas that cannot be reconciled within the worldview's own framework?

2. EXTERNAL CONSISTENCY

How well does the worldview match what we see in the real world? Is the worldview consistent with observational science? Does history unfold in the ways this worldview's teachings predict?

3. CONSEQUENCES OF CONSISTENT APPLICATION

What would (or could) happen if people always acted as if the worldview were entirely true? (Notably, the consequences of believing a message don't necessarily tell us whether that message is true. So evaluating a worldview's consequences may not matter on a **theoretical** level but clearly matters on a **practical** level as people live out their beliefs.)

Let's briefly apply these tests to check how secular Marxist worldviews compare with God's Word. As chapter 2 described, secular worldviews lack a consistent, ultimate foundation for concepts like truth, morality, and logic. Secular worldviews must borrow these ideas from outside of themselves, failing the internal consistency test. Secular worldviews that rely on evolution, as Karl Marx did, also run into problems with **external consistency** by contradicting observational science.[43] Classical Marxism also failed to accurately predict real-world history, leading to neo-Marxist revisions.

What about consequences? We can glimpse the consequences of Marxist-based worldviews by thinking about what happens when people redefine truth, morality, goodness, and human value in revolutionary terms. "Truth," according to neo-Marxism, is whatever the feelings and lived experience of oppressed groups dictates. "Morality" is whatever changes the power balance. "Goodness" can equate to violence (not to mention oppression) if that's what the revolution needs. As a result, everything from riots to book burnings to vandalism to the destruction of churches can now qualify as "social justice."[44]

Neo-Marxism also assumes a low view of certain humans—whomever neo-Marxism judges as *oppressors* based on discriminatory factors like gender and skin tone. Neo-Marxist movements that espouse radical environmentalism may even view *all* humans as a "blight on the earth."[45] Altogether, these shaky conceptions of truth, morality, and human value add up to a precarious social equation—as multiple historical case studies illustrate.[46]

In contrast, a biblical worldview alone passes all three tests. God's Word is internally consistent, providing a self-sufficient foundation for truth, morality, justice, logic, knowledge, scientific reasoning, human value, and corresponding human rights. Scripture not only aligns with observational science but also accurately records and predicts history.[47] When consistently applied, a biblical worldview also accords with human flourishing—as research,[48] history,[49] and lives transformed by the gospel repeatedly attest.

A biblical worldview sees all human beings as God's image bearers worthy of respect. It sees the natural environment as a gift to steward wisely. It sees economic assets as resources to give generously, invest diligently, and enjoy with contented thanksgiving. It sees our fallen world and sinful natures realistically, setting appropriate "guardrails" to prevent abuses while allowing optimal freedoms in accordance with our God-given designs. The very opposite of oppressive, a biblical view summons humans to abundant life in Jesus Christ.

ENDNOTES

1. *Merriam-Webster.com Dictionary*, s.v. “Conspiracy Theory,” accessed July 26, 2024, merriam-webster.com/dictionary/conspiracy%20theory.

2. Incidentally, the story of evolutionary origins is inconsistent with much observational data, so it should not be called a “theory.” See “Evolution: Not Even a Theory,” Answers in Genesis, AnswersInGenesis.org/theory-of-evolution/evolution-not-even-theory/.

3. See *Merriam-Webster.com Dictionary*, s.v. “Theory,” accessed July 26, 2024, merriam-webster.com/dictionary/theory.

4. For instance, an article in the journal *Social Identities* claimed that declaring “the Frankfurt School was involved in a deliberate and covert plot to undermine Western civilization” is a conspiracy theory (Rachel Busbridge, Benjamin Moffitt, and Joshua Thorburn, “Cultural Marxism: Far-Right Conspiracy Theory in Australia’s Culture Wars,” *Social Identities* 26, no. 6 [2020]: 722–738). Similarly, another article stated, “According to the conspiracy theory . . . the Frankfurt School implemented a slow takeover of ‘culture,’ seeking to undermine Christianity, family, and nation in favor of a new worldview and system of control, involving mass immigration, sexual liberation, and moral and aesthetic decline. Cultural Marxists, the conspiracy theorists believe, now control all areas of public life, including the media, schools, entertainment, the economy, and national and global systems of governance” (Joan Braune, “Who’s Afraid of the Frankfurt School? ‘Cultural Marxism’ as an Antisemitic Conspiracy Theory,” *Journal of Social Justice* 9, no. 1 [2019]: 1–25). These critiques illustrate the unhelpfulness of making sweeping, oversimplified claims (for instance, pinning everything solely on the Frankfurt School) in conspiratorial terms without appropriate substantiation, nuance, and qualification. A more helpful approach is to supply careful documentation that people can use to reason for themselves about which elements of the above claims are supported by data and which are indeed exaggerations or conjectures.

5. For instance, as chapters 5 and 6 note, the Frankfurt School thinker Herbert Marcuse strongly critiqued the Soviet Union; however, the neo-Marxist existentialist philosopher Jean-Paul Sartre vocally supported hard totalitarian communist regimes until the Soviet invasion of Hungary (Gary Gutting, *French Philosophy in the Twentieth Century* [Cambridge: Cambridge University Press, 2001], 126).

6. Table 1 in chapter 2 summarizes just a few of these. See also the discussion under objection 7 below.

7. Details and references are available in chapter 5.

8. For examples of one such inconsistency and how to avoid it, see Steve Golden, “What Are the Dangers of Quote Mining?” Answers in Genesis, March 1, 2017, AnswersInGenesis.org/is-the-bible-true/what-are-dangers-quote-mining/.

9. For discussions of whether Marxism is the most reasonable worldview in which to put one’s faith, please see chapter 2 and objection 9 below.

10. Interestingly, a biblical view—with its moral foundation and its emphasis on the importance of the physical as well as the spiritual, contrary to first-century gnostics—is what allows these observations to make sense in the first place. (And notably, to acknowledge certain accuracies within Marx’s ideas is not to miss their inaccuracies—for instance, a deterministic overemphasis on the role of material conditions at the expense of ideas and internal conditions.)

11. While the numbers are staggering in any calculation, estimates of exactly *how many* millions vary, depending on factors such as what types of deaths are included—e.g., civilian deaths from starvation versus political deaths of prisoners, protesters, dissidents, and others labeled “enemies of the state.”

12. Further explanation and references are available in the footnotes of chapter 2.

13. Ilya Somin, "Lessons from a Century of Communism," *The Washington Post*, November 7, 2017, washingtonpost.com/news/volokh-conspiracy/wp/2017/11/07/lessons-from-a-century-of-communism/. (Please read with appropriate discernment; reader discretion is advised due to some language.)

14. Regarding pricing, perhaps today's technological abilities for widespread monitoring, tracking, and data collection could help fill in certain details of consumer needs in the absence of a pricing system—but at significant costs to the type of privacy traditionally considered a right in many free countries. Digital surveillance of consumers has already cast a shadow on that right, as chapter 7 describes, but not without ongoing, well-justified pushback. And regarding worker incentives, soft-totalitarian incentivization methods (including social credit systems, which could also be proposed should automation substantially reduce the need for human workers) tend to entail types of manipulation, coercion, and control more characteristic of *dystopias* than *utopias*.

15. This is *not* a suggestion that Western nations be forcibly turned into theocracies but a reminder that individuals, families, and societies will generally flourish best the more closely they choose to align their mentalities and practices with God's Word.

16. E.g., Exodus 20:15–17 (c.f. Leviticus 25:23); Ecclesiastes 5:18–19; Ephesians 4:28.

17. A few famous historical examples of such reformers in England include William Wilberforce, Hannah Moore, and Lord Shaftesbury. More information is available in Eric Metaxas, *Amazing Grace: William Wilberforce and the Heroic Campaign to End Slavery* (Grand Rapids, MI: Zondervan, 2007); Eric Metaxas, *Seven Women: And the Secret of Their Greatness* (Nashville: Thomas Nelson, 2015); and David Furse-Roberts, *The Making of a Tory Evangelical: Lord Shaftesbury and the Evolving Character of Victorian Evangelicalism* (Eugene, OR: Wipf and Stock, 2019). See also Alvin Schmidt, *Under the Influence: How Christianity Transformed Civilization* (Grand Rapids, MI: Zondervan, 2001).

18. Of course, not innocent in the sense of being untainted by the curse of sin but innocent in the sense of not having committed a crime that deserves punishment from another sinful human being in order to uphold specific standards of justice established by a holy God.

19. While not the focus of the answer to this claim, it's worth pointing out that *fairness* is an important term to define. For instance, does "fairness" mean "equal *opportunity* for people to—if at all possible, under the relevant circumstances—work hard and get rewarded"? Or does "fairness" mean a right to *equal outcomes* for everyone, regardless of whether individuals choose to exercise responsibility in accordance with the opportunities available to them? If the latter is the case, would establishing equal outcomes across the board by coercive—even forceful or violent—means, regardless of the varied and complex reasons for the original differences in wealth, still qualify as fairness? What sorts of consequences would logically flow from life in such a society?

20. E.g., Matthew 25:31–46; John 13:34–35; James 2:8–16.

21. This response considers socialism as a whole, the way the term *socialism* is used in the objection, rather than evaluating individual policies sometimes associated or conflated with "socialism."

22. *Merriam-Webster.com Dictionary*, s.v. "Socialism," accessed July 26, 2024, merriam-webster.com/dictionary/socialism.

23. *Merriam-Webster.com Dictionary*, s.v. "Communism," accessed July 26, 2024, merriam-webster.com/dictionary/communism.

24. Regarding Marxism, an early analysis of the plight of the poor under communism is available in Nick Eberstadt, *The Poverty of Communism* (New York: Routledge, 2017, first published by Transaction Publishers in 1988). (Please read his remarks on abortion in communist countries with biblical discernment.) Regarding neo-Marxism, a table of studies suggesting that diversity, inclusion, and equity interventions either *decrease or fail* to increase "tolerance" is available in David Millard Haskell, "What

DEI Research Concludes About Diversity Training: It Is Divisive, Counter-Productive, and Unnecessary," Aristotle Foundation for Public Policy, February 12, 2024, aristotlefoundation.org/reality-check/what-dei-research-concludes-about-diversity-training-it-is-divisive-counter-productive-and-unnecessary/. See also Patrick Forscher et al., "A Meta-Analysis of Procedures to Change Implicit Measures," *Journal of Personality and Social Psychology* 117, no. 3 (2019): 522. Forscher et al.'s analysis of 492 studies involving over 87,000 participants suggests that implicit bias interventions are largely ineffectual.

25. For instance, chapter 5 described some important discrepancies between how God's Word and neo-Marxism understand the concept of "justice."

26. Chapters 2 and 5 flesh out these concepts in greater detail.

27. See also "Does the Bible Teach Socialism?" in Erwin Lutzer, *We Will Not Be Silenced: Responding Courageously to Our Culture's Assault on Christianity* (Eugene, OR: Harvest House Publishers, 2020).

28. Others have pointed this out in different terms. See also Axel Weber, "Why True Charity Can Only Blossom Under Capitalism," Foundation for Economic Education, September 19, 2023, fee.org/articles/why-true-charity-can-only-blossom-under-capitalism.

29. To acknowledge the importance of personal responsibility is not to imply that diligence is the only factor involved in wealth or that poverty is always easy to escape with enough effort and initiative.

30. An exception being that Jesus did not stand on the side of anyone in a sense that would involve partiality, as will be discussed below.

31. For instance, against the backdrop of a society which tended to comparatively devalue women, Jesus taught a Samaritan woman (John 4:7–26), traveled with women (Luke 8:1–3), and sent women as the first witnesses of his resurrection (Matthew 28:10).

32. A case can be made that Jesus was highlighting the ruler's need for a priority reset. The ruler's reaction shows that he was placing wealth before God, which is idolatry. The Gospels depict Jesus encountering various people of earthly means, nobility, or power (besides the hypocritical religious rulers, who also needed a priority reset) without commanding them to renounce their "privilege" or to change society's power balance. A Christ-follower who loves God will obey God's commands to love others (John 14:15), including by voluntarily practicing good works and generosity, as Zacchaeus did. None of this suggests the Gospels advocate for state control of resources, coercive wealth redistribution, or neo-Marxist conceptual redefinitions.

33. Because a previous section addressed the claim that socialism is all about helping people—which in itself is a Christlike goal—this section will primarily focus on the broader worldview of Marxism and neo-Marxism.

34. This does not negate—but rather establishes the broader context for—Jesus' evident concern with liberation from sin's earthly effects, as discussed below.

35. That is, effects like death and suffering which highlight the reality that we live in a sin-broken world. See Genesis 3:1–24; Romans 8:22; 1 Corinthians 15:21–26, 54–57.

36. See, for instance, Matthew 11:2–5.

37. This is true even though Jesus promoted voluntary giving as a way to love others and invest treasure in heaven—again, showing the importance of eternal priorities (Luke 12:32–34).

38. See Acts 10:34–35; Romans 2:11; Colossians 3:25; c.f. Exodus 23:3; Leviticus 19:15; Deuteronomy 1:16–17. Some may argue that God showed "partiality" by revealing salvation from sin and its effects to the Jews before the Gentiles, exemplified in Matthew 15:21–28. However, Romans 2:6–11 twice mentions "the Jew first and also the Greek" *in the context of God's impartiality*, affirming that God's impartiality is compatible with his revelatory, redemptive, and judicial timeline.

39. E.g., see John 4:46–54; Luke 7:1–10, 8:40–56. It's also interesting to note that in Luke 7, Jesus helped the centurion by healing this Roman's servant—presumably not for the purpose of thereby enabling the servant to take back power from the centurion and join a revolution against Rome.

40. For Zacchaeus, who apparently had been oppressing others (in the biblical sense of the word *oppression*), meeting Jesus transformed him into someone who voluntarily gave of his resources to correct the wrongs he'd personally committed. The gospel, not state coercion, changes hearts (Luke 19:1–10).

41. As the answer to objection 6 described, these practices are not the same as socialism, and socialism is not the best way to achieve them.

42. Notably, this answer assumes the theoretical reality and practical importance of logic, which is founded on a biblical worldview (more on that in chapter 2). Certain forms of neo-Marxism critique logic itself as oppressive and therefore as invalid. Besides the irony that this critique itself depends on the existence of logic, dismissing logic's relevance for human life and society entails clear practical problems. Even mere survival requires relying on certain principles of logic like cause and effect.

43. For more information, visit AnswersInGenesis.org.

44. Chapters 5 and 8 cite varied examples of headlines illustrating these consequences.

45. Notably, atheistic, materialistic worldviews do not provide foundational reasons for why we should care about the earth, the oppressed, or anything else. Such worldviews cannot explain immaterial concepts like "justice" except in terms of a material realm which is ultimately meaningless.

46. Totalitarian regimes of the twentieth century provide numerous examples of secularism consistently applied. Chapter 3 also offers the French Revolution as a case study of what logically happens when revolutionaries consistently live out a secular worldview—even with noble intentions, even in the name of the greater good, and even with declared (albeit foundationless) ideals of human rights, justice, and doing no harm.

47. For just a few examples, see AnswersInGenesis.org/bible-history/; Dan Hayden, "Fulfilled Prophecy," *Answers* 6, no. 2, April–June 2011, AnswersInGenesis.org/is-the-bible-true/4-fulfilled-prophecy/; and Clive Anderson and Brian Edwards, *Evidence for the Bible* (Green Forest, AR: Master Books, 2018).

48. For example, reports from the Institute for Family Studies (IFS) document how the biblical institution of marriage is linked to higher personal well-being and lower crime. (See Rafael Mangual et al., *Stronger Families, Safer Streets: Exploring Links Between Family Structure and Crime*, IFS, December 2023, ifstudies.org/ifs-admin/resources/reports/ifs-strongerfamilies-final-1.pdf; Brad Wilcox, "Who Is Happiest? Married Mothers and Fathers, Per the Latest General Social Survey," IFS, September 12, 2023, ifstudies.org/blog/who-is-happiest-married-mothers-and-fathers-per-the-latest-general-social-survey; and Jonathan Rothwell, "Married People Are Living Their Best Lives," IFS, February 9, 2024, ifstudies.org/blog/married-people-are-living-their-best-lives.)

49. The central role of a biblical worldview in the rise of modern science, medicine, and education, as well as in the abolition of Britain's legalized slave trade, offer just a few examples. E.g., see Alvin Schmidt, *Under the Influence: How Christianity Transformed Civilization* (Grand Rapids, MI: Zondervan, 2001).

APPENDIX C

KEY HISTORICAL FIGURES & EVENTS

This is a list of key figures and events discussed in the book. It is not meant to be an exhaustive catalog of all historical figures and events relevant to Marxism or today's neo-Marxist culture. Bold terms refer to other concepts, people, or events listed here or in the Glossary.

HISTORICAL FIGURES

BAILEY, ALICE (1880–1949)

An influential Theosophist who founded the Lucis Trust organization and advocated for a spiritualized version of "true communism." Bailey taught that a "planetary Hierarchy" of (deceptive) spiritual entities planned to lead humanity into an "**Age of Aquarius**" involving a more collectivistic world order. (See also **Theosophy**.)

BESANT, ANNIE (1847–1933)

A committed socialist, social Darwinist, and eugenicist who served as president of the Theosophical Society. (See also **Theosophy**.)

BLAKE, WILLIAM (1757–1827)

An English Romantic poet who believed the church is an oppressive force that suppresses "free" sexual expression. (See also Romanticism.)

BLAVATSKY, HELENA (1831–1891)

One of the most influential founding leaders of Theosophy. Blavatsky communicated with deceptive spiritual entities, taught a spiritualized version of evolutionary thinking, and helped popularize Eastern spiritual practices in the West.

DARWIN, CHARLES (1809–1882)

The English biology enthusiast who famously popularized the idea that all living things evolved naturally from common ancestors.

DIOCLETIAN (C. AD 245–316)

A Roman emperor who spearheaded the "**Great Persecution**" against Christians.

ENGELS, FRIEDRICH (1820–1895)

Karl Marx's friend, supporter, and coauthor of *The Manifesto of the Communist Party*.

FIRESTONE, SHULAMITH (1945–2012)

A neo-Marxist feminist who, believing that the family is the main source of society's problems, called for a sexual and socialist revolution that would create a new society without concepts such as marriage, childhood, or (to a large extent) sexual mores.

FOURIER, CHARLES (1772–1837)

A utopian socialist credited with coining the word *feminism*. (See also **utopian socialism**.)

FREIRE, PAULO (1921–1997)

A Brazilian neo-Marxist who had a (literally) radical impact on multiple countries' education systems. Believing that education either *sustains oppression or promotes revolution*, he essentially taught that schools should serve as neo-Marxist discipleship centers.

FREUD, SIGMUND (1856-1939)

The pioneering psychoanalyst who speculated that human behavior is largely controlled by unconscious processes and repressed motives—especially sexual ones.

FROMM, ERICH (1900-1980)

A German psychoanalyst and socialist who was involved in the **Frankfurt School**. (See also **psychoanalysis**.)

GRAMSCI, ANTONIO (1891-1937)

An influential neo-Marxist and leader of the Communist Party of Italy. While imprisoned in Southern Italy, Gramsci wrote down his beliefs that the mainstream groups in a culture use their power to subjugate other groups and that a successful *political* revolution would first require a type of *cultural* revolution.

HEGEL, FRIEDRICH (1770-1831)

A German philosopher who significantly influenced **Karl Marx**'s thinking when Marx was a university student. Hegel believed that ideas drive history and that the material world is part of a (capital-I) Idea in the process of coming to grips with itself as being "the Absolute." Marx later turned Hegel's reasoning around to suggest that *material realities* are the most important force driving history.

HORKHEIMER, MAX (1895–1973)

The **Frankfurt School**'s second leader, who headed the "Studies on Authority and Family" project that critiqued the family as an oppressive social construct.

LENIN, VLADIMIR (1870–1924)

The first leader of the Soviet Union and the head of the Russian communist group known as the **Bolsheviks**.

MARCUSE, HERBERT (1898–1979)

An influential member of the **Frankfurt School** who viewed "freedom" in terms of sexual licentiousness and seemed to advocate for a version of "tolerance" based on *intolerance*.

MARX, KARL (1818–1883)

The German philosopher best known for popularizing communism.

OWEN, ROBERT (1771–1858)

A utopian socialist who promoted a form of global socialism based on the abolition of the family. Owen stated these ideas had been endorsed by séance spirits. (See also **utopian socialism**.)

REICH, WILHELM (1897–1957)

A German psychoanalyst who briefly assisted the **Frankfurt School** and who viewed the concept of *oppression* through a Freudian lens. (See also **psychoanalysis** and **Sigmund Freud**.)

ROUSSEAU, JEAN JACQUES (1712–1778)

A Swiss-born philosopher who promoted the idea that feelings are the authority for truth—including the truth about who we are and how we should live.

SHELLEY, PERCY BYSSHE (1792–1822)

An English Romantic poet who experimented with a version of evolutionary thinking, endorsed "free love," and called for the overthrow of existing society. (See also **Romanticism**.)

SOLZHENITSYN, ALEKSANDR (1918–2008)

A Russian dissident who publicized the oppressiveness of Soviet **communism** through his Nobel Prize-winning book, *The Gulag Archipelago*.

TEILHARD DE CHARDIN, PIERRE (1881–1955)

An evolutionary paleontologist, Jesuit priest, and forerunner of New Ageism who believed a process called *planetization* would advance human evolution to an "Omega Point" of "godlike" consciousness.

KEY EVENTS

THE GREAT PERSECUTION (C. AD 303–313)

A period of especially severe pressure and violence against Christians in ancient Rome under **Emperor Diocletian**.

THE RENAISSANCE (1400–1600)

A cultural movement in Europe marked by the "rebirth" of interest in pagan philosophy.

THE PROTESTANT REFORMATION (1517–1600s)

A movement among European Christians marked by a desire to return to God's Word as the church's final authority.

THE "ENLIGHTENMENT" (MID 1600s–LATE 1700s)

A cultural movement in Europe marked by the widespread turn toward human reasoning rather than God's Word as the authority for truth.

THE FRENCH REVOLUTION (1789–1799)

A revolt by France's middle class against the French aristocracy, violently ending France's monarchical government.

THE RUSSIAN REVOLUTION (1917)

A series of events that forcibly transitioned Russia from monarchism to communism. In the initial "February Revolution," violent public protests drove the tsar to abdicate, leaving a "provisional government." Communist armies overthrew this government in the "October Revolution," resulting in a dictatorship under the **Bolshevik** party's leader, **Vladimir Lenin**.

THE CANDLELIGHT DEMONSTRATION (1988)

A peaceful protest against communism in Bratislava, where thousands gathered to light candles, pray, and sing—a risky event that helped to spark the **Velvet Revolution**.

THE VELVET REVOLUTION (1989)

A massive protest movement that helped to topple decades of hard **totalitarianism** in Czechoslovakia.

THE FALL OF THE BERLIN WALL (1989)

The event that marked the end of East German **communism** after weeks of peaceful protest marches—and years of prayer.

MAP OF KEY EUROPEAN CITIES

This map highlights key European cities mentioned in the book. It is not intended to be an exhaustive atlas of all places relevant to the history of neo-Marxism.

GERMANY

1 BERLIN

2 TRIER

3 FRANKFURT

4 BAUTZEN

CZECHIA

5 PRAGUE

SLOVAKIA

6 BRATISLAVA

ITALY

7 ROME

8 TURI

FRANCE

9 PARIS

AUSTRIA

10 VIENNA

SWITZERLAND

11 ST. PETER'S ISLAND

APPENDIX D

GLOSSARY

This guide provides explanations for selected key words used throughout the book. However, it is not an exhaustive catalog of all relevant terms. Bold terms refer to other concepts, people, or occurrences described here or in the list of historical characters and events.

ACCESS ECONOMY (SEE ALSO SHARING ECONOMY)

An economic system that emphasizes *access* to shared goods over *ownership* of private goods. Access to goods and services may be based on social credit. (See **social credit systems**.)

AGE OF AQUARIUS

A "New Age" when, according to Theosophist **Alice Bailey**, the "old forms of religion, politics, and of the social order" would give way to a more collectivistic "new order."[1] (See also **theosophy**.)

APOLOGETICS

The field of study and practice focused on logically defending a biblical **worldview**.

ATOMIZATION

A process that disconnects or distances humans from one another, producing a society of isolated individuals who are more vulnerable to manipulation and control.

AUTHORITARIANISM (DICTATORSHIP)

A system of governance where one person or elite group holds all the political power, without the people who are governed having a say in what happens.

BIODIGITAL CONVERGENCE

A widespread merging of technology with living things.

BIOTECHNOLOGIES

Technologies that utilize, engineer, or incorporate biological elements such as genes, cells, organs, and embryos. (Examples include genetic modification, artificial reproductive technologies, and **brain-computer interfaces**.)

BOLSHEVIKS

A group of communists in early twentieth-century Russia who followed the teachings of **Vladimir Lenin** and played a leading role in the 1917 **Russian Revolution**.

BOURGEOISIE

Karl Marx's preferred term for Europe's wealthy, business-owning class.

BRAIN-COMPUTER INTERFACES

Technologies in which a machine records a brain's activity as input for a computer program—or a computer inputs signals into a brain.

CANCEL CULTURE

A widespread societal tendency to suppress, shun, and silence people who don't conform to certain "community guidelines" prescribed by secular culture.

CAPITALISM

A socioeconomic system (usually contrasted with **communism**) where people can privately own and control their own resources in a free-market society.

Note: Some people take "capitalism" to mean an idolatrous *usage* of free-market systems, where business owners pursue money as the ultimate goal at the expense of everything else—including people. A biblical view provides the moral basis for condemning the idolatry, covetousness, greed, and exploitation associated with such usages. But biblical principles (e.g., mandates *against* theft and *for* generosity) also assume a socioeconomic system of private ownership and regulate how to righteously apply that system.

COLLECTIVISM

A view that emphasizes social *groups* (like states or communities) above the *individuals* belonging to those groups. Collectivism generally teaches individuals to view themselves primarily in terms of their groups, to never bring shame upon the group, and to place the group's needs first. Strong versions of collectivist thinking may be used to endorse **communism**. (For contrast, see **individualism**.)

COMMUNISM

A socioeconomic system where, instead of people privately owning the *means* (like tools, farms, and factories) of producing *goods* (like food and clothes), people theoretically share these means (and to some degree the resulting goods[2]) in common. During the early stages of communism as **Karl Marx** envisioned it, a dictatorship may control the means of production. Marx hoped for a final stage in which state control would no longer be needed, leaving a classless society where people have moved past the idea of owning private property. However, history's major communist revolutions have consistently produced long-term dictatorships.

COUNTER-HEGEMONY

An "alternative" system of power and cultural influence that a society's marginalized groups must set up, according to neo-Marxist **Antonio Gramsci**, to take back control from the dominant groups. (See also **cultural hegemony**.)

CRITICAL THEORIES

Modes of thinking informed by **neo-Marxism** (or similar ideas) that critique society in hopes of revolutionizing the existing social order. Critical theories, like **Marxism**, view society in terms of *oppressed* vs. *oppressor* groups. Typically, these theories label people as "oppressors" based on identifying features (like gender or ethnicity) rather than on personal actions or attitudes.

Note: Conventionally, "Critical Theory" is only capitalized when referring to the original blend of ideas from **Karl Marx** and **Sigmund Freud** as formulated by the **Frankfurt School**.

CULTURAL HEGEMONY

The dominance that a society's most powerful groups maintain over marginalized groups, according to the Italian neo-Marxist **Antonio Gramsci**. Theoretically, this domination happens because (1) the powerful groups have the most influence over mainstream culture, thinking, and civil life and (2) the wider society allows it. (See also **counter-hegemony**.)

DECHRISTIANIZATION

A campaign to remove Christian influence from society and replace Christianity with an alternative worldview, which happened during the **French Revolution**.

DEISM

The belief that a divine being created the world but does not relate to humans, cannot be known by them, and has not revealed truth through his Word.

ESG SCORE

A measure of how well a company or organization meets certain "environmental, social, and governance" criteria, like having a low carbon footprint or following particular "diversity, equity, and inclusion" policies.

FALSE CONSCIOUSNESS

The idea, according to the neo-Marxist thinker **Herbert Marcuse**, that society is fine as it is and cannot (or should not) be revolutionized.[3] Marcuse believed this idea to be false—hence the term *false consciousness*.

FREIE DEUTSCHE JUGEND (FREE GERMAN YOUTH LEAGUE)

The official youth organization of East Germany's communist government.

HERMETICISM

A varied set of unbiblical spiritual ideas supposedly based on writings by a combined Greek and Egyptian deity.

INDIVIDUALISM

A view that primarily emphasizes *individuals* rather than the *groups* to which those individuals belong. Individualism generally teaches people to value independence. Strong versions of individualist thinking may be used to endorse the unbiblical idea of prioritizing the self above all else. (For contrast, see **collectivism**.)

MARXISM

The system of thinking endorsed by **Karl Marx**, including Marx's philosophical, historical, and socioeconomic ideas and their underlying worldview assumptions.

Note: Marx's writings were not always consistent or complete, so "Marxism" is not a unified system of thinking. Also, different variations of Marxism have developed as different people interpreted and applied Marx's thinking in different ways.[4]

MORALISTIC THERAPEUTIC DEISM

An influential worldview that teaches that God mainly wants people to be happy and do good to others. This worldview misses the essential gospel truths that all humans are sinners who need salvation, which is found only in Jesus Christ.

NEO-MARXISM

A system of thinking (with many variations) that revises and expands on **Karl Marx**'s ideas—especially his view that history is the story of group conflicts demanding the revolutionary reorganization of society. While Marx believed humanity's problem lies in oppression between *economic groups*, neo-Marxist movements attribute the problem more broadly to oppression between *cultural groups*.

PRESUPPOSITIONS

Statements that we can't necessarily *prove* are true but must *assume* are true as starting points for our thinking.

PROBLEM-POSING

A method of education promoted by the Brazilian neo-Marxist **Paulo Freire**, where teachers relate academic subjects to problems that demand (revolutionary) action. (For instance, instead of simply teaching science, science teachers might present a historical lack of gender diversity in science jobs as a problem for students to reflect about changing.)

PROLETARIAT

The working class, which **Karl Marx** believed must revolt against the **bourgeoisie**.

PROPAGANDA

A type of communication that persuades by appealing to something other than logic (or by misusing facts).

PSYCHOANALYSIS

An approach to psychology based on the (largely discredited) teachings of **Sigmund Freud**, who speculated that certain unconscious processes drive much of human behavior.

ROMANTICISM

A movement among certain artists, writers, and thinkers in eighteenth- and nineteenth-century Europe. With a focus on praising nature, emotion, beauty, and the human individual, this movement emphasized the worship of creation rather than the Creator (Romans 1:25).

SHARING ECONOMY (SEE ALSO ACCESS ECONOMY)

An economic system that emphasizes the *sharing* of certain goods and services over the private *ownership* of those goods. For instance, people may access ride-sharing services rather than owning cars themselves.

SOCIAL CREDIT SYSTEM

A system in which individuals are assigned "social credit scores" based on their behaviors. Engaging in "good" behavior increases one's social credit score, while "bad" behavior decreases it. Higher social credit scores grant people certain privileges, while lower scores can result in the loss of privileges.

SOCIALISM

A political theory or socioeconomic system that, according to the *Merriam-Webster Dictionary*'s definitions of the terms,[5] looks very much like communism.

THE FRANKFURT SCHOOL (AKA THE FRANKFURT INSTITUTE FOR SOCIAL RESEARCH)

A group of intellectuals originally based in Frankfurt, Germany, who combined ideas from **Karl Marx** and **Sigmund Freud** to develop the philosophical movement known as Critical Theory. (See **critical theories**.)

THE GENERAL WILL

The (faulty) final authority for truth according to **Jean Jacques Rousseau's social contract**. The General Will refers to a collective consensus based not on what most people *want* so much as on what's supposedly *good for* them.

THE GLOBAL BRAIN

A hypothetical future network of minds, devices, the internet, and artificial intelligence systems, all interconnected through technologies such as **brain-computer interfaces** to supposedly produce a form of "godlike" global consciousness.

THE SOCIAL CONTRACT (ROUSSEAU)

A sociopolitical system proposed by **Jean Jacques Rousseau**, where people give up certain individual freedoms and bind themselves to obey the **"General Will."**

THEOSOPHY

An occult religion incorporating aspects of Eastern spirituality, founded in the late 1800s by a small group of people, including **Helena Blavatsky**.

THERAPEUTIC (PHILOSOPHICAL SENSE)

A term relating to the belief that life is all about being happy, comfortable, and worry free.

THERAPIZATION

A process by which mainstream society comes to adopt the **therapeutic** mindset that life's highest purpose is to be happy, comfortable, and worry free.

TOTALITARIANISM

A system of governance that results when someone or something tries to take God's place as the authority for truth. Totalitarian regimes seek to control not only people's outward actions (as dictatorships do) but also their inner thoughts and emotions.[6]

Note: Rod Dreher differentiates *hard totalitarianism*, which controls by using force and violence, from soft totalitarianism, which controls by using other forms of manipulation (such as appeals to comfort, safety, and security).[7]

TRIVIALIZATION

A process that simplifies humanity's God-given rationality and distracts people to pursue the insignificant, making society more vulnerable to manipulation and control.

UTILITARIANISM

An ethical decision-making system that claims that the "right" thing to do in any given situation is whatever will bring the "greatest good" to the most people. (Usually, the *greatest good* is equated with *happiness*.)

UTOPIAN SOCIALISM

A varied branch of communist thinking characterized by the hope that a restructured society would create "heaven on earth." Some versions of this thinking predated **Karl Marx**'s writings.

WOKE

An adjective describing a mindset that views the world through a neo-Marxist perspective. This viewpoint sees certain sociocultural groups as oppressed by more powerful groups and calls for a social revolution to address and reverse this power imbalance.

WORLDVIEW

The set of "big picture" beliefs we use to interpret and explain the world around us. These beliefs shape how we answer major questions like "Where did everything come from? Why are we here? How do we know right from wrong? What happens when we die?"

ENDNOTES

1. Alice Bailey, "The World Situation," in *Esoteric Philosophy: A Treatise on the Seven Rays*, vol. 2 (Lucis Trust, 1942), 631, accessed July 2024, lucistrust.org/online_books/esoteric_psychology_volume_ii/chapter_iii_humanity_today/1_the_world_situation.

2. People may still be able to purchase and own things (at least certain types of things) in many communist societies; however, society's wealth and material resources are theoretically to be shared in common.

3. Other Marxists and neo-Marxists have used the term *false consciousness* in various nuanced and sometimes ambiguous ways. See Inanna Hamati-Ataya, "False Consciousness," in *Encyclopedia of Political Thought* (Chichester, UK: Wiley Blackwell, 2015), 1225–1228.

4. These points were mentioned on a wall display at the Karl Marx House Museum in Trier, Germany (see chapter 2).

5. See *Merriam-Webster.com Dictionary*, s.v. "Socialism," accessed July 29, 2024, merriam-webster.com/dictionary/socialism, and *Merriam-Webster.com Dictionary*, s.v. "Communism," accessed July 29, 2024, merriam-webster.com/dictionary/communism.

6. Rod Dreher, *Live Not by Lies: A Manual for Christian Dissidents* (New York: Sentinel, 2020), 8 (ebook version).

7. Dreher, *Live Not by Lies*, 7 (ebook version).

JESUS IS VICTOR